BRITISH TECHNOLOGY AND EUROPEAN INDUSTRIALIZATION

BRITISH TECHNOLOGY AND EUROPEAN INDUSTRIALIZATION

The Norwegian textile industry
in the mid nineteenth century

KRISTINE BRULAND

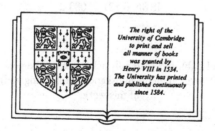

The right of the
University of Cambridge
to print and sell
all manner of books
was granted by
Henry VIII in 1534.
The University has printed
and published continuously
since 1584.

CAMBRIDGE UNIVERSITY PRESS

CAMBRIDGE

NEW YORK   NEW ROCHELLE   MELBOURNE   SYDNEY

Published by the Press Syndicate of the University of Cambridge
The Pitt Building, Trumpington Street, Cambridge CB2 1RP
32 East 57th Street, New York, NY 10022, USA
10 Stamford Road, Oakleigh, Melbourne 3166, Australia

First published 1989

Printed in Great Britain at the University Press, Cambridge

British Library cataloguing in publication data

Bruland, Kristine
British technology and European industrialization:
the Norwegian textile industry in the mid nineteenth century.
1. Norway. Textile industries. Technology transfer from Great Britain
I. Title
338.4'7677'009481

Library of Congress cataloguing in publication data

Bruland, Kristine.
British technology and European industrialization: the Norwegian
textile industry in the mid nineteenth century/Kristine Bruland.
p. cm.
Bibliography: p.
Includes index.
ISBN 0-521-35083-2
1. Textile industry – Norway – History – 19th century.
2. Textile industry – Great Britain – History – 19th century.
I. Title.
HD9865.N93B78 1989
338.4'7677'00948 – dc19   88-22822

ISBN 0 521 35083 2

The author and publisher gratefully acknowledge the generous financial
support of NAVF (Norges allmennvitenskapelige forskningsråd) in the publication
of this work.

CE

CONTENTS

TABLES

FIGURES

FIGURES

PREFACE

This book is based on my D. Phil. thesis which was presented at Oxford in 1986. I am very grateful to my supervisor Peter Mathias (now Master of Downing College, Cambridge), whose interest and astute comments helped me immeasurably, as also did his writings, which made a number of important issues clear to me during the research. I would also especially like to thank Francis Sejersted, who supervised the work while I was researching in Norway, and my examiners, Patrick O'Brien and John Harris, particularly for very helpful advice on revising the study for publication as a book.

In studying the transfer of textile technologies from Britain to Norway in the mid nineteenth century this work has relied heavily on business records of Norwegian textile firms. I owe a considerable debt, therefore, to those who assisted me in locating and understanding these records, in particular Merete Skogheim of the Norwegian Technical Museum, Oslo, Odd Halvorsen of the Halden Historical Collection, Arne Slivenes of the Bergen City Archive, and Christopher Harris, who drew my attention to the Wallem archives in Bergen University Library. I am grateful also for the encouragement and help, especially early in my research, given by Kari Hoel, and by Even Lange of the Business History Centre, Oslo. From the firms themselves, I would like to thank J. W. Fenton, former director of the Arne Fabrikker, Bergen; the staff and directors of A/S Solberg Spinderi; and the staff and directors of the Nydalens Compagnie. Trine Parmer, Lars Thue, Jan Ramstad, and K. B. Minde gave me access to their own research, for which I would like to thank them. For comments on work in progress I am grateful to Nick Crafts, and to participants in the Economic History Seminar, Oxford, and the Technical Change Seminar at the Department of Science and Technology Policy, University of Manchester. I would also like to thank Keith Brown, of the University of Oslo, who first encouraged me to study in England.

I owe a particular debt of thanks to British Petroleum (Norway) a.s., who founded the BP Norwegian Scholarship at Balliol College, which I held between 1982 and 1986. Without the kindness and generosity of British Petroleum and its representatives in Stavanger, Oslo and London, this research would have been utterly impossible. In particular I would like to thank Alan Yeo, Ian Barrett, Peter Blundson and Thomas Taylor.

Finally, I want to thank my husband Keith Smith for very important comments, suggestions and help in the writing of this book; I dedicate it to him.

LOCATION OF FIRMS

Oslo   Nydalen Spinnery
        Vøien Spinnery
        Hjula Weavery
        Christiania Sailcloth Factory

Drammen Solberg Spinnery

Halden   Halden Spinnery

Bergen   Rosendahl & Fane
        M.B. Wallem & Sons
        Arne Fabrikker

0   300 km
0   200 miles

N

SWEDEN

Trondheim

NORWAY

Bergen   Oslo
        Drammen
        Halden

Kristiansand

Aberdeen
SCOTLAND

1

TECHNOLOGY
AND EUROPEAN GROWTH

Underlying this study is the idea that we still know relatively little about the technological basis of European economic growth in the mid nineteenth century. The technologies employed within continental Europe changed sharply as it industrialized, but how did this happen? The following chapters are concerned with this aspect of European industrialization; they are in large part an empirical study of a pattern of technological diffusion, describing the acquisition and adaptation of British textile technologies by a peripheral European economy, Norway, from the early 1840s to around 1870. However, the focus of the study is not as narrow as this summary might suggest, for the empirical study is intended to throw some light on a wider, and to my mind very important, issue in the economic history of Europe.

Explaining the process of industrialization which occurred throughout much of Europe from around the middle of the nineteenth century has long been a key problem for economic history, yet its treatment remains unsatisfactory; for, although the literature on the topic is already very large, important questions remain unresolved. Continental industrialization involved new forms of enterprise in the creation of new industries or the transformation of existing ones, and a broad yet profound process of technological change. But what mechanisms generated, diffused and adapted these technologies? How did continental entrepreneurs and managers acquire the technological capacities first to operate the new technologies and secondly to do so at levels of efficiency sufficient to withstand competition from the world's technological leader, Britain? In fact we know relatively little about this, and in particular the nature, extent and effects of technology export have yet, in my view, to be adequately explored. What role was played by exports of machines and equipment from Britain, through the activities of British engineering firms, in the spread of industrialization through Europe from the 1840s? How significant, for continental industrialization, was the repeal of the prohibitions on the export of machinery from Britain in 1843? The existing literature on the economic history of continental European industrialization which will be discussed in the next chapter, is in the main organized around two rather different problem areas. The first, following the pioneering and

1

profoundly influential work of Alexander Gerschenkron, attempts to describe and account for the different economic and institutional mechanisms through which industrialization occurred. The second problem area deals with the spread of technology and technological knowledge through the interregional and international movement of individual entrepreneurs and technicians during what might be called the 'first phase' of industrialization, that is, during the period from about 1760 to about 1840.

Later periods and problems, however, have been relatively neglected; in particular the acceleration of European industrialization from the 1840s, and the technological details of how this occurred, deserve more attention. In Germany, for example, as Trebilcock has remarked, 'the motive power which had been accumulating since the late eighteenth century was translated into a definite forward surge between 1850 and 1914', with growth rates of net national product increasing sharply.[1] In France, a similar surge occurred in the period from the 1840s to the 1860s.[2] Russia saw a particularly rapid growth in the number of industrial enterprises from 1850, notably in textiles.[3] Among the smaller economies of Europe – Belgium, Switzerland, Scandinavia – it was in the years after 1845 that industrialization took hold, survived and prospered. Despite important structural divergences between the continental European economies undergoing the process of economic change, and the regional differences within them,[4] industrial change was nonetheless very widespread and of very great historical significance. Although we know a great deal about the quantitative outlines of this change,[5] we still know surprisingly little about the details of how it happened, and little in particular about the process of enterprise formation and technological change which were the practical basis of the growth of new industries.

If we are to fill these gaps in our knowledge of the history of European industrialization then we need to give more attention to an important avenue of inquiry, namely the study of the acquisition of new technologies at enterprise level within the industrializing economies. After all, industrialization involves structural change by virtue of the creation of new industries, and these in turn rest on new enterprises actually deploying new technologies. But how was this possible? How did continental entrepreneurs and enter-

[1] Clive Trebilcock, *The Industrialization of the Continental Powers, 1780–1914* (London, 1981), p. 45.
[2] M. Lévy-Leboyer, 'Capital investment and economic growth in France, 1820–1930', P. Mathias and M. M. Postan (eds.), *The Cambridge Economic History of Europe. VII: The Industrial Economies: Capital, Labour and Enterprise*, Part 1 (Cambridge, 1978), pp. 266–7.
[3] O. Crisp, 'The pattern of industrialisation in Russia', in *Studies in the Russian Economy Before 1914* (London, 1978), p. 37.
[4] See S. Pollard, *Peaceful Conquest: the Industrialization of Europe, 1760–1970* (Oxford, 1981), where the regional character of European industrialization is emphasized.
[5] See, for example, N. Crafts, 'Gross National Product in Europe 1870–1910: some new estimates', *Explorations in Economic History*, 20 (1983), pp. 387–401; 'Patterns of development in nineteenth-century Europe', *Oxford Economic Papers*, 36 (1984), pp. 438–58.

prise managers learn about, acquire and operate the new technologies of the industrial economy?

When posing such questions, one must necessarily consider the impact which prior British industrialization had on later continental developments, particularly from the 1840s. Did British technological leadership underpin, facilitate or enhance change elsewhere, and if so, how? If technologies originating in Britain were put to work elsewhere, was this through imitation of Britain by continental industrializers, on the basis of domestic resources, or was there a direct *diffusion* – perhaps via the export of equipment – of British technologies from the UK? The latter question leads in turn to a consideration of the importance of the removal, in 1843, of the prohibitions on the export of machinery from Britain.

Britain had forbidden the emigration of skilled artisans from the early eighteenth century, and from 1750 had enacted a range of regulations prohibiting the export of machinery: 'By 1785 the tools and machinery used in the cotton, woollen and silk textile industries, as well as the tools and utensils used in the iron and steel manufacture, had been banned from export.'[6] The regulations were in fact never completely effective, for some equipment could be exported under licence, and the prohibitions could otherwise be subverted by smuggling, by industrial espionage, and by general flows of technological information.[7] Farnie remarks that 'the repeal in 1843 of the Act of 1786 forbidding the export of machinery gave legal sanction to what had become a customary practice in defiance or in evasion of the law'.[8] Nevertheless the Act did constrain the access of foreigners to British techniques and, by the same token, the size of the market available to the British capital goods industry. But the European market for machinery in the early nineteenth century was expanding, and thus prohibitions in effect protected an infant machine-making industry on the continent. This latter point was repeatedly made in the submissions to the Select Committee of 1841: '... the impossibility of getting it from England made machine-making a very good speculation in France, and machine makers have very much improved within the last ten years', remarked one witness.[9] Other witnesses emphasized the growing importance of the machinery trade as a whole, pointing out that '... the partial prohibition tends to deprive English machinists not merely of the

[6] M. Berg, *The Machinery Question and the Making of Political Economy, 1815–1848* (Cambridge, 1980), p. 205.

[7] P. Mathias, 'Skills and the diffusion of innovations from Britain in the eighteenth century', *The Transformation of England* (London, 1979), pp. 28–9; A. Birch, 'Foreign observers of the British iron industry during the eighteenth century', *Journal of Economic History*, 25 (1955), pp. 23–33; M. W. Flinn, 'The travel diaries of Swedish engineers of the eighteenth century as sources of technological history', *Transactions of the Newcomen Society*, 31 (1957–9), pp. 95–115; J. R. Harris, 'Industrial espionage in the eighteenth century', *Industrial Archeological Review*, 7, 2 (1985), pp. 127–38; D. Jeremy, *Transatlantic Industrial Revolution* (Oxford, 1981), pp. 40–1.

[8] S. Farnie, *The English Cotton Industry and the World Market, 1815–1896* (Oxford, 1979), p. 56.

[9] Evidence of G. Withers, quoted in S. Pollard and C. Holmes (eds.), *Documents of European Economic History. Vol 1: The Process of Industrialization, 1750–1870* (London, 1968), p. 325.

benefits of their inventive activity, but of the trade in unprohibited, as well as that for prohibited machines'.[10] In recommending repeal of the prohibition the Committee in effect accepted these arguments, and therefore accepted also the view that Britain should attempt to achieve a dominant position in machinery supply to the world. The repeal came into force in 1843.

From that time, therefore, the technological environment faced by European entrepreneurs presumably changed sharply as British machines and equipment became legally available. But how did this affect the pace and direction of continental industrialization? How did it affect the ability and willingness of European entrepreneurs to deploy British techniques? If we are to answer such questions then we need to know much more than we do about how British engineering enterprises responded to the repeal, that is, about the extent to which they searched for European markets after 1843, about the nature of the goods and services they offered, about the competition among them, and so on. From the other side – the demand side – it seems to me that there are two broad questions. Firstly, there is the question of how market seeking by British engineering firms altered and perhaps eased problems of enterprise formation and technological innovation for European entrepreneurs. Secondly, there is the question about the conditions underlying differential responses by entrepreneurs in various parts of the continent.

This study takes an enterprise-oriented approach to such questions, for answering them requires, in my view, not a general European-wide survey or analysis, but rather an examination of particular industries and, if possible, particular firms. I have chosen to concentrate on the construction of a mechanized textile industry in Norway, a development which began in earnest in approximately 1845, and which was an important component of Norwegian industrialization at that time. Norway was then, as to some extent it remains, a small, marginal, peripheral European economy. It is therefore remarkable that as early as the 1840s it was able to deploy and operate, in the textile industry, what might now be called 'state of the art' technologies. How was this possible? In attempting to answer this question, the focus of this study is not on the Norwegian industry as a whole, but rather on ten firms engaged in various aspects of textile production (spinning, weaving, sail-cloth making, etc.), with a particular emphasis on one firm, a large integrated spinning and weaving establishment. This large firm was the Hjula Weavery, run by an important Norwegian entrepreneur, Halvor Schou. On the British side, the focus is wider for, as I shall show, these Norwegian firms acquired technology through business relationships with several hundred British enterprises engaged directly or indirectly in technology supply. My objective is essentially to describe the process of technology acquisition by the large integrated firm, Hjula Weavery, with reference to other firms where appropriate and possible. The primary sources for this study, which are described fully in the bibliography, are taxation records, fire insurance records (which

10 *Second Report From the Select Committee on Machinery*, 7 (1841), p. 277.

give an insight into the changing nature of the capital stocks of the firms), and firms' correspondence and invoice archives. The invoice records enable us to relate changing capital stocks to sources of technology acquisition. The correspondence archives, which in the case of Hjula Weavery are unusually complete, permit a detailed insight into the number of British machine makers or suppliers active in the small Norwegian market, the nature of their activities, and the technological problems with which they and their Norwegian customers dealt. The central theme of this work is the scale, complexity and importance of the interaction between the Norwegian firms and the large number of British textile engineering firms and machinery-supplying agents who supplied the technology on which Norwegian textile industrialization was based. On the basis of the empirical study, two broad arguments are advanced.

1 Mechanization of the Norwegian textile industry was a process of direct technological diffusion. Underlying the possibility of this diffusion were two major internal economic transitions. In Norway, there was the emergence and consolidation of a capitalist economy, with a high proportion of national income entering foreign trade and an outward-looking entrepreneurial class. In Britain there was a transition of a different kind, essentially a structural change within an already solidly established market economy; in the early nineteenth century an important division developed between final-output producing sectors of the economy, and a capital goods industry producing the means of production for the former. In particular the emergence of a machine-making industry in Britain was an event of critical importance. For Britain, this development institutionalized process changes in technology as the province of a particular specialized industry. For Norway, and for other European industrializers, it altered the nature of technology acquisition, particularly after 1843. This is, perhaps, the key point of the study – that outward-looking, market seeking activity by British textile engineering firms and machinery suppliers went a long way towards solving the problems of acquiring the new industrial technologies for countries such as Norway. These British engineering firms, I shall show, played a key role, indeed a decisive role, in Norwegian textile industrialization. This leads me to argue that the literature on European industrialization has not differentiated sharply enough between two stages in the spread of industrialization. In the first stage the agent of international diffusion was the individual craftsman, artisan, engineer or entrepreneur. In the second stage, relatively neglected within European historiography, the vehicle was the machine manufacturing enterprise.

2 The diffusion of textile industrialization to Norway should not be understood in terms of *imitation* of British practice. This is because imitation – a frequently used concept in the history of industrialization and also in the

economics of technological change – seems to me to imply a degree of autonomy in the imitator. That is, it implies replication of the British experience with domestic resources. Now Norway certainly replicated British technical practice, as I shall show, but it did so on the basis of technological 'packages' supplied directly from Britain by British textile engineering firms. The contribution of these firms was very great indeed. They provided flows of technical information; they acquired or supplied machinery and shipped it; they supplied ancillary equipment; they supplied construction expertise; they recruited and supplied skilled British operative and managerial labour for Norwegian firms (and frequently paid the families of such workers, on behalf of emigré operatives, during their periods of work in Norway). Sometimes these 'packages' were put together by British agents of Norwegian firms who also operated as important channels of diffusion. It follows that Norwegian textile industrialization was not so much an imitation as an *extension* of British developments following the development of a differentiated capital goods industry in the UK. More precisely, I suggest that the key concept should not be imitation but *interaction*, between a Norwegian entrepreneurial class who, though possessing commercial and marketing skills, in many cases lacked relevant technical and engineering skills, and British textile engineers whose search for markets provided the techniques and equipment which Norwegian entrepreneurs put to work.

After a consideration of the relevant literature, the following chapters will describe the internal changes in the British and Norwegian economies in the first half of the nineteenth century, and then go on to analyze the multifarious aspects of the process of technological diffusion which these changes made possible. The diffusion of textile technology to Norway will be discussed under the following headings:

1 the flow of technological information,
2 the acquisition and sources of capital equipment,
3 the roles of British textile engineers and machinery-supplying agents in the transfer of technology to Norway,
4 the roles of British workers and managers in the Norwegian textile industry,
5 interrelations among Norwegian firms in the diffusion of British technology.

Clearly it is impossible to draw general conclusions from an examination of a small number of firms in one small European economy. However there are indications from the sources used for this study that its propositions concerning the demiurgic role of British machinery suppliers may be of wider application, and of wider relevance to the study of European industrialization. That is to say, the experience of these Norwegian firms may well be representative of a more general European experience. Certainly it is a simple matter to show that technology exports from Britain to Norway were but a minor part of a major export effort by British textile engineers, and there are small but suggestive links between the Norwegian firms studied here and their counterparts elsewhere. This wider export activity will be described in the final chapter. The question of whether the comprehensive technological input to Norwegian firms by British engineers was replicated elsewhere must remain open, but the general impression which emerges from the Norwegian material is that this was a standard, probably routine business procedure of British textile engineering firms. It seems to me therefore very likely that the Norwegian experience is indeed representative, in which case this study suggests questions about our understanding of the technological basis of European industrialization as a whole, as well as perhaps signposting some routes for further research. The central questions which emerge from this study all concern the role of the British capital goods industry. Was the emergence of this industry the key to the extension of British industrial methods to Europe? Did it supply, in other countries and perhaps other industries, the same all-inclusive technological packages which it offered to the Norwegian textile industry? If so, then we will have made an important step in understanding how the technologies of British industrialization spread so rapidly throughout Europe. But we can only know the answer to such questions through detailed studies of firms and industries, by looking at the economic history of technological change from the perspective of the firm. Paul Uselding has remarked that: 'The promise of the unification of business and technological history is that it can illuminate the large and central questions of capitalistic evolution by marshalling relevant evidence on how the prime institution of that system, the business firm, originates and manages elements of novelty, i.e. technology.'[11] It is to this task that this book aims to contribute.

[11] P. Uselding, 'Business history and the history of technology', *Business History Review*, 54 (1980), p. 443.

2

THE HISTORIOGRAPHY OF EUROPEAN INDUSTRIALIZATION

The emergence of a mechanized textile industry in Norway was a component of wider industrial growth in that country. But this in turn was, of course, part of a general spread of industrialization throughout Europe from the late eighteenth century. This process was, arguably, the decisive historical event of the modern period, for it involved far more than changes in production methods and levels of output, important though these were. The industrialization process also involved, perhaps was ultimately caused by, major changes in social and economic organization, and it led to significant shifts in regional structures, patterns and levels of trade, and the distribution of both inter- and intra-national political power. Moreover, this process was not a once and for all affair. On the contrary, it installed, throughout Europe and North America, a new economic regime within which the emergence and spread of new technologies have been pervasive. This large-scale historical process has given rise to two broad areas of inquiry relevant to this study. One is historical: the economic history of the industrialization of nations and regions. The other is analytic: the economics of technological change.

Broadly speaking, the literature relevant to early industrialization and the international diffusion of new technologies falls into three categories:

1 Economic histories of the spread of industrialization, or reflections on the problem of industrialization from an historical standpoint. Such works are typically wide in scope, examining all of Western Europe, and frequently including discussion of Russia and Eastern Europe.
2 Case studies of the diffusion of particular technologies, either intra- or internationally, historical or contemporary.
3 Theoretical analyzes, often involving mathematical modelling, of intra-firm, intra-sectoral, economy-wide and international diffusion within the general economics literature on technological change.

What follows is not an exhaustive survey of the literature within these categories, but rather a discussion of the general approaches which have been taken within them, particularly with respect to the problem of technological diffusion and industrialization.

THE ECONOMIC HISTORIOGRAPHY OF THE SPREAD OF INDUSTRIALIZATION

From an historical point of view the industrial transformation of Europe has two important aspects, one frequently emphasized and the other, I shall suggest, somewhat inadequately treated in the literature. In the first place there is the fact of British priority, and therefore the question of whether the 'British model' – that is, the sequence of coal, metals, textiles, and mechanical engineering as a path to industrial development – was a predominant feature of the pattern of European industrialization. While it is not particularly difficult to see why accelerated growth in Britain might impel growth elsewhere, it is an interesting question as to whether European industrialization 'occurred as an outgrowth of a single root with mutations caused by varying circumstances', as Pollard has put it,[1] emphasizing an underlying unity of experience, or whether the empirical differences highlighted by Crafts's recent research justify his view that 'there were different paths to maturity for nineteenth-century Europe', and that 'there are strong signs of differences of transition between the pioneer industrializer, Great Britain, and the other countries'.[2] Cameron has echoed this: 'there was not one model for industrialization in the nineteenth century – the British – but several'.[3] But a second key feature of European development, to be distinguished from the general economic effects of Britain's leadership on the structural pattern of European development, was that it frequently involved the transfer of specific technologies from Britain to its European 'followers'. Sidney Pollard in fact argued in personal correspondence with Cameron that this was what he had in mind when suggesting that 'the industrialization of Europe took place on the British model ... Perhaps I could admit at once that the British origin is not meant to imply a model in the sequence or speed, but in the kind of technology and social institutions created.'[4] This point was emphasized in Pollard's book *Peaceful Conquest*:

Industrialization ... meant the imitation and absorption, at first or second hand, of the technology pioneered in Britain. This is because in some important sense the acceptance of the new technology appeared to be critical: without it, no industrialization as we understand it could take place, but once it was adopted successfully on a wide enough basis, nothing appeared to be able to prevent the region concerned from 'taking off'.[5]

---

[1] S. Pollard, *Peaceful Conquest. The Industrialization of Europe 1760–1970* (Oxford, 1981), p. v.

[2] N. F. R. Crafts, 'Patterns of development in nineteenth-century Europe', *Oxford Economic Papers*, 36 (1984), pp. 453–4.

[3] R. Cameron, 'A new view of European industrialization', *Economic History Review*, 38 (1985), p. 23. See also P. O'Brien and C. Keyder, *Economic Growth in Britain and France, 1780–1914* (London, 1978), p. 18; P. O'Brien, 'De we have a typology for the study of European industrialization in the nineteenth century?', *Journal of European Economic History*, 15, 2 (1986), pp. 291–334.

[4] *ibid.*, p. 9.   [5] S. Pollard, *Peaceful Conquest*, p. 142.

In what follows I want to suggest that the historical literature, with the exception of that part which deals with very early industrialization, has not focussed in adequate detail on whether or how this actually occurred. In approach, Europe-wide histories of industrialization tend to be concerned more with the structural and institutional transformation of the European economies than with the specific processes of technological diffusion, in particular at enterprise level, which underlie industrialization.[6] There are two distinct ideas underlying this emphasis. The first is the notion that the rate of technological change is in some sense dependent upon social structure, therefore political and social change should be in the foreground of any history of industrialization. The second idea rests on the necessity of 'preconditions' or 'prerequisites' for industrial growth. Growth requires entrepreneurs to promote it, with some degree of social acquiescence in their values and activities; investment, hence finance, hence a banking system are required; new labour skills are needed and so on. In this approach, emphasis is placed on the mechanisms and institutions through which these preconditions are satisfied. I shall discuss some examples of each of these approaches.

The idea that the technological dynamism of Europe is the effect of capitalism *qua* new social system has a long history. Its most powerful proponent was unquestionably Marx; from early writings such as the *Communist Manifesto*, to *Capital* many years later, he argued consistently that the structure of capitalism is distinctive in that it is the first economic system characterized by a ruling class driven by internal competition to have a vested interest in technological change as opposed to preservation of the technological *status quo*. Although this idea is really only a starting point for Marx, who develops a sophisticated analysis of technology on the basis of it,[7] it continues to play a major role in some histories of European industrialization. Particularly in Marxist works, the dissolution of the feudal economy and the formation of capitalist relations of production are treated as the key to any historical analysis of technology.

Perhaps the clearest recent example of this approach is Berend and Ranki's *The European Periphery and Industrialization*. Berend and Ranki place considerable emphasis, both in describing and in explaining industrialization, on the 'socio-political prerequisites of change', by which they mean the 'laying of the groundwork of modern capitalist relations of production'.[8] Their discussion of Norway, for example, stresses the dissolution of communal landholding and the formation of a free-holding peasantry, the absence of a feudal

---

[6] See, e.g., I. Berend and G. Ranki, *The European Periphery and Industrialization 1780–1914* (Cambridge, 1982); A. Milward and S. Saul, *The Economic Development of Continental Europe 1780–1870* (2nd Edition, London, 1979); S. Pollard, *Peaceful Conquest*; C. Trebilcock, *The Industrialization of the Continental Powers* (London, 1981).

[7] See, e.g., N. Rosenberg, 'Marx as a student of technology', in *Inside the Black Box. Technology and Economics* (Cambridge, 1982), pp. 34–54.

[8] Berend and Ranki, *European Periphery*, p. 28.

aristocracy, and the legal dismantling of feudal trading privileges and the guild system. 'Thus,' they conclude, 'by the second half of the nineteenth century, Norwegian society had removed the medieval obstacles to capitalist development.'[9] This process is systematically traced in the other European economies with which Berend and Ranki are concerned.

The central problem with this kind of work, quite apart from its historical inaccuracy – as the next chapter will show, Norway was distinctly capitalist a good deal earlier than the second half of the nineteenth century – arises from the fact that it is at best a very partial explanation. The overcoming of 'obstacles' is not the same thing as the actual achievement of industrialization, and the latter by no means automatically flows from the former.

Of course the Marxian tradition is not the only framework for discussing the general propensity of economic systems to technological change. Perhaps the most relevant non-Marxian formulation is that of David Landes in his *Unbound Prometheus*.[10] Landes speaks of the foundations of European tcch- nical progressiveness in terms of a conjunction of rational calculation (that is, a culture which places a high value on the rational adaptation of means to ends), and on the other side a 'faustian spirit of mastery'. By the latter I take him to mean that nothing was out of bounds to scientific and technical exploration, and that such exploration was positively valued. Both of these features were, in Landes's picture, part and parcel both of the European scientific revolution and of the conduct of economic life.

These approaches, as noted above, do little to explain the actual course of technological change, and neither Landes nor Berend and Ranki stop at this point. Their discussion of general preconditions leads to the examination of further, more detailed, 'prerequisites' of growth and change. Here there is a very wide literature which shares a similar general orientation. This literature derives from the classic, indeed the founding, discussion of the 'prerequisites' of industrialization, namely Alexander Gerschenkron's *Economic Backward- ness in Historical Perspective*.[11] There would probably be wide assent to Lars Sandberg's remark that Gerschenkron provided 'the most intellectually satisfying framework currently available for analysing the early stages of European industrialization'.[12]

Underlying Gerschenkron's work are two key organizing ideas. The first is that all industrialization processes are similar in terms of outcome (that is, they give rise to basically similar economic or rather industrial structures). The second, and probably even more influential idea, is that these industrial- ization processes required a similar set of functional 'prerequisites'. Differing

[9] *ibid.*, p. 33.
[10] D. Landes, *The Unbound Prometheus. Technological Change and Industrial Development in Western Europe from 1750 to the Present* (Cambridge, 1969).
[11] A. Gerschenkron, *Economic Backwardness in Historical Perspective* (Cambridge, Mass., 1962).
[12] L. Sandberg, 'Poverty, ignorance and backwardness in the early stages of European industrialization. Variations on Alexander Gerschenkron's grand theme', *Journal of European Economic History*, 11, 3 (1982), p. 675.

degrees of backwardness among countries led to these prerequisites being met in different ways, or to 'substitutes' being found for them. It is differences in terms of satisfaction of prerequisites which account for the emergence of different paths to industrialization.

Gerschenkron's two organizing ideas are connected. With the first he essentially accepts the validity of Marx's famous remark that 'the more developed country only shows to the less developed its own future'. 'There is little doubt,' Gerschenkron remarks, 'that in the broad sense this generalization has validity.'[13] Thus industrializing countries are in some manner on broadly similar paths to broadly similar ends. The problem with this assertion is, of course, that considerable diversity seems to characterize the experience of European development in the nineteenth century. One way of looking at Gerschenkron's work, therefore, is to see it as an attempt to construct a uniform analytical understanding from this apparent diversity, to understand certain empirical differences in terms of the way essentially invariant problems are overcome.

This invariance is based on the fact that diverse industrialization processes were based on uniform historical preconditions. 'Certain major obstacles to industrialization *must* be removed and certain things propitious to it *must* be created before industrialization can begin.'[14] Now it is important to be precise about what Gerschenkron means by this, for I shall argue below that his understanding of the nature of 'prerequisites' has had significant – and in some ways harmful – effects on subsequent economic histories of European industrialization. In talking of 'prerequisites', Gerschenkron had in mind the following: 'What is meant ... is not the common sense notion that in order to start an industrial plant certain very concrete things are needed. The concept refers to certain long-run historical changes.'[15] The pattern of industrialization made possible by these long-run changes is based on five preconditions:

1 the availability of capital for investment, and 'an increase in the volume of fixed capital',
2 the exploitation of economies of scale,
3 changes in technology,
4 the 'transformation of agricultural labourers and small artisans into factory workers',
5 the emergence of entrepreneurs, within a stable commercial environment, and with reasonable standards of commercial honesty.

Now the prerequisites are nothing but the historical changes which allowed this pattern to occur; they are the historical changes which resulted in rural-urban migration, an entrepreneurial culture, an appropriate framework of contract law, a higher rate of technological innovation, and so on. Gerschenkron's argument is that the 'English model' is by no means the only way

---

[13] Gerschenkron, *Economic Backwardness*, p. 6.   [14] *ibid.*, p. 31.   [15] *ibid.*, p. 31.

for these changes to occur. Unfortunately he does not spell out precisely what he means by the English model, but it is usually taken to involve relatively low rates of initial investment, further investment financed by retained profits, a gradual evolution in technological level and complexity, the indigenous emergence of an entrepreneurial class, and a process of agricultural revolution and enclosure leading to rural-urban migration and the formation of an urban labour force. These considerations led Gerschenkron to the conclusion that:

> one way of defining the degree of backwardness is precisely in terms of the absence, in a more backward country, of factors which in a more advanced country served as prerequisites of industrial development. Accordingly, one of the ways of approaching the problem is by asking what patterns of substitutions for the lacking factors occurred in the process of industrialization in conditions of backwardness.[16]

The main 'substitutions' discussed by Gerschenkron are (1) the role of an innovating banking structure in the provision of industrial finance (in particular the role of the Crédit Mobilier in France, and the role of investment banks in Germany), (2) the role of the state in finance (especially in Russia), (3) the role of the state in substituting for the entrepreneurial function, (4) the role of specific types of capital good in substituting for an appropriately large and skilled labour force (and hence the use of capital goods of a type not seemingly justified by the structure of relative factor prices). (5) Gerschenkron emphasizes the importance of what he calls 'ideologies of delayed industrialization', by which he means the ideas associated with, e.g., Saint-Simon in France and Friedrich List in Germany. These ideas provided a rationale for the activities of bureaucratic elites which substituted for the entrepreneurs of British experience.

Gerschenkron's work has had substantial, though not always acknowledged, impact on the historiography of European industrialization and technological change,[17] although this impact has not been so much on specific ideas as it has been on shaping the scope of subsequent work. By that I mean that historians, in describing the industrialization of Europe, concentrate – in what might be called a 'Gerschenkronian' fashion – more on the prerequisites of industrialization and technological change than on the process by which it actually occurred. This is particularly the case with general histories of industrial development, either of Western Europe – such as those by Milward and Saul and Trebilcock – or of peripheral Europe, such as that by Berend and Ranki, or integrated works such as Pollard's *Peaceful Conquest*.[18] After discussing general prerequisites these works invariably move on to a discussion of the factors emphasized by Gerschenkron: labour supply, the role of the state, the influence of foreign trade, the provision of capital and the

---

[16] *ibid.*, p. 46.
[17] Although Pollard, *Peaceful Conquest*, is quite explicit in his acknowledgement of Gerschenkron's influence.
[18] See Footnote 6 above.

banking system, etc. What is strikingly absent is any systematic account of the process of technology acquisition; rather, these works offer an account of the different development 'paths' in each area listed above. Berend and Ranki, for example, offer no discussion whatsoever of the technology transfer process. Pollard, despite the fact that he emphasizes that technological diffusion is what industrialization is all about, gives the topic five pages (out of 450) in which he emphasizes the role of British emigrés, all prior to 1830, and devotes one page to the diffusion of the Watt engine, focussing on the importance of accompanying skilled labour in order to get the machine to work. Milward and Saul devote a chapter of extreme generality to the topic, discussing technological change in a number of sectors, without at any point indicating how this occurred. Trebilcock, though finding much to admire in Gerschenkron, is doubtful about whether Gerschenkron's ideas are widely applicable,[19] and this leads him to a rather wider discussion of technological issues than most authors of general histories; at one point he suggests that technological diffusion rather than industrialization is the appropriate concept in analyzing Western Europe.[20] However, with the exception of five excellent pages on the diffusion of British armament techniques to Spain, there are only a dozen or so isolated references in a work of 500 pages, and no systematic treatment at all.

If this absence of a serious treatment of technological change and diffusion is surprising in general histories of industrialization, it is even more so in histories of technological change itself. Here the classic work is Landes's *Unbound Prometheus*, mentioned above; a more recent contribution is Kenwood and Lougheed's *Technological Diffusion and Industrialization Before 1914*.[21] Both are specifically histories of technological change and diffusion. Yet Landes, in a very substantial chapter on the 'continental emulation' of early British industrialization, closely follows what we might call the Gerschenkronian agenda, devoting considerable space to political and institutional change, to the entrepreneurial climate, to investment requirements, to the activities of emigré technicians, to the role of the state. Technology itself actually plays a very minor role. When Landes came to trace the technological evolution of the major continental industries his discussion concentrates on regional location, growth rates, power intensity and power sources, and types of output.[22] There is simply no discussion of the sources of technology acquisition, nor of the actual problems of innovation, operation and diffusion, nor of how they were solved by enterprises. It is suggested that a European machine-making industry was developed in the 1820s, but there is no account of how this happened or of what products it produced, nor of how it affected technology acquisition and industrial

---

[19] Trebilcock, *Industrialization of the Continental Powers*, Ch. 6.   [20] *ibid.*, p. 129.
[21] A. Kenwood and K. Lougheed, *Technological Diffusion and Industrialization Before 1914* (London, 1982).
[22] Landes, *Unbound Prometheus*, pp. 158–83.

development. In relation to textiles it is noted, for example, that 'some [European machine makers] even tried their hand at textile equipment, but it was soon recognized that this was the kind of product best left to specialists'.[23] But there is nothing on who or where these specialist firms were, or on their impact on the technological basis of the textile industry. It is claimed that textile firms 'often maintained machine departments large enough to stand on their own'[24] but no evidence is offered to back this claim, nor is there any discussion of its significance. Landes's book as a whole is of deservedly famous complexity and scope, but in a history of technological change the absence of a detailed treatment of enterprise acquisition of technologies seems to me to be a strange omission.

Similar problems can be found in Kenwood and Lougheed's work. Once again, despite the title of the book which suggests an explicit study of technological diffusion, we are in Gerschenkronian territory. 'Prerequisites' are discussed almost exclusively, with the only direct discussion of technological diffusion coming in the form of a brief (one page) outline of an epidemic model of diffusion,[25] with nothing about how epidemic models are actually used in the economics literature. Quite apart from the fact that their discussion of epidemic models is inadequate (they fail to mention, for example, why economists are interested in the mathematical structure of epidemics, or what general problems epidemic models are meant to explain) they do not acknowledge that there is a more important class of non-epidemic models in the literature.[26] About two thirds of the book discusses 'preconditions' for the diffusion of industrial technology, and under 'spread' there is an account concentrating on international trade (which can in fact operate as much to inhibit diffusion as to promote it) and the role of investment banks and the state.[27]

So, to sum up, the principal weakness of this literature lies in its treatment of the technological level itself. What we have are histories of technological change and industrialization in Europe in which the process of technological change is conspicuous by its absence. There are, it seems to me, two broad reasons for this. One lies in the nature and influence of what I have called the 'Gerschenkronian agenda'. The key problem here is that Gerschenkron defines his prerequisites as 'certain long-run historical changes', in opposition to 'the common sense notion that in order to start an industrial plant certain very concrete things are needed'. Now it is certainly necessary to be cautious about common sense notions, but the fact is that industrialization does require the starting of industrial plants, and this moreover is a quite specific process with its own internal logic and problems. 'Very concrete

[23] *ibid.*, p. 183.   [24] *ibid.*, p. 184.
[25] Kenwood and Lougheed, *Technological Diffusion*, p. 7.
[26] It is some years since Probit models supplanted epidemic models as the basic analytical approach to diffusion. See, e.g., P. Stoneman, *The Economic Analysis of Technological Change* (Oxford, 1983), Ch. 7.
[27] Kenwood and Lougheed, *Technological Diffusion*, Ch. 11.

things' are indeed needed, although a reading of Gerschenkron and those influenced by him does not reveal what they are. No doubt it is unfair to lay these criticisms at the door of Gerschenkron himself, but the fact remains that, however important his prerequisites, prerequisites is *all they are*. They are necessary conditions at best, and by no means sufficient ones.

There may however be another reason for the particular emphasis of these general economic histories. This is that the authors are constrained by what the specialist research literature tells them. Although in one respect this literature is rich and detailed, it can nevertheless be argued that there are significant gaps, particularly in terms of case studies of technological diffusion involving mid nineteenth-century industrializers.

HISTORICAL CASE STUDIES OF TECHNOLOGICAL DIFFUSION

The central emphasis of the literature on the early spread of industrialization is on the role of human agents as carriers of technological knowledge, and the importance of the emigré technician, engineer or skilled worker is generally acknowledged. Even today, large areas of technological knowledge are not formally codified, and this was even more the case in the late eighteenth and early nineteenth centuries. This placed a premium on the experience of individual workers, and a range of studies has confirmed the centrality of their contribution to the diffusion of a number of technologies. Robinson, for example, showed their crucial role in Russia in the eighteenth century,[28] while Mathias has presented a view of the process for western Europe as a whole.[29] He points out that the flow of artisans and entrepreneurs in early industrial Europe was complex and multilateral. Nevertheless,

with the basic mechanization of the textile industry after 1770, the growth of deep mines and large-scale metal fabrication, and the associated growth of engineering, it was principally British engineers and artisans who sponsored diffusion of these new techniques abroad. This was particularly true of machine-making and mechanical engineering generally.[30]

The eighteenth century saw a substantial flow of formal technological knowledge through technical societies, magazines and encyclopaedias, and visits to Britain by foreigners. Yet it was primarily human skills which diffused the new technology, and it was problems in their supply which underlay what Mathias calls the 'critical *technical* blockages holding back the

28 P. E. Robinson, 'The transference of British technology to Russia, 1760–1820', in B. Ratcliffe (ed.) *Great Britain and Her World 1750–1870* (Liverpool, 1975).
29 P. Mathias, 'Skills and the diffusion of innovations from Britain in the eighteenth century', in *The Transformation of England* (London, 1979), pp. 21–44.
30 *ibid.*, p. 23.

spread of the new innovations'.[31] At the same time there were strong interconnections among the technological advances of the period, which made it difficult to abstract any particular technical advance in isolation for application elsewhere.

These conclusions were confirmed by Harris in a study of attempts to deploy English steel-making technology in France. Despite considerable experimentation based on formal descriptions of English techniques, early success depended heavily on English entrepreneurs; in attempting to develop indigenous steel and file-making capacity the French government had, in the words of one manufacturer, 'the mortification of spending great sums without achieving its goal of establishing manufacture of this kind'.[32] The central reason for this lay in the fact that 'the skilled workmen were still the true metallurgists of Yorkshire', and such workmen were more important in a practical sense than the early industrial scientists such as Réaumur and Berthollet in France.[33] Like Mathias, Harris emphasizes the interconnection of different phases of technical change, but concludes that the fundamental obstacle to the development of high-quality steel production in France was 'that the French did not bring over and domesticate many, if any, really specialized English workers in steel'.[34]

For textiles, the importance of the skilled British worker in the development of the French textile industry, especially during the late eighteenth century, was shown conclusively by W. O. Henderson.[35] These ideas are echoed in the most detailed recent study of technological diffusion, David Jeremy's *Transatlantic Industrial Revolution*,[36] which examines the diffusion of textile technologies between Britain and North America from 1790 to 1830. Once again the importance of skills is emphasized, for example by the fact that: 'At Philadelphia a disassembled spinning mule confounded interested parties for four years and was eventually shipped back to Britain in 1787, leaving Philadelphians none the wiser but angrier.'[37] Jeremy employs a four-stage analysis of international diffusion, an expansion from a two-stage process originally suggested by Myra Wilkins.[38] These stages are:

---

[31] *ibid.*, p. 33. See also J. R. Harris, *Industry and Technology in the Eighteenth Century: Britain and France* (Published Inaugural Lecture, University of Birmingham, 1971), where this point is also made.

[32] J. Harris, 'Attempts to transfer English steel techniques to France in the eighteenth century', in S. Marriner (ed.) *Business and Businessmen. Studies in Business, Economic and Accounting History* (Liverpool, 1978), p. 213.

[33] *ibid.*, p. 227.   [34] *ibid.*, p. 227.

[35] W. O. Henderson, 'English influence on the development of the French textile industries, 1750–1850', in *Britain and Industrial Europe 1750–1850* (Leicester, 1972), pp. 10–36.

[36] D. Jeremy, *Transatlantic Industrial Revolution. The Diffusion of Textile Technologies Between Britain and America, 1790–1830s* (Oxford, 1981).

[37] *ibid.*, p. 76.

[38] M. Wilkins, 'The role of private business in the international diffusion of technology', *Journal of Economic History*, 39 (1974), pp. 166–88.

1 a phase of 'build-up' of technological potential, during which skills, plans, technical information and so on become available. These create conditions of feasibility for technology transfer.
2 the construction of pilot plants which demonstrate the technical and commercial feasibility of the new processes.
3 the internal spread or diffusion of the new processes.
4 the modification of the imported technology to accord with local conditions.

The period with which Jeremy deals is of course, like those of Mathias and Harris, prior to the repeal of the prohibitions on the export of machinery from Britain. The prohibitions were not difficult to evade, but in the build-up of potential the availability of skilled labour was nonetheless very important, and Jeremy is notably successful in tracing the activities of labour recruiters (on behalf of American enterprises), as well as the subsequent careers of those they recruited. Samuel Slater, for example, 'the Arkwright of America', was recruited from the Jedediah Strutt mill in Derbyshire to construct a carding machine in Rhode Island; it was he who made the Arkwright process, which depended heavily on managerial and machine operative skills, commercially feasible in the USA. Slater set up a number of enterprises in southern Massachusetts, and his businesses were, in Jeremy's words, 'the single most fruitful node of technology diffusion in American cotton manufacturing before 1812'.[39] Jeremy traces the diffusion of four textile technologies (cotton spinning, power-loom cotton weaving, calico printing and woollen manufacture), his most important conclusion being: 'that for a new technology still partially understood or not yet reduced to verbal or mathematical forms, the experienced practitioner must be the most efficient form of international diffusion'.[40]

It is important to note, however, that all of the studies mentioned above focus on the period prior to the emergence of a developed capital goods industry in Britain. Yet, as Mathias has pointed out, this was in many respects the most important development of the British economy in the first half of the nineteenth century:

From 1815 onwards the capital goods industries (from small beginnings) grew faster as an industrial sector than the consumer goods industries ... Platts of Oldham, leading a rapidly expanding textile machinery industry, for example, equipped European and New England mills. By the 1850s they were installing capacity in India.[41]

Where such an industry exists, then process innovations are of course its products, which could be expected to have a higher degree of formal organization and codification than the cases described above. Problems of, for example, construction or assembly of equipment become no longer the

---

[39] D. Jeremy, *Transatlantic Industrial Revolution*, p. 90. For a detailed account of Slater's career in America, see J. Prude, *The Coming of Industrial Order. Town and Factory Life in Rural Massachusetts 1810–1860* (Cambridge, 1983).
[40] D. Jeremy, *Transatlantic Industrial Revolution*, p. 262.
[41] P. Mathias, *The Industrial Revolution and the Creation of Modern Europe* (Oxford, 1986).

responsibility of the end-user but of the product supplier, and this could be expected to have significant effects on the ability to deploy a new technology and hence on the pace and scale of diffusion. The most notable example of such a capital goods supplier in early industrialization is of course the firm of Boulton & Watt. Their international marketing was based on the objective of securing patent protection prior to sale, but in return for this they would agree 'to supply engines at agreed prices, to furnish drawings of millwork, to find mechanics, and to ship the goods'.[42] In fact patent rights were difficult to secure and to enforce, but as Tann points out:

A more successful approach to foreign marketing was achieved by the firm's making available certain engineering services, which influenced the operation of the pull mechanism. For both the foreign and British customer a crucial factor in the innovation decision was access to a skilled mechanic, preferably one trained at Soho, to erect the engine, to train men to operate it, and perhaps even to remain in charge of it.[43]

This factor had in fact been an important constraint in the diffusion process of the Newcomen engine from the 1720s.[44] Jennifer Tann has shown that labour supply was integral to the international sale of the Watt engine. Purchasers therefore were buying not simply a machine but a 'package' of equipment, information and technical skills. It turned out, however, that buyers were so prone to poaching these skilled mechanics that Boulton & Watt turned to supplying, not their own engineers, but specially recruited workers whose recruitment was specific to particular orders, 'with every expectation that the man would remain abroad'.[45] These 'packages' sometimes extended further, into the supply of machinery as well as its power source, with Boulton & Watt in effect becoming a design and production engineering consultancy involved in the supply of integrated technology packages.

But the role of the capital goods enterprise was not confined to the international diffusion of the steam engine, and became of great importance in the diffusion of cotton technology. Mathias has pointed out that:

The conclusion of this process [i.e. of the development of a UK capital goods industry] was that developments within the British economy – the differentiation process which brought an independent engineering industry into existence and the build-up of forces which encouraged the flow of capital abroad – actively encouraged the progress of industrialization in some other countries abroad where appropriate conditions of profitability existed.[46]

---

[42] J. Tann, 'Marketing methods in the international steam engine market: the case of Boulton and Watt', *Journal of Economic History*, 38, 2, p. 368.
[43] *ibid.*, p. 374.
[44] E. Robinson, 'The early diffusion of steam power', *Journal of Economic History*, 24 (1974), p. 97.
[45] J. Tann, 'Marketing methods', p. 376.
[46] P. Mathias, *The First Industrial Nation* (Second Edition, London, 1983), p. 232.

Platts of Oldham, for example, who were mentioned above, played an important role in Japan, through their agents Mitsui & Co. Saxonhouse examined the 'superfast' diffusion of mule-spinning technology in Meiji Japan, asking why it was that the industry developed so rapidly. His study identified two primary causal factors: first, a high degree of cooperation among Japanese textile firms, leading to very rapid intra-industry diffusion of best-practice technique, and secondly, equipment acquisition from one major supplier, namely Platts.[47] But to what extent did similar processes occur in Europe? It is surprising that we know so little, practically nothing in fact, about this. Henderson's studies of Britain's role in European industrialization, which extend into the mid and late nineteenth century, are in practice organized largely around the role of individual engineers and entrepreneurs in the early phase of industrialization, and, although he repeatedly emphasizes the importance of British machinery, there is a relative lack of emphasis on the period during which British machine-making firms became active.[48] Yet, as the following chapter will show, the textile machinery industry was already large by the time the Select Committee on the Exportation of Machinery reported in 1841; Kirk has pointed out that much of the industry's subsequent growth was a consequence of exports, although the main emphasis of his study is on the late nineteenth and early twentieth centuries.[49] Given the generally important role of textile manufacture in early industrialization outside the UK, Kirk also noted that 'it may be pertinent to ask what was the role of the English machinists in developing these industries?'.[50] Later chapters of this study address precisely this question for the period after 1843, when British machine-making firms could imitate the earlier 'packaging' role of Boulton & Watt.

THE ECONOMIC ANALYSIS OF DIFFUSION

This section will not survey the large contemporary literature on the economics of the diffusion of innovations,[51] but simply outline the types of questions which it seeks to answer, and hence suggest its limitations for the historical analysis of diffusion. Current theory concerns itself with two problems, the pace of diffusion and its time path. In terms of rate, the problem can be expressed as follows: if a new technique is not economically superior to an existing technique, then it will not diffuse. But suppose a new

47 G. Saxonhouse, 'A tale of Japanese technological diffusion in the Meiji period', *Journal of Economic History*, 39 (1974), pp. 149–65.

48 W. O. Henderson, *Britain and Industrial Europe, 1750–1870* (Leicester, 1965); also *The Industrial Revolution on the Continent. Germany, France, Russia, 1800–1914* (London, 1967).

49 R. M. Kirk, *The Economic Development of the British Textile Machinery Industry, c. 1850–1939* (Salford, 1983).

50 *ibid.*, p. 6.

51 For such surveys, see, e.g., S. Davies, *The Diffusion of Process Innovations* (Cambridge, 1979); E. Mansfield, *The Economics of Technological Change* (New York, 1979); and Stoneman, *The Economic Analysis*.

technique is strongly superior to existing techniques (for example, its fixed and variable costs are less than the variable costs of the existing technique), why, then, does it not diffuse immediately? Why do not all potential adopters take it up at once? The second problem concerns the path of diffusion, which is normally argued to follow a sigmoid or S-shaped curve. This implies that the number of new adopters increases initially at a slow rate, that the rate then increases, and that finally it decreases. So diffusion occurs at a non-instantaneous rate, and that rate changes over time. Why, the literature asks, should diffusion paths take this form?

Two broad classes of models have been proposed and explored in answer to the questions raised above: epidemic models, which treat diffusion by analogy with the progress of an infection, and Probit models, which analyze the different characteristics of adopters.[52] These models have two features which make them unsuitable for historical analyses. First, they assume the economic superiority of the new technique, which involves the further implicit assumptions that potential users actually have the capacity to assess new techniques and put them to work, and that calculating the profitability of a new technique is unproblematical (both in terms of calculation technique and absence of uncertainty). These assumptions are rarely if ever appropriate in historical analysis, and applicability of the theory is therefore sharply limited. Secondly, as a consequence of the first feature, the models analyze only the demand side of technological change, rather than the factors determining supply of new technologies, and the interaction between suppliers and potential users in determining applicability of a technique. The latter also is inappropriate for historical analysis. These critical points have been most forcefully made, perhaps, by Nathan Rosenberg. Although Rosenberg accepts that 'the diffusion of innovations is essentially an economic phenomenon, the timing of which can be largely explained by expected profits',[53] he places considerable emphasis on developments at the technological level which affect the post-innovation economics of the technique. Five types of activity in particular affect the possibility and pace of diffusion:

1 the continuity of inventive activity (i.e. the extent to which post-innovation improvements occur),
2 development of technical skills among users,
3 development of skills in machine making (i.e. among suppliers of the new equipment),
4 development of complementary inputs,
5 competitive improvements in 'old' technologies.

[52] For epidemic models see E. Mansfield *et al.*, *The Production and Application of New Industrial Technology* (New York, 1977), Ch. 6; for Probit models, P. David, *A Contribution to the Theory of Diffusion* (Stanford, 1969).
[53] N. Rosenberg, 'Factors affecting the diffusion of technology', in *Perspectives on Technology* (Cambridge, 1977), p. 191.

This approach is potentially a very fruitful one in the analysis of the international diffusion of technologies. In particular there is the fact that technologies are often highly specific to particular environments, and may not be economically viable outside them. Making them profitable may well involve the kinds of supplier and user learning and development outlined by Rosenberg; this, it seems to me, is the (unstated) approach which underlies the more successful historical studies of diffusion – such as Jeremy's account of textile technology diffusion in the USA – and it is the approach which will be adopted in this study.

But also important to this study is the emphasis placed by Rosenberg on the importance of the capital goods industry in both innovation and diffusion. In the brief survey of case studies above, I noted that many studies concentrate on the early period of industrialization prior to the emergence of a capital goods industry in Britain. This leads to a justified emphasis on the role of emigré technicians, skilled workers and entrepreneurs as the carriers of process innovations. However when a capital goods industry develops product innovations, these become process innovations within the equipment-using industries. The effect is to shift the burden of developing process innovations on to specific enterprises specializing in these tasks. Rosenberg, like Mathias, stresses the historical importance of this:

In both the US and the UK in the nineteenth century, technological change became institutionalised in a very special way – that is, in the emergence of a group of specialised firms which were uniquely oriented toward the solution of certain kinds of technical problems. The rapid rate of technological change was completely inseparable from these capital goods firms. In fact I would regard the emergence of such firms as the fundamental institutional innovation of the nineteenth century from the point of view of the industrialization process.[54]

The capital goods industry in effect packages information, skills and equipment, and in so doing significantly reshapes the innovation decision for firms and hence the diffusion environment both nationally and internationally. But this is more than a matter of buying machines; Mira Wilkins in particular has argued that the diffusion process should not be identified simply with the transfer of techniques. As she puts it:

It is worth considering the difference between mere transfer and the absorption of technology within the host country. A company can export capital goods. In one country the machines installed might be allowed to break down and eventually fall into disrepair; in another country, the same machines might be used efficiently in modern industry, copied, adapted, and produced locally.[55]

Wilkins defines 'absorption' in terms of efficiency of use of the new technology (that is, the ability to use it as efficiently as the best-practice producer), and the ability to produce it domestically. It seems to me that this

[54] N. Rosenberg, 'Economic development and the transfer of technology: some historical perspectives', in *Perspectives on Technology* (Cambridge, 1977), p. 152.
[55] Wilkins, 'Private business', p. 171.

definition is too restrictive; absorption could just as well be the ability to deploy a technology on a continuing basis within enterprises which are viable in the long run. And they need not be produced domestically, especially in a small economy which may not be able to support a mechanical engineering industry of sufficient size. Nevertheless, underlying 'absorption', as Wilkins points out, are not only exporters of technology but 'private companies within the host country that can digest the technology'.[56] It is this two-sided process which will be studied empirically in the following chapters.

CONCLUSION

This chapter has argued, first, that general economic histories of European industrialization have neglected the technological level of the process; the question of how industries and firms changed their technological basis has been downplayed in favour of, for example, emphasis on financial systems, state involvement, and other 'prerequisites' of industrialization. Secondly, empirical case studies have concentrated largely on the early industrialization of the eighteenth and early nineteenth centuries, and have (correctly) emphasized the role of individual emigration in technology diffusion. This leaves open the question of how later industrialization occurred, an important omission, since recent work by Crafts suggests that, for most European economies, the transition to industrialization and higher levels of income occurred primarily after 1850.[57] What was the technological basis of this? Empirical studies such as those by Saxonhouse and Kirk, and historical and theoretical points of the kind made by Mathias and Rosenberg suggest that the machine-making sector of the capital goods industry may play an important role. Yet there remains a gap in our knowledge concerning the precise activities and significance of such firms in the mid and late nineteenth century, particularly in terms of their effect on the diffusion of industrialization. This is the problem which will be addressed in later chapters of this study, where the role of British textile engineers and equipment suppliers will be shown to be central to the development of skills and capabilities in the Norwegian textile industry, and thus to the existence of the industry as such.

[56] *ibid.*, p. 171.
[57] See N. F. R. Crafts, 'Patterns of development in nineteenth-century Europe', *Oxford Economic Papers*, 36 (1984), pp. 438–58.

3

BRITAIN AND NORWAY, 1800–1845
TWO TRANSITIONS

Norwegian textile industrialization occurred within the context of change and transition in both the British and Norwegian economies. In Norway the growth and development of a market economy, and in Britain an important structural change within the world's leading market economy, established conditions for a transfer of technology between the two. These changes produced, on the one hand, the capacity to generate a process of outward technology transfer and, on the other, a fertile environment for the reception and use of foreign techniques. This chapter deals with the contours of these changes, necessarily in outline, for a full treatment of the changes in economic activity in Norway, let alone in Britain, at that time would be a substantial task. The aim here is more modest; it is simply to describe some of the preconditions for technology transfer. If, in the previous chapter, I have been critical of the Gerschenkronian approach to the 'prerequisites' of industrialization, that is because of the incompleteness of such approaches. It is not because there are no prerequisites. We are concerned here, therefore, with some of the conditions which made technological diffusion possible between these two economies; later chapters will describe in detail how it actually occurred.

NORWAY IN THE EARLY NINETEENTH CENTURY

In considering Norwegian economic development it should be borne in mind first and foremost that we are dealing with a country which is large in size, yet very small in population. Although the population increased by over 50 percent between 1801 and 1845, it was still less than one and a half million.[1] As late as 1890, nearly 70 percent of the population lived in 'sparsely populated rural areas', and was relatively evenly distributed across a large, mountainous, inhospitable land mass. The economic significance of this, particularly for the textile industry, lay in the difficulties posed for the creation of an integrated internal market. This had definite effects on enterprise decisions; Halvor Schou (an important textile entrepreneur whose

[1] Statistisk Sentralbyrå, *Historisk Statistikk 1968* (Oslo, 1969), p. 33.

activities will be discussed extensively below) at one point decided against capacity expansion on marketing grounds, for increased sales would have required a substantial network of agents due to the dispersed nature of the market. Peter Jebsen, another textile manufacturer, attempted to solve the problem by taking his own boat around the isolated settlements of the coastal region.[2]

Perhaps the key distinguishing feature of the Norwegian economy in the preindustrial period was that it was characterized by a substantial and increasing degree of openness; the level of foreign trade was in many respects exceptional for such a peripheral economy. At the beginning of the nineteenth century, for example, about a third of domestic grain consumption was imported.[3] The export sector was significant in size from the mid eighteenth century, and grew strongly in the first half of the nineteenth century. This expansion was based on two important commodities – fish and timber – and a service, maritime transport. Probably the best recent estimates of Norwegian trade levels at that time come from Hovland, Nordvik and Tveite, who suggested that:

the export sector of the Norwegian economy including shipping constituted between 20 and 30 percent of total output in the years 1750–1850. Probably 30 percent of total output was exported in the boom years after 1800. In the 1830s and 1840s exports made up about 20 percent of output. The subsequent vigorous expansion after 1850 brought the share of exports in GNP close to 30 percent by 1870.[4]

A second important characteristic of preindustrial Norway was that both the level of trade, and its commodity and geographical composition, were affected by Norway's somewhat anomalous political and constitutional position. From the mid seventeenth century to 1814, Norway was part of a 'twin kingdom' of Denmark and Norway. However the king was Danish, the capital was Copenhagen, and the administrative bureaucracy was predominantly though not exclusively Danish. As Bergh *et al.* pointed out:

The configuration of political forces ... created a very particular division of labour. Norway on the one hand sold timber, fish and metals, partly to Denmark, but primarily to other countries, in order to provide the state with foreign exchange. On the other hand the country constituted an important market for Danish agricultural products, manufactures, and not the least, for Danish culture.[5]

The Napoleonic wars marked a turning point in the relationship with Denmark. The Danish and Swedish monarchies backed opposing sides, Denmark allying itself with France, and Sweden with Britain and Russia.

[2] *Hjula Weavery, Papers and Correspondence, Kopibok 1855–1858*, 9 November 1856 (Norsk Teknisk Museum Archives). Jebsen: S. Grieg, *A. S. Arne Fabrikker* (Oslo, 1946), p. 56.

[3] L. Jörberg, 'The Nordic countries 1850–1914', in C. Cipolla (ed.) *Fontana Economic History of Europe. The Emergence of Industrial Societies – 2* (London, 1977), p. 431.

[4] E. Hovland *et al.*, 'Proto-industrialization in Norway, 1750–1850: fact or fiction?', *Scandinavian Economic History Review*, 30, 1, p. 47.

[5] T. Bergh *et al.*, *Growth and Development: the Norwegian Experience 1830–1980* (Oslo, 1980), p. 4.

This had direct consequences for Norway. In the first place it was physically isolated from Denmark by the British naval blockade, while at the same time its trading relations with Britain were restricted. In the second place, both Britain and Russia, in treaties at Abo in 1812 and Stockholm in 1813, promised Norway to Sweden for services rendered. The prize was claimed by the Swedish Crown Prince Carl-Johan in late 1813, although popular resistance in Norway led him to adopt, from 1814, a conciliatory policy based on the acceptance of the so-called 'Eidsvoll constitution', which had been drawn up by Norwegians who had hoped to avoid his rule. This meant that Carl-Johan governed Norway in union with Sweden, rather than via amalgamation or incorporation. Norway was in practice governed by a Norwegian cabinet and administered by a bureaucracy staffed almost entirely by Norwegians. It had its own currency – the Norwegian daler – and was independent of Sweden in matters of public finance.[6]

On the one hand this implies that nineteenth-century Norway, despite its unusual constitutional position, can be considered as an independent economic unit. The textile entrepreneur Halvor Schou emphasized this in a letter to Sir William Fairbairn concerning the space allotted to Norwegian industry at the Industrial Exhibition in London in 1862:

I beg you to bear in mind that Sweden and Norway are two separate kingdoms, that, though they are united under one king with one common Foreign Department, they have separate governments, finances and legislations. Neither of the two nations wish to have their industrial production mixed together, and you will save us from much trouble and unnecessary squabble if you can settle this matter so that you give to each of us a certain space independant of another [sic.][7]

On the other hand, the events surrounding the Napoleonic wars had a significant impact on Norway's economic development. Exports of timber, for example, had grown strongly from 1800, but the closing of the British market in 1807 – after the Danish alliance with France – led to a marked decline in exports, from almost a million cubic metres in 1805 to under 600,000 in 1815–19.[8]

After the Kiel treaty in 1814, which settled Norway's future with Sweden, free access to the Danish market was closed off, and Norwegian iron exports in particular suffered from a 50 percent tariff. Quite apart from the structural changes which attended economic growth, therefore, the Norwegian economy faced difficult problems of adjustment in the first quarter of the nineteenth century as a result of the European conflict. This was no doubt a principal component of the search for wider markets by the Norwegian export

---

6 A detailed account is given in Per Maurseth, *Sentraladministrasjonens historie. Bind I, 1814–1844* (Oslo, 1979). See also T. K. Derry, *A History of Modern Norway 1814–1872* (Oxford, 1973), Chs. 1 and 2.

7 Hjula Papers, Kopibok, 1861–1863, 28 June 1861.

8 F. Hodne, *An Economic History of Norway, 1815–1870* (Bergen, 1975), p. 42.

industries mentioned above, and an increasing openness of the economy. I turn now to a brief description of these major industries.

The Norwegian staple industries

The Norwegian export trade was based, in the main, on timber, fishing and shipping, whose early nineteenth-century development will be outlined in this section.

Timber

Norway is heavily forested with fir and pine, has suitable river systems for the internal transport of timber, and – in contrast to the other major Scandinavian timber producers – several ice-free ports. Output grew rapidly in the late eighteenth century, but contracted sharply under, first, the British blockade during the Napoleonic wars, and secondly, the post-war British tariff which gave preference to Canadian timber. By 1816 Norwegian timber exports to Britain were at their lowest level since the mid seventeenth century. This was partly a result of a tariff levied on pieces of timber rather than lengths: Norwegian logs tended to be shorter, and thus faced a higher effective tariff. As noted above, exports declined sharply in the early part of the century, recovering slowly to the 1805 level by the 1840s.[9] Then, a general expansion of world demand, and a reduction in British duties, led to a revival of the industry in mid century, followed by a major boom. Exports reached a peak of 2.3 million cubic metres in 1873.

The performance of the timber industry was of considerable importance for the entire southern Norwegian economy, prosperity or recession in the industry having marked effects on the region.[10] Three linkages between timber and the wider economy were particularly important. First, timber development required and generated substantial investment in transport infrastructure, for example in river alteration for the transport of wood. Secondly, the approximately 3,000 sawmills (700 involved in the export trade) were an important vehicle for the import and development of mechanized methods. Finally the fortunes of the shipping industry were closely bound up with the export trade in timber.[11]

Fishing

Fishing was perhaps the most important of the export staples.[12] Recent estimates suggest that up to 15 percent of the total workforce took part in the annual fishing season off the west coast. Up to 90 percent of the total catch

---

[9] A. Schweigaard, *Norges Statistik* (Christiania, 1840), pp. 90–1.
[10] Hovland *et al.*, 'Proto-industrialization', p. 48.
[11] S. Dyrvik *et al.*, *Norsk Økonomisk Historie 1500–1970, Band 1, 1500–1850* (Bergen, 1979), Ch. 16; F. Sejersted, 'Aspects of the Norwegian timber trade in the 1840s and 1850s', *Scandinavian Economic History Review*, 16, 2 (1968), pp. 137–54; F. Sejersted, *Fra Linderud til Eidsvold Værk*, 3 Vols. (Oslo, 1973).
[12] T. Solhaug, *De Norske Fiskeriers Historie, 1815–1880* (Bergen and Oslo, 1976).

was exported, and fish products made up between 45 and 50 percent of total commodity exports. The whole range of North Sea and Atlantic fish were caught, and, since they had to be preserved for export, this led to substantial shore-based activity by which the catch was smoked, salted or wind-dried.

Between 1815 and 1830, there was general growth in output and exports, with an approximate doubling of the trade in cod and herring.[13] As with timber, there were important linkage effects; Hovland *et al.* list the most important as follows:

a The provision of lodgings for the predominantly itinerant labour force of the industry, and the construction of facilities for on-shore processing.
b The supply of equipment. Although many fishermen made their own gear, they nevertheless required a supply of materials – rope, thread for netting, canvas for sails, etc. But there was also a considerable amount of specialized production of fishing inputs, particularly by sail-makers. These came to include major textile enterprises, some of which will be referred to below. The supply of nets came to be organized through the first example of a 'putting out' system in Norway, based in Bergen and organized by local merchants using the fishing and farming workforce during the winter months.
c Boats were a major item of equipment, and were the product of highly specialized producers. Most of the fishing was inshore, and open boats of various types were used; mid century production was approximately 5,000 per year.
d Finally, barrels and cooperage. Virtually all output was exported in barrels, which was of course the product of a specialized trade, with town merchants acting as intermediaries between coopers and fishermen.[14]

Shipping

Norway's shipping industry was bound up with its general openness and the particular fortunes of the export staples. After a hesitant period at the beginning of the century, the industry grew strongly from 1830, both in vessels and tonnage; the latter grew at compound rates of about 5–6 percent per year,[15] and by 1880 Norway possessed the third largest mercantile marine in the world. This growth appears to have been based on the conjunction of particularly favourable supply factors, especially the ready availability of large numbers of competent seamen and skippers, with the expanding demand resulting from the sharp growth in world trade from mid century. Norwegian maritime success appears to have rested on two main factors: cheap labour, and what Hodne calls 'the advantage of a second-best technology'.[16] The Norwegian industry was based on simple forms of sail, and they continued to rely on this long after competitors had moved to steam.[17] The typical

[13] Derry, *History of Modern Norway*, p. 102.
[14] Hovland *et al.*, 'Proto-industrialization', pp. 47–52.
[15] Statistisk Sentralbyrå, *Historisk Statistikk*, p. 363.
[16] Hodne, *Economic History of Norway*, p. 103.
[17] T. Bergh *et al.*, *Growth and Development: the Norwegian Experience 1830–1980* (Oslo, 1980), pp. 76–80, argue that the failure to make the transition to steam hampered the subsequent

Scandinavian commercial device was to buy ships at the very end of their working lives, very cheaply, and then simply keep them running, using small and low-paid crews. The tactic was so successful that it was still being used at the beginning of the second world war, when substantial quantities of Australian grain were still being carried to Britain and Germany in second-hand sailing ships under Scandinavian ownership.

Artisanal manufacture in Norway

An important feature of the Norwegian economy in the early nineteenth century was the integration of the export staple industries with the agrarian sector. Norway was a predominantly rural economy in which the farming population also carried out seasonal work in fishing and timber. This work-force was also responsible for a range of handicraft manufactures, from tools and implements to clothes. Even where technical improvements were adopted in farming, the implements were often home-made. With hand-threshing machines, for example, 'Jacob Sverdrup based the instruction at his pioneer agricultural school on the hypothesis that his pupils would have to make the improved equipment for themselves'.[18] Much Norwegian textile and equipment manufacture came through the system known as 'Husfliden', which can perhaps best be translated as 'homecrafts'.[19] An important implication of this is that, in general, artisanal enterprises producing small manufactures for local markets were absent in Norway. In particular, Norway lacked the handicraft-based textile manufacture which existed elsewhere in Europe.[20] Hovland *et al.* remark that:

The scattered and unreliable source material makes it difficult to grasp the structure and extent of domestic textile production. But one thing seems fairly clear: the existence of alternative employment opportunities such as fishing or forestry was a serious obstacle to textile handicraft production within the rural economy ... textile production had to compete in the labour market, and the export sectors were able to pay higher wages than could be earned in handicraft textile production.[21]

On the one hand the 'husfliden' system meant that the emerging textile industry of the early nineteenth century, and indeed the mechanical engineering industry which also grew strongly from the 1840s, faced little if any competition from artisanal enterprises. On the other hand, the absence of

development of the industry. But this could only really be called a failure if steam offered greater profits, which has not been demonstrated.

18 Derry, *History of Modern Norway*, p. 101.

19 For a general description of home-based manufacture of implements, see Eilert Sundt, *Om Husfliden i Norge* (Oslo, 1975).

20 See S. Grieg, *Norsk Tekstil Vol. 1* (Oslo, 1948), p. 176. Norway differed from Sweden in terms of the scale of handicraft manufacture: see Lennart Schön, 'Proto-industrialization and factories: textiles in Sweden in the mid-nineteenth century', *Scandinavian Economic History Review*, XXX, 1 (1982), pp. 57–99.

21 Hovland *et al.*, 'Proto-industrialization', pp. 53, 56.

handicraft production meant that demand was met by imports, and the emerging Norwegian textile sector – whose development will be described in the next chapter – thus found its main competition in already industrialized foreign producers rather than a significant indigenous unmechanized industry.

Norwegian economic growth and industrialization

The above sketch of the Norwegian economy in the first half of the nineteenth century indicates an acceleration of export-led growth which set the stage for industrialization itself. General increases in market-oriented economic activities, the opening-up of export markets and the sharp growth in the export staple industries, combined with dramatic demographic changes,[22] are indications of an economic transition which provided a favourable climate of commercial and economic opportunity for an emergent entrepreneurial class. The openness of the economy involved a growing import of manufactures, in particular textiles as Table 3.1 shows.

Table 3.1 *Imports of cotton and wool manufactures to Norway*
(tons)

	Cotton	Wool
1830	90	93
1835	136	138
1840	187	151
1845	375	229

Source: Statistisk Sentralbyrå, *Historisk Statistikk 1968*, pp. 270–1

The import figures suggest rapidly growing demand for textile manufactures, and hence a commercial opportunity for Norwegian textile entrepreneurs if they could either substitute for existing imports or meet further increases in demand from domestic resources. However, given the openness of the economy this would have to be done in competition with advanced producers. Therefore the mechanized production of textiles in Norway required the acquisition of technological capabilities of a fairly high order; but, precisely because the principal competition was with advanced foreign producers, one route to competitiveness lay in the transfer or diffusion of technology from abroad. That this was possible at all resulted from developments in the British economy which will be described briefly in the following section.

[22] See, e.g., M. Drake, 'Norway', in W. R. Lee (ed.) *European Demography and Economic Growth* (London, 1979), pp. 284–318; T. Moe, 'Some economic aspects of Norwegian population movements 1740–1940: an econometric study', *Journal of Economic History*, 30, 1 (1970), pp. 267–70.

TEXTILE GROWTH AND MECHANICAL ENGINEERING IN THE UK, 1800–45

In the long run, industrialization rests on the development of capital goods industries: iron and steel, energy industries, the production of power equipment, machinery and so on. Such industries played an important role in Britain well before the industrial revolution of the late eighteenth century; shipbuilding and metals production in particular were carried out on a large scale.[23] Their role in early textile industrialization, however, may have been slight; in the main buildings were small (although water frame mills became very large by the beginning of the nineteenth century), power sources consisted often of human energy, and techniques were simple. The early technological advances in spinning and weaving do not appear to have required formal engineering skills: 'Kay's flying shuttle, Arkwright's water frame, Hargreave's spinning jenny, Crompton's mule, and Roberts's power loom, all belong to this period, and the inventive activity required to produce them was of the severely practical kind which owed nothing to science or mathematics.'[24] Moreover it is important to note that, with the exception of Roberts's inventions, which in fact began in the mid 1820s and were produced within a major mechanical engineering enterprise, all of the eighteenth-century inventions were developed by individuals, rather than within specialized machinery enterprises. Kirk and others have suggested that among early cotton textile enterprises, 'many preferred to construct their own machinery rather than purchase'.[25]

However, the supply of machinery, and hence the development of the mechanical engineering industry, was strongly affected by the changing scale

Table 3.2 *Index of growth in real net output for textiles,*
1770–1842
(5 year moving averages, 1800 = 100)

1770	76	1820	199
1790	89	1827	288
1800	100	1832	360
1810	118	1837	463
1815	127	1842	612

Source: P. Deane and W. A. Cole, *British Economic Growth, 1688–1959* (second edition, Cambridge, 1978), p. 213

[23] P. Mathias, *The First Industrial Nation* (Second Edition, London, 1983), p. 110.
[24] A. Burstall, *A History of Mechanical Engineering* (London, 1963), p. 229.
[25] R. M. Kirk, *The Economic Development of the British Textile Machinery Industry, c.1850–1939* (Salford University, Ph.D thesis, 1983), p. 1. For an account of the development of the Roberts automatic mule, see K. Bruland, 'Industrial conflict as a source of technical innovation: three cases', *Economy and Society*, 11, 2 (1982), pp. 91–121.

of the textile industry. The growth of British textile output was exceptionally rapid from the late eighteenth century, as Table 3.2 indicates.

The figures imply a compound annual average rate of growth of real output of just under 3.5 percent. Most estimates of capital formation, though often necessarily tentative, show capital equipment or the value of the fixed capital stock increasing at a somewhat faster rate. Table 3.3 shows estimates for equipment.

Table 3.3 *Capital equipment in cotton, 1811–46*

1817	6.6	–
1819–21	7.0	14
1829–31	10.0	55
1844–6	19.5	225

Sources: S. Chapman, 'Fixed capital formation in the British cotton manufacturing industry', in J. Higgins and S. Pollard (eds.) *Aspects of Capital Investment in Great Britain, 1750–1850. A Preliminary Survey* (London, 1971), p. 75; Deane and Cole, *British Economic Growth 1688–1959* (second edition, Cambridge, 1978), p. 191

Spindleage increased at roughly 8 percent per year, which is consistent with Blaug's estimates of the rate of growth of total capital from 1834.[26] Power looms obviously increased at a faster rate, but this was accompanied by scrapping of virtually the entire stock of hand looms between 1830 and 1860.

Now such growth in demand for capital equipment would imply, if the division of labour is indeed a function of the extent of the market, the development of specialized equipment manufacture. And in fact this occurred; although the early growth of the textile industry was, technologically speaking, a relatively simple matter, the development of the industry quite rapidly led to a major expansion in machinery and power requirements. Advances in iron founding and in engineering led to the provision of cast iron, wrought iron and some steel parts. The pioneering and influential work of Henry Maudslay (1771–1831) facilitated the emergence of a specialized mechanical engineering sector: 'Not only did he produce greatly improved lathes and other machine tools, but he also pioneered precision engineering and mass production, with his standard true-planes, measuring machines, gauges and screw-making tackle.'[27] As Musson and Robinson showed, a wide variety of craftsmen – foundrymen, blacksmiths, instrument makers, clock and watchmakers, and so on – moved into the mechanical engineering

[26] M. Blaug, 'The productivity of capital in the Lancashire cotton industry during the nineteenth century', *Economic History Review*, 2nd Series, 13 (1961), p. 359.

[27] A. Musson, 'The engineering industry', in R. Church (ed.) *The Dynamics of Victorian Business. Problems and Perspectives to the 1870s* (London, 1980), p. 90.

industry,[28] this movement being facilitated, Musson has argued, by the fact that machine tool production was standardized, 'ready-made' and mass produced much earlier than has been generally acknowledged.[29] This made it possible for firms to engage in what Musson calls 'the standardized manufacture of other products':

By the second quarter of the nineteenth century, if not earlier, Manchester had become the most important centre of engineering in the country. Scores of engineering firms sprang up there in the late eighteenth and early nineteenth centuries, making water wheels, steam engines, boilers, textile machinery, machine tools and eventually railway locomotives ... Manchester became the centre not only of the revolution in the cotton industry, but also of that in engineering associated with it.[30]

By the 1840s, therefore, Lancashire was in fact the home of a substantial machine building industry. A more precise picture of its size emerges from the survey of major manufacturing towns in Lancashire carried out by the Select Committee on the Exportation of Machinery in 1841. Although it did not distinguish between textile and non-textile enterprises, we can reasonably assume that a large part of the industry was producing textile machinery (see Table 3.4).

Table 3.4 *Mechanical engineering establishments in eleven Lancashire towns, 1841*

Location	No. of firms	Employment[a]	Capital (£000)	Horsepower employed
Manchester	26	5430	400	404
Salford and Patricroft	9	2520	240	244
Stockport	8	500	40	50
Ashton	8	1155	85	122
Rochdale	13	720	80	113
Burnley	5	210	30	40
Bury and Heywood	7	740	70	76
Bolton	7	2250	220	225
Preston	7	930	100	127
Blackburn	6	720	50	73
Oldham	19	2207	200	337
Total	115	17382	1515	1811

[a] Defined as 'Number of hands which each establishment is capable of employing'.
Source: *Select Committee on the Exportation of Machinery*, Vol. VII (1841), Appendix 2, p. 230

[28] A. Musson and E. Robinson, *Science and Technology in the Industrial Revolution* (Manchester, 1969), Ch. 13.
[29] Musson, 'Engineering industry', p. 91.   [30] *ibid.*, pp. 91, 94.

The 1851 Population Census of Great Britain showed approximately 48,000 workers engaged as 'Engine and Machine Makers', located mainly in Lancashire and Cheshire, the West Riding, London, Staffordshire, Warwickshire, Northumberland and Durham, and Lanarkshire and Renfrewshire.[31]

Moreover the textile component of the mechanical engineering industry grew solidly throughout the nineteenth century. Saul points out that:

in 1907 it was the largest single branch of engineering and an overwhelmingly dominant force in world trade. In 1913 about 40,000 men were employed, over three-quarters of them by six very large manufacturers of cotton machinery in Lancashire.[32]

Now of these six firms mentioned by Saul, it is important to note that four were founded before 1843, when the prohibitions on the export of machinery were repealed. Dobson & Barlow of Bolton and Asa Lees of Oldham were founded in the 1790s, Platt Brothers of Oldham in 1821, and John Hetherington of Manchester in 1837. Other important firms founded in the first half of the nineteenth century included Parr, Curtis & Madeley, who were described in 1851 as 'the most extensive makers of cotton spinning machinery in Manchester',[33] Sharp, Roberts & Co., who developed the automatic mule, and Fairbairns, who employed between 1,000 and 2,000 men. With the exception of Sharp, Roberts & Co., all of these firms were, as we shall see below, active in the development of the Norwegian textile industry after 1843.

The implications of the development of this substantial and active mechanical engineering sector, focussing on textile machinery, have been given surprisingly little attention by historians; as Saul noted, 'the neglect of textile engineering is puzzling: it hardly gets a mention anywhere, not even by Clapham'.[34] Indeed there is no full-scale economic history of the development of the capital goods industry in Britain. The relative neglect of the textile machine-making industry, and in particular of its international activities, which has only recently begun to be remedied in the works of, for example, Farnie, Kirk, and Saxonhouse and Wright,[35] is of considerable importance in limiting our understanding of the development of the British textile industry, and also of the history of its competitors. The basic reason for this, as noted in the previous chapter, is that the products of a specialized

31 *ibid.*, p. 98.
32 S. B. Saul, 'The market and the development of the mechanical engineering industries in Britain, 1860–1914', in S. B. Saul (ed.) *Technological Change: the United States and Britain in the 19th Century* (London, 1970), p. 142.
33 Musson, 'Engineering industry', p. 94.
34 Saul, 'Mechanical engineering industries', p. 142.
35 D. Farnie, 'Platt Bros. and Co. Ltd of Oldham, machine makers to Lancashire and the world', *Business History*, 23 (1981); Kirk, *Textile Machinery Industry*; G. Saxonhouse and G. Wright, 'New evidence on the stubborn English mule and the cotton industry, 1878–1920', *Economic History Review*, 2nd Series, 37, 4, pp. 507–19.

capital goods industry form, in effect, process innovations for the end-using industry. As Rosenberg has argued, this institutionalizes technological development and change as the province of a particular industry.[36] Both price and non-price competition within the machinery industry are likely to have marked effects on the technological level and capabilities of other industries using their machines and equipment. For that reason it seems reasonable to suggest that the development of such capital goods industries marks a crucial transitional phase in the development of industrial economies in general, and of Britain in particular, during the early nineteenth century. This can be thought of in terms of structural change within the manufacturing sector. But such a transition has wider economic effects, which derive from the fact that British machine-making firms did not confine their profit-seeking activity to Britain. As Mathias has put it:

The engineering industry had developed initially in the textile areas in response to the needs of the mill owners for machine builders and repairers. Many of the most famous firms had been completely sponsored in their early years in this way. But once specialized as an industry in its own right its leaders claimed the right to export markets of their own. Engineer after engineer argued thus before the Parliamentary Committees on the Export of Machinery in 1824 and 1843.[37]

In seeking markets abroad as well as at home such firms were led to develop and market their machinery and equipment in ways which made it possible for technically inexperienced foreigners to absorb, quite rapidly, a technology which had taken many years to develop in Britain. The effect of this was to expand the scope of industrialization and to accelerate its progress outside the UK. The long-standing neglect of these issues by historians is all the more strange when their importance in political and economic debate in early nineteenth-century Britain, particularly in the policy dispute over the export of machinery, is remembered. Berg has pointed out that:

The debate hinged on the recognition of machine making as the pivot of the whole system of production. Previously, free trade had always been conceived in terms of manufactured commodities. The actual process of manufacturing had not been looked on as the market product in its own right. Now contemporaries saw that the tools, machines, sources of power, and exportable consumer goods were also attractive in foreign markets.[38]

Subsequent historical studies on textile machinery have, as Kirk put it, 'exclusively focussed on the technical characteristics of the equipment to the neglect of the machinery-supplying industry'.[39]

The authors referred to above have all shown that British textile machine makers were very active in international markets. But the bulk of the

[36] See Footnote 53, Ch. 1, p. 21, above.   [37] Mathias, *First Industrial Nation*, p. 232.
[38] M. Berg, *The Machinery Question and the Making of Political Economy, 1815–1848* (Cambridge, 1980), p. 205.
[39] Kirk, *Textile Machinery Industry*, p. 3.

empirical studies of the engineering industry are concentrated on the late nineteenth and early twentieth centuries, and do not address the question of the impact of market-seeking by British firms on non-British economies during their early and mid-nineteenth-century industrialization. We still have no detailed description of the activities of British machine makers in any mid-nineteenth-century industrializing country, nor any account of how such countries were able to absorb and internally diffuse the new technology from Britain. It is these processes which are the focus of the remainder of this study, which will show, through a description of the process of technological diffusion between the British and Norwegian economies, that the internal transition noted above in the British economy was the basic facilitating process behind Norwegian textile industrialization.

4

ACQUISITION OF TECHNOLOGIES
BY NORWEGIAN TEXTILE FIRMS

The primary purpose of this chapter is to provide a detailed quantitative account of the scale of technology transfer, in terms of machinery and equipment supply, from Britain to the Norwegian textile firms studied here. Subsequent chapters will be concerned with how this transfer occurred, and with how technological problems within the diffusion process were solved.

The scale of technology transfer is established here in the following way. Using fire insurance records, I have assembled data which gives a detailed quantitative description of the evolving capital stock and complement of techniques accumulated by various firms within the Norwegian textile industry between 1845 and 1870, concentrating on machine stocks. That is, I use the fire insurance records first to establish the changing fixed capital of a number of firms. Then these fixed capital stocks are disaggregated into plant, power equipment, machines and so on. The machinery component of fixed capital is then further disaggregated into particular machine types – that is, preparatory and finishing, spinning and weaving equipment – for each firm. Finally, by referring to extant invoices and firms' purchase records, I establish the degree to which, for two of the bigger firms, these machine stocks consisted of imports from Britain. I show that, within a rapidly growing fixed capital stock, the growth of what I call 'direct production equipment' formed the predominant part, and that, with only extremely minor exceptions, this equipment originated in Britain. This leads to the conclusion that the scale of the diffusion of textile techniques from Britain to Norway was therefore very large.

We begin, however, with an outline description of the background and development of the Norwegian textile industry, and then descriptions of the particular firms which are examined in this study.

DEVELOPMENT OF THE NORWEGIAN TEXTILE
INDUSTRY[1]

As the previous chapter noted, Norway did not have a substantial domestic production of textiles in the pre-industrial period. High levels of imports

---

[1] This section draws on Grieg's pioneering narrative account of the Norwegian textile industry: S. Grieg, *Norsk Tekstil*, Volume 1 (Oslo, 1948).

meant that the putting-out system which played such an important role in other parts of Europe did not emerge in Norway, and the role of merchants in the establishment of the industry came not through putting-out but through their participation in factory-based enterprises.

However most of the early development of textile production in Norway occurred within state-owned enterprises, often involving the provision of work for convicts or paupers. Early establishments included the Correction and Manufacturing House (1682–1721) in Bergen, which produced for the army and was exempted from import duties on raw materials, the Christiania Linen spinnery (1785–1811), and the Enighedsfabrikken (1785–97) which was granted permission to import, duty free, a stocking frame from England in its first year of operation, and which taught women and children the art of spinning as well as providing a more general education. Probably the first

Table 4.1 *Formation of firms in the Norwegian textile industry*

Year	Names of firms
1813	Halden Spinnery
1814	Ludvig Mariboe (Lilleborg in 1829)
1818	Solberg Spinnery
1826	Haugvaldstad cloth factory
1835	Berner
1839	Svaes cotton weavery
1844	Bluhmer & Tschudy; Christiansen
1845	Wallem; Ellendalen Spinnery; Nydalen Spinnery; Rosendahl & Fane; Vøien; Heimbeck & Torkildsen; Vestfossen; Halstadelven; Lilloe (Høie in 1850); Myhrebøe; Frølich; Olseveveriet
1846	Arne Fabrikker; Schjølberg
1847	Sellegrod; Weil; Dahm; Høeg
1849	Brenneriveien; Christiania Mechanical Weavery; Nøsted; Brænne
1850	Lampe; Møller
1851	Hambro
1852	Hansen & Co; Hixon
1853	Rokken; Devold; Jørstad
1854	Mørch; Bergen Steam Weavery; Akerselven cloth factory
1855	Nicholaysen; A/S Fuglesangs Sønner
1856	Hjula Weavery; Foss Spinnery; Lillehammer; Christiania Sailcloth Factory; Breien
1858	Salhus
1860	Krog
1867	Leerfossen
1869	Kverndalen
1870	Aalgård

Source: Grieg, *Norsk Tekstil, passim.*

mechanized factory in Norway was the state-run Wool and Linen Manufactory at Kongsberg (1809–24). The preparatory and spinning machinery was constructed by a Mr Wilson, who had learnt his trade in Scotland. Working with him as a machine builder at Kongsberg was A. Gellertsen, who later became a director of the Solberg Spinnery, one of the firms which will be examined below. These are only a few of the state-run establishments prior to the 1840s; Grieg refers to fifteen such enterprises: one established in the seventeenth century, ten in the eighteenth century, and four between 1800 and 1832.

In the early nineteenth century, however, a number of small private textile firms were started. Grieg writes of twenty-nine firms established by 1845. Many were short lived, but among the few which survived were the Solberg Spinning Mill, which was established in 1818, and the Halden Spinning Mill established in 1813.

As noted in the previous chapter (see Table 3.1) the substantial growth of manufactured cotton imports to 1845 indicated the existence of a significant and growing market. Associated with this was the fact that from 1845 the number of entrants into the Norwegian textile industry grew sharply, as Table 4.1 indicates.

For such a small economy, this creation of fifty-four textile enterprises over half a century or so appears to be a very vigorous programme of enterprise formation, and suggests that Norwegian entrepreneurs grasped with alacrity the commercial and technological opportunities which opened up in the 1840s.

Output grew rapidly; as with Britain, a good indicator of changing output is raw cotton imports.[2] These also grew sharply from the mid 1840s as Table 4.2 indicates. The picture, therefore, is one of a rapidly expanding industry, both in terms of output growth and of numbers of firms. Since imports of

Table 4.2 *Norwegian imports of raw cotton, 1840–60 (tons)*

1840	138
1845	257
1850	797
1855	1202
1860	2053

Source: Statistisk Sentralbyrå, *Historisk Statistikk* (Oslo, 1968), Table 156, pp. 271–3.

---

[2] See, e.g., P. Deane and W. A. Cole, *British Economic Growth 1688–1959* (Second Edition, Cambridge, 1978), Table 15, p. 51; and N. F. R. Crafts, *British Economic Growth During the Industrial Revolution* (Oxford, 1985), Table 2.4, p. 23.

cotton manufactures ceased growing from 1845, and declined from the mid 1850s, a general process of import substitution is indicated.[3]

Firms and capital growth

Obviously a number of aspects of such growth could be discussed: economic preconditions and context, financial bases, and so on. But, since the focus of this study is on technological development, I want to go on to consider the technological basis of this output growth. The remainder of this chapter begins to address this question by examining the nature of the changing fixed capital stock of the industry, and the sources of supply of the machinery component of fixed capital. Rather than deal with the whole industry, however, I propose to concentrate on a limited number of firms. Various criteria have been used to select these firms. On the one hand they have been chosen to give a reasonable cross-section in terms of firm size, geographical location, and activity within the overall textile process. On the other hand, choice has been governed to some extent by the availability of source material, particularly concerning technology acquisition.

Since they will be referred to extensively in subsequent chapters, these firms will be described briefly here. They are as follows:

1 *Halden Spinnery* was established in 1813 in the Southern Norwegian border town of Halden, by the entrepreneur Mads Wiel. Wiel's family were engaged in the timber and shipping trades, and as merchants. He took an active interest in manufacturing processes, particularly those such as tobacco processing and rope making, where mechanization could be introduced into processes for which local demand was strong. The Halden factory was the first mechanized textile mill of a modern type in Norway; waterpowered, using machinery initially from the Danish firm of C. A. Nordberg, production began with cotton spinning in 1815. This was followed by wool spinning and dyeing two years later; subsequently the firm engaged in cotton weaving, stocking knitting, and the printing of English cloth. Wiel's death in 1835 was followed by an unsettled period during which ownership changed several times and production stopped for periods, although investment in new machinery continued to occur. In 1850 the firm was taken over by a consortium of four merchants, who undertook to sell only Halden-produced thread in their shops. Halden generally employed between fifty and sixty workers.

2 *Solberg Spinnery* was established in 1818, in the countryside outside the port of Drammen, about twenty-five miles south of Oslo on the Oslofjord. Initially there were four partners, three of whom were merchants and shopkeepers, while one, A. Gellertsen, was a machine builder and engineer

3 F. Sejersted, *En Teori om den Økonomiske Utvikling i Norge i det 19 Århundre* (Oslo, 1973), pp. 50–4.

who was at that time working at the state wool manufactory at Kongsberg. Gellertsen was soon required to give up this post because of his Solberg connection. The central figure in the firm was Haavald Helseth, and all of the early partners were associated with a dissident political and religious movement whose leader, Hans Nielsen Hauge, later became a partner in the firm. According to Grieg, the firm began as a kind of cooperative, with the partners supplying their own cotton, paying to have it spun, and selling it in their own shops. Early machinery was built by Gellertsen, though equipment was purchased from Cockerills in Belgium in the early 1840s. In the early 1820s production was low, with output of between 1,000 and 1,400 lbs of spun yarn per year. But the firm expanded sharply in the 1840s, and by 1846 was spinning 600 lbs of yarn per day. During the 1840s, Solberg employed twenty-five to thirty workers; from the late 1850s, sixty to seventy. The firm still exists, still uses its original nineteenth-century buildings, and is an extremely successful spinner and weaver of high-quality cotton fabric.

3 *Nydalen Spinnery* was established in 1845, on the Akerselven river running through Oslo, by Adam Hjorth, a merchant and shopkeeper, H. Gulbrandson, a merchant who undertook to sell the yarn produced in the factory, O. Gjerdrum, a civil servant, and Olav Roll, an engineer who designed the mill (and who also designed the Hjula works, to be discussed below). The technical side of the enterprise was largely in the hands of Hjorth, who had worked in a textile mill in Manchester, and who travelled frequently to England. Production began in 1847 with 7,000 water-powered spindles and 150 workers. By 1856 there were 450 workers, and by the mid 1870s, 740. The enterprise expanded steadily, and by 1856 had 21,000 spindles; production was generally of coarse-count yarns.

4 *Vøien Spinnery* was established in 1845 by Knud Graah, a Dane, who in the 1830s had come to Oslo where he worked in shops selling yarn and fabrics, and his brother-in-law N. O. Young, who was active in a range of manufacturing and processing enterprises such as distilling, brewing, rope making, tobacco processing and so on. He also owned two ships. They bought the property in 1844 and built the factory, which was water-powered. Graah subsequently took sole control, and managed the enterprise single-handed for sixty-three years. He visited England on a number of occasions and used English managers. The mill expanded steadily, from 2,400 spindles in 1846, to 5,544 ten years later, to 8,080 in 1868. From seventy workers at the outset, employment expanded to 120–50 during the 1850s and 1860s, and to about 200 by the mid 1870s. Production was mainly of low-count yarns and calicoes. Until 1856 Graah also owned a small weavery.

5 *Rosendahl & Fane*, established in 1845, began as a water-powered spinning mill with thirty-five workers, producing about 50,000 lbs of yarn per year. Later the firm diversified into weaving, and in 1860 into rope making. During

the 1850s the firm produced fish-net yarn, coarse thread, and rope. It normally employed between forty and eighty workers.

6 *M. B. Wallems Sønner* [M. B. Wallem and Sons] was established in 1845 in Bergen by two brothers, J. N. and Daniel Wallem. It lasted only four years, going out of business in 1848. Nevertheless it was the first important industrial enterprise in Bergen; in fact the mechanized rope production at Wallem led to a lawsuit from a surviving rope makers' guild. The factory was steam-powered, and produced fish-net and sailcloth yarn, and linen yarn, as well as rope.

7 *Arne Fabrikker* was established in 1846 by Peter Jebsen, who came from Schleswig to Bergen in 1842 and worked in textile retailing. He spent about six months in Manchester in 1845, and bought machines there with which he returned to Bergen. The factory began production as a water-powered weavery in 1846, with thirty-six looms; by the following year it had ninety-six, and a year later, 128. In 1849 Jebsen diversified into cotton and hemp, and in 1850 into dyeing and bleaching. Jebsen's brothers worked as managers for him, and he was active in railways and shipping, and in politics. In the mid 1850s the spinning mill was destroyed by fire, and the replacement mill of about 12,000 spindles became steam-powered. A second spinnery was built in 1863, and a new weaving mill in 1867. In 1863 Arne merged with the woollen firm Hansen & Co. Production began with 150 workers, and employment by the mid 1860s was 450.

8 *Brenneriveien Weavery* was established in 1849, and *Hjula Weavery* in 1856, both by the entrepreneur Halvor Schou. Schou came from a family prominent in Norwegian commercial life; in particular they owned a major brewery (which still exists). Schou was educated abroad, at a school for business in Lübeck, and began work for the family brewery; shortly afterwards he set up the Brenneriveien enterprise. Brenneriveien was, in effect, a pilot plant for the much larger Hjula operation; powered by a small 10 horsepower steam engine, it was engaged in cotton weaving and bleaching. Hjula, constructed between 1854 and 1856 on the Akerselven river in Oslo, was water powered, and operated on a much larger scale. Apart from the Brenneriveien equipment, and a range of new looms, Schou also installed seventy looms which he had bought from Knud Graah's weavery. After steady expansion, Schou diversified into cotton spinning, and from the mid 1860s into woollen spinning and weaving. Employment grew steadily from about 180 workers at the inception of the plant to nearly 600 by the mid 1870s. This integrated enterprise was one of the largest in Norway, and will form the centrepiece of the discussion in subsequent chapters. Besides his very active management of the Hjula enterprise, Schou was active in Norwegian public life on taxation committees, in railway promotion, and in government finance (he negotiated a major state loan, for example, with Baring Bros. in the mid 1850s).

9 *Christiania Sailcloth Factory* was established in 1856. Its early partners included O. M. Hauge, a leading merchant, who sold the products of the mill, Christian Brinch, a shipping entrepreneur, and H. Heyerdahl, who dealt with technical matters. Heyerdahl was an engineer who had worked in Britain on railway construction during the late 1840s. The factory produced sailcloth, linen yarn, fish-net yarn and also engaged in hemp spinning and rope making. By the early 1870s it had about 600 workers.

What follows is based on fire insurance records, from which it is possible to construct a picture of the net stock of equipment. Unfortunately the Norwegian industry lacks the estimates of spindleage and motive power which were collected in Britain under the provisions of the Factory Act of 1833, and lacks also the estimates by contemporary observers of working capital which can be found in Britain. Thus it is not possible to construct an account of the capital productivity of the industry of the kind pioneered by Blaug for the British industry.[4] But it is possible, however, to trace the contours of a major programme of technological diffusion.

Capital stock of the Norwegian textile industry

First, a description of the fire insurance records from which the capital stock estimates have been derived. These consist of protocols, currently held in official State Archives in Oslo and Bergen, compiled by Norges Brannkasse, the state-owned fire insurance corporation. In them the replacement value of new plant and equipment is specified. Firms could add to and subtract from their insured stock at any time, and most did this fairly frequently as their capital stocks grew. But the Brannkasse also required all firms to update their overall insurance cover (i.e. to respecify their entire insured stock) at ten year intervals, and this occurred, during the period of this study, in 1846, 1856 and 1866–7. Valuations were in Specie Daler, which had an exchange rate of approximately 4 SD = £1Stg through the period from 1845 to 1870. Interpretation of fire insurance records such as these is complicated by a number of well-known problems.[5] First, there is the question of whether or not valuations are realistic. This is perhaps not a serious problem since there are incentives for insurance enterprises not to over-value insured property, and for firms not to be under-insured. Then there is the problem of depreciation, which is usually treated in variously unsatisfactory ways in nineteenth-century insurance records and business accounts. Finally, there is the problem of the extent to which valuations reflect real magnitudes when price

---

[4] M. Blaug, 'The productivity of capital in the Lancashire cotton industry during the nineteenth century', *Economic History Review*, Second Series, 13, pp. 358–81.

[5] S. D. Chapman, 'The reliability of insurance valuations as a measure of capital formation', in J. Higgins and S. Pollard, *Aspects of Capital Investment in Great Britain, 1750–1850* (London, 1971), pp. 89–91.

levels are changing. In this case, with most of the equipment being imported and a roughly constant exchange rate, the appropriate price index(es) for deflating the capital stock series would have to be drawn from British machinery prices, which were rising during the boom years of the 1850s and fell during the 1860s; a precise index relevant to the Norwegian capital stock would be very difficult to construct. However, although all of these can be difficult problems where attempts are being made to estimate the real values of capital stocks, they are not necessarily serious where the aim is to depict relatively large and short-run changes in equipment stocks. It is the latter exercise which is carried out here.

Within the Brannkasse records, entries typically describe the insured items in some detail. However the entry for any particular year does not describe in full the entire insured stock of the firm: entries normally consist of additions to, and from time to time deletions from, the insured capital stock at the last entry, plus a total (that is, a figure which incorporates previous items). These totals, which were entered at irregular intervals, have been assembled in Table 4.3 which shows changing values of plant and equipment at intervals for various firms, in sterling.

The picture which emerges is of a rapid growth of capacity, with strong net investment taking place. However there are significant divergences between firms. The early established firms such as Halden and Solberg grew only slowly, while those established in the mid 1840s often grew very rapidly indeed; the Vøien enterprise almost doubled its insured capital stock between 1845 and 1850, and then doubled again over the following twenty years. The insured capital stock of the Hjula enterprise increased by over 75 percent in the fifteen years to 1870; Christiania Sailcloth grew by 25 percent in the 1860s, and by 78 percent between its foundation and 1870. Some firms grew by merger: Arne Fabrikker grew rapidly in the late 1840s and early 1850s, then contracted somewhat from 1857, but in effect doubled its size in 1863 by merging with the Hansen enterprise. A number of firms had fires during the period and found it necessary to reconstruct; with the Arne enterprise in 1853, and Halden and Solberg in 1854, it can be seen that this occurred rapidly, suggesting ready access to new equipment and finance. Table 4.3 covers firms engaged in different types of activities – spinning, weaving of sailcloth and domestic fabrics, and integrated activities – but even so there appears to be wide variation in the size of firms. Vøien and Solberg, for example, were both specialized spinning firms, yet Solberg's insured capital stock was less than half, for some periods less than a third, of Vøien's. Scale did not appear to have log-run effects on profitability; Vøien collapsed during the 1930s, whereas Solberg rode out the storm and still exists. (The Vøien mill itself, however, on a spectacular waterfall site, still exists; the main spinning rooms are now a fashionable restaurant.) Among the integrated firms, until its merger with Hansen, Arne was considerably smaller in scale than Hjula, as was the Rosendahl enterprise. These differences cannot, it

Table 4.3 Fixed capital stocks for eleven firms, 1845–70 (£ Sterling)

Year	Halden (1813)	Solberg (1818)	Nydalen (1845)	Vøien (1845)	Rosendahl (1845)	Wallem (1845)	Hansen (1852 later Arne wool)	Arne (1846)	Br.Veien (1849) Hjula (1856)	Christiania Sailcloth (1856)
1845				7050						
1846	3940	6975	7036			3245		1945		
1847			2572.5	9347.5				2805		
1848	4250(1)				3185					
1849								4022.5	3257.5	
1850								8870	3910	
1851				13910	3555				4740	
1852	5625	5000					1945	10462.5		
1853							1747.5 / 2700	2850 / 7785	6740	
1854	25	7500		18442.5		3680	3180	11435	7247.5	
1855'	5765(2)	9340(3)					12982.5 / 4952.5			
1856	6667.5(4)	5340		19827.5	4080		5060	12987.5	20845	

Table 4.3 (cont.)

Year	Halden (1813)	Solberg (1818)	Nydalen (1845)	Vøien (1845)	Rosendahl (1845)	Wallem (1845)	Hansen (1852 later Arne wool)	Arne (1846)	Br.Veien (1849) Hjula (1856)	Christiania Sailcloth (1856)
1857				21915				14022.5	21717.5	
1858		112227.5					5782.5			28505(5)
1859							7837.5	12837.5		40690
1860				23220			9180		26090	43592.5
1861				26714						38375
1862										4007.5
1863								24227.5		42331
1864				28013					30720.5	46123.5
1865									31650	48892.5
1866				29996	7005				33980	
1867	8490				9520					35264.5
1868		9387.5		29935	10367.5			24520	36982.5	49677.5
1869										
1870										50945

Horizontal lines indicate a merger or amalgamation.

Sources: *Brankassa, Branntakstprotokoller*, State Archives Oslo and Bergen, various volumes.

Plus: (1) *Fredrikshald Budstikke* 22 Oct 1848.

(2) *Smaalenenes Amtstidende* 14 Sept 1854. The two divergent entries for Halden occur because of a fire on 13 Sept 1854 which destroyed the entire plant. It was immediately reconstructed.

(3) The two entries for Solberg relate to a fire which destroyed one building in late 1853. The first valuation, of £7500, was in January 1854; the second, after rebuilding and reequipment, was in October.

(4) Loose note found in Halden archives.

(5) L. Thue, 'Fattigutter med to tomme hender?' in J. Myhre and J. Østbert (eds.), *Mennesker i Kristiania* (Oslo, 1979), p. 137.

seems to me, be ascribed easily to geographical location, to ownership or management types, or to differences in types of product (Solberg was for example producing similar counts of yarn to Vøien; Arne and Hjula had roughly similar product lines), and seem to suggest fairly wide variation in the efficient scale of operation.

The profile of machine acquisition

This section describes the particular types of machinery acquired by firms in the development of the Norwegian textile industry; I shall then go on to disaggregate the total capital stock figures into these broad equipment types. The technology of cotton manufacture involves four stages of production: preparatory, spinning, weaving and finishing. Analogous processes exist in woollen manufacture. These stages will be described briefly, since they govern the equipment requirements of enterprises.[6]

Stage one: preparatory
Within this stage raw cotton is first sorted and 'picked', i.e. has foreign bodies removed. It may then be dyed. This is followed by 'carding', a two part process in which the cotton fibre is brushed or combed into a roughly parallel alignment, and then made into a continuous rope or sliver. This is performed by hand, or mechanically with a 'carding engine'. This sliver is then stretched and doubled with a 'drawing frame' to make it more even, and it is then ready for spinning into yarn.

Stage two: spinning
A wide variety of techniques are then available to spin the cotton into a narrow twisted thread. The basic distinction is between intermittent spinning (using the jenny, the mule, or one of the mule derivatives) and continuous spinning (using the throstle or ring frame). Coarse and fine yarns differ in thickness and in number of twists per inch. The spun thread may then be bleached or dyed.

Stage three: weaving
In the weaving stage, the spun yarn is first prepared according to whether it is to be warp (that is, the strong length-wise threads which form the basis of the weave) or weft (that is, the yarn, carried by the shuttle, which forms the material of the woven cloth). Warps are strengthened by being sized; this is a mechanical process using various types of dressing machines. Wefts are appropriately packaged, then the cloth is woven on one of a very wide variety of looms. It can then be bleached or dyed.

---

[6] For a wider description of these processes and associated machinery, see D. Jeremy, *Transatlantic Industrial Revolution* (Oxford, 1981), pp. 5–7 and glossary, on which this section draws.

Stage four: finishing

For cotton goods the primary finishing process is printing with patterns of various colours. But there are other finishing processes based on altering the texture of the cloth. Warps or weft can be cut, to raise a pile, as in – for example – velveteen. Or the cloth can be hammered, using a 'beetling machine', which gives a linen-like appearance to the cloth. With a 'calender', heat and pressure are applied to produce a glazed finish. Finally, cloth would normally be pressed.

A wide range of machines and equipment were available to carry out these technical functions, as well as the many sub-processes which might be involved. It was by acquiring these machines, and the know-how to operate them, that Norwegian firms absorbed the new textile technology from the 1840s.

Against this background of particular processes within textile production, Table 4.4 examines the composition of the fixed capital stock for various Norwegian firms, particularly in terms of machinery types. I am concerned to establish the importance of direct production machinery, as opposed to buildings or power equipment, within the insured capital stocks. This can also be done using fire insurance sources. By examining the overall insurance revaluations which occurred, as noted above, at roughly ten year intervals, we can develop a picture of the internal composition of changing capital stocks. In Table 4.4 this is done for various firms for the years 1846, 1856 and 1867/8, in terms of the types of direct production equipment described above, plus power sources, ancillary equipment (such as boilers, belting, and so on), and buildings.

The final column of Table 4.4 calculates the percentage of the total fixed capital stock made up of direct production machinery and equipment. It is clear from Table 4.4 that the relative importance of machinery varied slightly between firms, in terms of the proportion it comprised of the total fixed capital stock. But in aggregate it is also clear that production equipment was the biggest single component of the fixed capital stock of the textile enterprises. Of a total fixed capital stock of £168,511 in 1867–8, just over 51 percent, or £86,198, comprised spinning machinery, looms, and preparatory and finishing equipment. The only firms exhibiting values markedly lower than 50 percent were Wallem in 1846 and Hjula in 1856, but in each case this is because the firm had only been recently established and buildings loomed large in fixed capital because the full complement of production equipment had not been built up. In later years, Hjula's machinery proportion grew to match those of other firms in the industry. The general conclusion to be drawn from this is that the acquisition of machine stocks was a major part of fixed capital formation in the Norwegian industry.

Table 4.4 Composition of fixed capital stocks for selected firms (£Stg)

Year/firm	Total	Prep&fin	Spin.mch	Looms	Water	Steam	Ancil.	Buildings	% Machines
1846–48									
Halden	3940	2032.5	750		250		157.5	750	70.6
Solberg	6975							1117.5	
Nydalen	7036	2196	1125		875	250	50	2542.5	47.23
Wallem	3245	992.5	295			330	90	1537.5	39.7
Rosendahl	3185	900	462.5	30	400		85	1307.5	43.7
Arne	1945	340			235		10	360	68.9
Vøien	9347.5			1000					
1856–58									
Halden	6667.5								
Solberg	11317.5	4712.5	2390		90	250	400	3027.5	62.8
Nydalen	n.a.								
Rosendahl	4080	1200	495	300	412.5		107.5	1565	48.9
Arne	12987.5	2530	1600	2740	575		925	4392.5	52.9
Vøien	19827.5	8605	5250		1125		762.5	3585	69.9

Table 4.4 (cont.)

Year/firm	Total	Prep&fin	Spin.mch	Looms	Water	Steam	Ancil.	Buildings	% Machines
Hansen & Co	5060	1330	300	687.5	125		372.5	2120	45.8
Hjula	20845	875		4012.5	450	225	2607.5	12112.5	23.5
Christiania Sailcloth	28505								
1867–68									
Halden	8490	2622.5	1250		1000		612.5	3005	45.6
Solberg	9387.5	3972.5	1887.5		862.5		215	2450	62.4
Nydalen	n.a.								
Rosendahl	9520	3305	1610		900		255	3435	51.6
Arne	24520	7272.5	1140	5802.5					60
Vøien	29935	10619	6905		900		3388	8130	58.5
Hjula	36982.5	8551	623.5	6927	600	162.5	5121	14946.5	43.5
Christiania Sailcloth	49677.5	14351	4945	4414	919	1150	10067	12710	47.7

Key:

Prep&fin:	Preparatory and finishing equipment	Water:	Water wheels, turbines and transmission equipment
Spin.mch:	Spinning machinery	Steam:	Steam engines and transmission equipment
Looms:	Looms	Ancil:	Ancillary equipment (e.g. belting, lathes, lighting, etc.)

Sources: *Branntakstprotokoller* [State Fire Insurance Records], State Archives, Oslo and Bergen, various volumes.

Sources of technology acquisition

Where did Norwegian textile firms acquire the machine stocks described above? From the early 1840s, imports of machinery into Norway accelerated, as Table 4.5 shows. A significant part of these imports originated in Britain, as Table 4.6 indicates. The two series cannot be compared directly, but with an exchange rate of approximately 15 Kr = £1 they suggest a British share of Norwegian imports varying between 60 and 90 percent. The important point here, however, is not simply the proportion originating in Britain but the sharp acceleration in machinery trade after 1843, which emerges clearly from both tables.

Table 4.5 *Imports of machinery by Norway, 1841–65*
(thousand Kroner)

1841	28
1847	93
1850	322

Source: Statistisk Sentralbyrå, *Historisk Statistikk 1968*, Table 156, p. 272

Table 4.6 *Machinery and millwork exports to Norway, 1843–50 (£)*

1843	1392
1844	2483
1845	9449
1846	15518
1847	5270
1848	5727
1849	4187
1850	12175

Source: *Parliamentary Papers*, 1854–5, LII, p. 226

The predominant British influence in Norwegian machinery imports remained for many years; Table 4.7 shows the British share of imports of machinery and steam engines for the fifteen years after 1850, and it can be seen that the British share remained consistently substantial.

The link between this machinery trade and the pattern of textile capital equipment acquisition described earlier in this chapter is that almost without exception the machine stocks of Norwegian textile firms were imported. It is possible to confirm this by tracing the purchase of specific machines. On the one hand this can be done using fire insurance records to note the acquisition

Table 4.7 *British share of Norwegian imports of machines and steam engines,*
1851–70 (Specie Daler)

Year	Imports from Britain	Total machinery imports	British share of total (%)
1851	20433	27842	73.4
1853	4455	5339	83.4
1854	n.a	42843	
1855	87950	108593	81.0
1856	119808	136494	87.8
1857	106967	119335	89.6
1858	37375	40412	92.5
1859	n.a.	82399	
1860	n.a.	168634	
1861	38929	48601	80.1
1862	49514	60183	82.3
1863	45277	66695	67.9
1864	55607	76349	72.8
1865	69684	96023	72.6

Sources: 1851–8: *Statistiske Tabeller for Kongeriket Norge*, Departementet for det Indre; 1859–65; NOS, *Tabeller vedkommmende Norges Handel og Skibsfart*, Departementet for det Indre.

of specific techniques; since entries normally consist of additions to the previously insured stock. This makes it possible to describe patterns of machine acquisition. This is done in Appendix A, which shows the detailed build-up of machinery, and is consistent with Table 4.4. But machine acquisition can also be traced through enterprise records, specifically through invoices, and this of course enables us to uncover exact sources of machinery supply. This is done, in Table 4.8, for two firms, Arne Fabrikker and Hjula Weavery, for which relatively complete invoice files remain. I have examined every single extant invoice to these firms, plus all correspondence referring to invoices or definite acquisitions and am thus able to trace the numbers and precise types of equipment purchased by these firms to 1870. The pattern of acquisition shown via these invoice records is broadly consistent with the fire insurance based Table 4.4 above, and with Appendix A.

Table 4.8 traces the acquisition of 673 items of all types of preparatory, spinning, weaving and finishing equipment over the period concerned. In addition there are nineteen other items of capital equipment, usually to do with power supply. Of this total of 692 pieces of equipment, no less than 689 are covered by invoices from British firms of textile engineers or machinery supplying agents. Two items came from Germany and one was domestically produced. Given British dominance of the world textile industry, pre-

Table 4.8 *Acquisition of textile techniques by Arne Fabrikker and Hjula Weavery, 1850–70*

	Looms	Spinning machines	Prep.&fin. and other textile machines	Total textile machines	Steam boilers	Steam engines	Turbines	Other machines and equipment
Hjula								
1850	40			40				
1851	14		4	18				
1852	6			6	1			
1853	52			52				
1854								
1855	37		1	38				
1856								
1857	12		2	14				
1858	27			27	1			1
1859	70		8	78				
1860	24		4	28				
1861								
1862	12		2	14				
1863	8	2	15	25				1
1864	4		4	4				
1865	8		8	16				
1866	9		3	12				
1867	4	1	9	14				
1868	4	2	8	14				1
1869	16			16				
1870	8	3	5	16				
Total for Hjula Weavery				432				

Total non-textile equipment: 5

Table 4-8 (cont.)

	Looms	Spinning machines	Prep.&fin. and other textile machines	Total textile machines	Steam boilers	Steam engines	Turbines	Other machines and equipment
Arne								
1855	10			10				
1856	8	5	14	27				
1857			4	4				
1858	10			10				
1859	20			20				
1860								
1861								
1862	32	2	12	14				
1863			25	57			2	1
1864	13	1	10	24	2		1	2
1865			(1 German) 3	3	(1 Norwegian) 2			
1866	10	2	4	16			1	1
1867	20	2	8	30	1			
1868	10		(1 German) 2	12				
1869			12	12			1	
1870			2	2				
Total for Arne Fabrikker				241				

Total non-textile equipment: 14

Sources: Firms' invoices, or correspondence confirming receipt, for years indicated; orders where receipt can not be clearly verified are not included.

dominance of British equipment among Norwegian imports might be expected, but this degree of technical dependence is nevertheless overwhelming. It indicates a *prima facie* case that the Norwegian textile industry was constructed through a major programme of technology transfer, or technological diffusion, from Britain to Norway. But what were the informational, organizational and human channels through which this transfer flowed? We turn to these questions in the following chapters.

5

FLOWS OF TECHNOLOGICAL INFORMATION

The process of equipment acquisition described in the previous chapter incorporated and was based upon flows of information concerning a wide range of technological developments and opportunities. This chapter begins the examination of these multi-faceted flows. For Norway, as for most late industrializing countries, three broad types of technological knowledge are relevant to the industrialization process. First, there is the transfer and dissemination of knowledge concerning the general range, scope and structure of technical advances being made abroad. This type of knowledge has its principal effect, it might be suggested, not so much through particular applications as through its role in the formation of a general industrial culture. Secondly, there is knowledge concerning the specific techniques which are available abroad. Finally, there is knowledge concerning the actual acquisition, construction (that is, setting-up), operation, maintenance and management of equipment.

Here we consider two important channels through which the first two of these types of knowledge spread into the Norwegian textile industry.

Information flows, particularly in the final category noted above, will remain an important theme of subsequent chapters, which will consider flows at a more detailed level, and the specific agents through which they occurred. But for the moment we are concerned first with Norwegian technical societies, and secondly with foreign travel by Norwegian entrepreneurs, as a means through which information on technical possibilities was diffused.

TECHNICAL SOCIETIES AND TECHNICAL LITERATURE

Perhaps the most important vehicles for the diffusion of general technical and industrial knowledge in Norway – as indeed in other countries – were the libraries, journals and educational activities of private technical societies, three of which were founded in the 1830s and 1840s.[1] They were:

[1] These societies are described in K. Fasting, *Teknikk og Samfunn. Den Polytekniske Forening 1852-1952* (Oslo, 1952), and B. Melby, *Oslo Håndverks- og Industri Forening* (Oslo, 1952).

1   *Christiania Håndverk Forening* (Oslo Crafts Society), founded in 1838.
2   *Den Tekniske Forening* (The Technical Society), founded in 1847.
3   *Polyteknisk Forening* (Polytechnic Society), founded in 1852.

In Kristiansand in 1848, P. J. Lilloe, a cotton entrepreneur who three years earlier had begun the enterprise which became the Høie mill, helped to found a craft society (the Kunstflidforeningen) with the aim of promoting domestic industry.[2] In later years, societies were founded in other parts of the country; the *Bergens Forelæsningsforening* (Bergen Lecture Society), for example, founded in 1868, carried out a modest programme of lectures of a popular character and set up a small library.[3]

The first of the Oslo groups, the Crafts Society, was founded with a political rather than a technical aim; it was a coalition of artisans, whose objective was to preserve such guild privileges as remained in Norway, and to prevent or at least contain the liberalization of trade and labour laws. In this the society failed utterly, since restrictions on entry to crafts were relaxed the very next year in the new Artisan Laws of 1839. The survival and subsequent influence of the society derived from its abandonment of its primary aim, and a concentration instead on the means through which it had hoped to achieve the aim. These, as set out in Article 2 of the Society's constitution, were 'To exhibit and lend generally useful and technical papers, drawings and models. Library. Meetings.'[4] Throughout the central decades of the nineteenth century the society kept up a modest programme of activity in these areas, until in 1871 falling membership encouraged it to merge with the more industrially oriented Teknisk Forening.

Founded in 1847, the Teknisk Forening was concerned not with craft production but with industrial processes, and with the implications for Norway of the new technology being developed abroad. The latter was specifically mentioned in the constitution of the group, which spoke of fostering 'Accessible and scientific lectures, exhibit of samples of first class Norwegian work, as well as the exhibition of foreign products which exemplify highly developed technique or which are suitable for production in Norway'.[5]

The original invitation to prospective members spoke in rather grandiose terms of furthering 'fruitful cooperation between science, practical insight, art and capital . . . to create the basis for the flowering of Norwegian society'.[6] In general the society attempted to extend knowledge of the new technology beyond those who might have been directly affected by it, and this was reflected in its membership, which included virtually the entire professoriate of the university, most of the ministers of the government, most of the higher

[2] O. Wicken, *Mustad Gjennom 150 År, 1832–1982* (Oslo, 1982), p. 9.
[3] A. Mohr Wiesner, *Bergens Forelæsningsforening 1868–1918 En femtiårsberetning* (Bergen, 1918), pp. 5, 14.
[4] Melby, *Håndverks-*, p. 26.   [5] *ibid.*, p. 31.   [6] *ibid.*, p. 32.

civil servants, and most of the municipal leaders and bigger businessmen. Industrial membership, although ostensibly confined to 'håndverksmestere', or craft masters, was also available to journeymen and apprentices, on the recommendation of a master. In 1848 the Teknisk Forening's membership of approximately 600 included 300 artisans, ten government ministers, fifty military officers (including several generals), and a number of artists. Significant numbers of the emerging entrepreneurial class were members, including most of the important textile and engineering entrepreneurs. Among those relevant to this study were Knud Graah (Vøien Spinnery), Adam Hjorth (Nydalen Spinnery), O. M. Hauge (Christiania Sailcloth Factory), Captain Steenstrup (Akers Mechanical Workshop), J. Jensen (Myrens Workshop), and O. Onsum (Kværner Workshop).[7] Two major textile entrepreneurs, Halvor Schou (Hjula Weavery), and H. Heyerdahl (Christiania Sailcloth), became members of the board in 1871, when the Håndverk Forening and the Teknisk Forening merged to become the Norsk Håndverk og Industri Forening (Norwegian Craft and Industry Society).

Apart from its general activities, the Teknisk Forening was distinguished by an active programme of exhibitions, which began with an invitation to potential exhibitors at its first meeting in 1848. The society took a central role in industry exhibitions in Christiania in 1851 and 1854 (at the latter, weaving techniques in particular were exhibited), and also arranged for Norwegian participation in world exhibitions in London, Paris and Stockholm in the 1850s and 1860s.

Perhaps the most important of the societies for the transfer of detailed technical information was the Polytechnic Society, founded in 1852. Its activities emphasized lecture courses for engineers and workers, and an extremely ambitious programme of publication. These activities were conducted, moreover, at quite an advanced level, and membership of this society thus required and generated a considerably higher level of specific technical competence than the Technical Society. Accordingly its membership was more restricted, rising from approximately fifty in 1852, to 150 in 1870, and to 600 by 1900. But its seventy-six members in 1863 included the textile entrepreneurs Graah, Hjorth, Heyerdahl and Schou.[8]

The Polytechnic Society conducted an active programme of meetings and lectures, averaging twenty-five meetings per year in the last half of the nineteenth century. By 1874, 287 meetings had been held on detailed aspects of the new technology, with most of the lectures being published either in the Society's journal *Polyteknisk Tidsskrift*, or in *Foreningsprotokollen* (the society's minutes).[9] Early meetings on textiles and engineering are shown in Table 5.1.

Reports from abroad were a characteristic part of the Polytechnic Society's work. It is important to note that, of the six founders of the society, five had significant foreign experience. Perhaps the most important was Oluf Roll, a

[7] *ibid.*, p. 32.   [8] *ibid.*, pp. 154–5.
[9] *Oppgave Over Foredrag og Diskussioner Den Polytekniske Forening (1854–1905)* (Oslo, 1905).

Table 5.1 *Some technical society meetings: textiles and engineering*

Year	Meeting No.	Topic	Publication
1855	21	Spinning materials	PT, pp. 270ff
1856	56	Further on spinning materials	PT, pp. 382ff
1857	70	Cotton and cotton spinning mills	PT (1858), pp. 14ff
1858	113	Portraits of Brunel and Stephenson	FPII (1859)
1863	152	Notes from a journey to England	PT, pp. 30ff
1863	154	Effects of heat on steam engines	PT, pp. 40ff

(PT = *Polyteknisk Tidsskrift*; FP = *Foreningsprotokollen*)

civil engineer educated not only in Oslo but also at the Hannover Polytechnic and the Ecole des Arts et Métiers in Paris; he went on to build the Hjula, Vøien and Nydalen textile mills.[10]

Among the formal aims of the society was the acquisition of a library of books and journals on technical matters. The contents of this library can be traced in two ways: first, early acquisitions can be found in the library of the Norwegian Technical Museum, which took over the society's library; secondly, later acquisitions were listed from time to time in *Polyteknisk Tidsskrift*. A range of works on engineering and textiles were acquired: Scott's *Practical Cotton Spinner* (1851), Templeton's *Millwrights and Engineers Companion* (1852), *The Engineer's and Machinists Assistant* (1843), (which contained 'plans, sections and elevations of steam engines, spinning machines, mills for grinding', etc.), various works by Ure, including *Recent Improvements in Arts, Manufacture and Mines* (1846), Appleby's *Illustrated Handbook of Machinery and Iron Work*, the American Engineering Society's *Collection of Drawings in Detail of the Most Approved Construction of American Machinery* (1852), and so on. Early journals included *The Artizan*, published from 1844, and *Appleton's Mechanical Magazine*. By the late 1860s the society was acquiring between forty and fifty books per year, and was subscribing to the *Proceedings of the Society of Engineers*, the *Proceedings of the Institution of Mechanical Engineers, Engineering*, and *The Civil Engineer and Architect's Journal*. Perhaps the most notable activity of the society was the publication of *Polyteknish Tidsskrift*, which came out fortnightly. This was a 'daring venture', since '... the early days were made difficult not simply by the undeveloped technical and industrial character of the country, but also by the limited number of people competent to understand the topics and issues addressed'.[11] Nevertheless the journal survived, subsidized for a time by a scientific society in Trondheim, and then by a stipend from the government from 1863. From 1859, the journal was paid to print patents for the

---

[10] *Teknisk Ugeblad*, 8 April 1902, p. 4.   [11] *ibid.*, p. 11.

government, although these grew only slowly from seven per year in 1859 to thirty per year by 1870. It is difficult to know to what extent the dissemination of patent information was important to the diffusion of new technology. Certainly few of the patents related to textiles; only five between 1857 and 1870, of which three are local patents for foreign processes (an Italian loom, a sewing machine, and a bleaching and dyeing process patented by William and John Banks of Manchester). In general, domestic innovative activity in textiles appears to have been low. The only name to appear which is related to any of the firms studied here is Jonathan Ballard, an Englishman who worked at the Vøien mill, who was granted a patent for a method of joining broken leather straps in 1862.[12] More important, perhaps, were the foreign reports carried in *Polyteknisk Tidsskrift*. Over the last fifty years of the nineteenth century there was hardly an issue which did not carry a report on foreign news, or a description of some foreign development, or a translation of a foreign article. These ranged from general accounts of developments in the UK, such as a survey of the cotton industry in 1854 (reprinted from *Literary and Scientific Monthly Lectures*), or a consideration of thirty years of technical development (translated in 1864 from a speech to the Institute of Civil Engineers in England), to quite specific discussions of dyeing techniques, or new sewing machinery (with drawings).[13]

A final important activity of the Polytechnic Society was its advocacy and lobbying for a state-supported system of technical education. In 1865, for example, it proposed to the government the setting up of a Polytechnic School;[14] this matter was raised again as a formal proposal in 1868 and 1871.[15] The society's case, which was unsuccessful until the 1870s, was based on the argument that Norway's need for skilled manpower was not being met, and that there was in effect excess demand for technically skilled people: 'The real need for a polytechnic school can be seen from the fact that each year a large number of men from this country go to technical-scientific schools abroad, and that all, after completing courses and returning, immediately find jobs.'[16]

With the possible exception of some activities of the Polytechnic Society, it appears that the role of the technical societies in the diffusion of the new technology was mainly within the first of the types of information flow outlined above. That is, they transmitted information concerning the general nature and scope of technical development abroad. Although from time to time specific technical developments and topics were discussed, these were by no means sufficient to transmit a working knowledge of the technology of a particular industry. The lecture and publication programmes of the societies were in general of wide scope rather than of narrow focus. By disseminating

12 *Polyteknisk Tidsskrift*, September–October 1862, p. 160.
13 *Polyteknisk Tidsskrift*, 17, 19 October 1854; September–October 1862; Second issue, 1864; second issue, 1865.
14 *Polyteknisk Tidsskrift*, 1878, p. 5.   15 *Teknisk Ugeblad*, 8 April 1902, p. 5.
16 *Polyteknisk Tidsskrift*, 12, 1854, p. 190.

such information within a fairly heterogeneous but socially influential group of members – including some in positions of authority and influence – their primary contribution appears to have been the creation of a general awareness of the importance of industrial culture and development, rather than the development of specific technical skills. This accords with David Jeremy's argument that, for the United States, 'inanimate sources of technical information were inadequate as a vehicle of technology diffusion' prior to 1830. The main reason for this was that publications, even when quite detailed, often omitted important operating information. This 'forced Americans to rely more on immigrant artisans than on any other method of transferring the technology'.[17] As we shall see, this experience was replicated, fifty years later, in Norway. But that should not imply that the flow of general technical information was unimportant.

FOREIGN TRAVEL BY NORWEGIAN ENTREPRENEURS

In the early years of the nineteenth century, the embryonic Norwegian textile sector obtained technical information and equipment primarily through Denmark, Sweden and Belgium. Much of this was presumably an indirect flow from Britain, which was the major source of technical developments in those countries. The role of such figures as William Cockerill, for example, in the development of Belgian textile production is well known.[18] Cockerills were in fact important suppliers to early Norwegian enterprises; a director of Solberg Spinnery, H. Helseth, visited Cockerill plants in Belgium and Holland in 1841, and ordered equipment from the firm.[19] The following year Helseth visited the Nääs spinning mill in Sweden. An early Norwegian plant, the Halden Spinnery, which was founded in 1814, looked to the Nordberg machine-making firm in Copenhagen, not only for information and machines, but also for skilled workers and engineers, such as Gellertsen, who became a founder director of the Solberg Spinnery.

This state of affairs changed fairly dramatically in the 1840s, however, as Norwegian entrepreneurs began to look directly to Britain for the supply of equipment and technical information. This led to a series of visits to Britain by virtually all of the important Norwegian textile entrepreneurs in search of information and the new technology.

Of course by the mid nineteenth century, visits to Britain were a well-established part of European entrepreneurial practice – the 'grand tour' in reverse, as it were.[20] As Robinson put it, referring to the late eighteenth century:

[17] D. Jeremy, *Transatlantic Industrial Revolution* (Oxford, 1981), p. 72.
[18] See, e.g., D. Landes, *The Unbound Prometheus* (Cambridge, 1978), pp. 158–9.
[19] H. Helseth, *Hovel Helseths Selvbiografi* (Oslo, 1924), p. 25.
[20] P. Mathias, 'Skills and the diffusion of innovations from Britain in the eighteenth century', in *The Transformation of England* (London, 1979).

Prussian, Bavarian, Hanoverian nobles, Russian princes and counts, French marquises, and a medley of Swedes, Danes, Portuguese and Spanish notables pushed their way into Birmingham button factories, swooped elegantly round chemical works, paper mills, munitions foundries or shipyards, and reported their findings back to their ministers at home.[21]

Norwegian business travel was firmly part of this wider European practice. The Norwegian parliament specifically discussed such visits, and agreed on their desirability, in 1836 and again in 1854; accordingly they directly subsidized such visits with stipends. The stipends were available, however, only to those who could not otherwise afford the trip; Halvor Schou, of Hjula Weavery, travelled at his own expense. He took the view that the stipends, even where they were available, were too small. Writing in the newspaper *Morgenbladet* in 1873, he argued that they were an example of the government's 'half measures', and argued that 'the step ought fully to be taken ... when such stipends are too small, they do not fulfil their purposes'.[22] Nevertheless, with few exceptions, the entrepreneurs behind the enterprises studied here visited England, often very frequently, from the 1840s. Early in his career, for example, Halvor Schou began to visit the UK, and between 1854 and 1870 there are only four years in which his correspondence files do not refer to a visit. These files contain a voluminous correspondence with about twenty British firms with whom Schou had direct contact during his journeys. As far as can be ascertained, he was the most frequent visitor to England of the Norwegian entrepreneurs, although this appearance may simply derive from the fact that his correspondence archives are more complete than those of other entrepreneurs.

In some cases visits to England appear to have played a central role in decisions by Norwegian entrepreneurs to enter the textile industry in the first place. Adam Hjorth, of the Nydalen Spinnery, began his career working in a shop, travelling abroad for the owner, presumably on purchasing trips. It has been suggested that this brought him into contact with the British textile industry, and sparked his ambitions in this field. In 1845 he visited Manchester, on what Grieg suggests was his second trip to England, specifically to study cotton manufacture.[23] Haugholt writes that Hjorth spent 'a period as a common worker', presumably at this time.[24] Also during this visit he met, for the first time, another fledgling Norwegian entrepreneur, Knud Graah of the Vøien Spinnery.[25] Like Hjorth, Knud Graah had worked in Oslo before visiting Manchester earlier in the 1840s; '... it was during this trip, under the

---

[21] E. Robinson, 'The transference of British technology to Russia, 1760–1820: a preliminary survey', in B. M. Ratcliffe (ed.) *Great Britain and Her World 1750–1914* (Manchester, 1975), p. 3.

[22] Quoted in S. Grieg, *Norsk Tekstil, Vol. 1* (Oslo, 1948), p. 573.   [23] *ibid.*, p. 293.

[24] K. Haugholt, *Aftenposten*, 17 August 1963.

[25] O. Mørch, *A/S Knud Graah & Co.og A/S Vøiens Bomuldsspinderi 1846–1921* (Oslo, 1921), p. 13.

munication'.[55] The travel patterns of Norwegian textile entrepreneurs, on the other hand, appear to have been predominantly a matter of the second category of technical information flow; they suggest a widespread awareness not only of the general trend of technical development in the UK but also of the economic implications of those trends. More importantly they disclose an awareness of the commercial possibilities of the new technology, and a willingness to search out particular techniques. Visits by Norwegian entrepreneurs appear to have been focussed fairly narrowly on specific technical issues, and for that reason to have been a fruitful channel for the diffusion of innovations. But, even so, that in itself was not enough to actually set the new technology into operation; that required actual acquisition as well as considerably more detailed information flows, capabilities and skills relating to the setting up and operation of technologies. I turn now to how these specifically technological problems were solved.

[55] Quoted in N. Rosenberg, 'Economic development and the transfer of technology: some historical perspectives', in *Perspectives on Technology* (Cambridge, 1977), p. 155.

(and the surrounding district) and Hull, followed by Antwerp and Riga on the way home. (The firm had purchased spinning equipment in Antwerp in 1845, and one of the partners, C. Christiansen, lived there.) He particularly sought a water wheel, and obtained estimates from James Lille & Son of Manchester, from Wren & Berend, from Fairbairn & Co., and from S. and I. Witham. From Leeds he wrote to Christiansen that 'I have made enquiries in workshops in Manchester and places around', and that the Witham quotation, which was by far the lowest, was 'recommended by various mill owners (I asked them), so I have ordered a water wheel with axle wheel for £204'.[33] A week later he wrote that he had bought a carding machine and other equipment, 'because several spinning mills have lately stopped working and one can get machines quite cheap'. In fact his list also included a fifty-six spindle spinning machine, a polishing machine, a lathe, and a substantial quantity of ancillary equipment – cards, eleven gross of bobbins, belting and so on, a total of thirty-five separate items. He was accompanied throughout the visit by an English foreman called Booth, who appears to have made the purchasing decisions; in a letter to his brother from Leeds, Rosendahl remarked that: 'I have had no reason to be dissatisfied with Booth, and I hope to be able to send him back again.'[34] This visit led to a further range of purchases, from a number of firms, which will be discussed in the next chapter.

The establishment of the Wallem firm was also preceded by an important visit to the UK in mid 1845, during which Wallem acquired most of the equipment needed for his mill. During this visit Wallem kept a small notebook and diary, in which his objectives and tasks were set out, and in which details of purchases and contracts were noted down. The list of approximately fifty items to be covered included first a wide range of machinery and equipment acquisition, including a steam engine with piping and transmission equipment, a winding machine, and various types of ancillary equipment. A later entry in the notebook, written in excellent English and in a hand other than Wallem's, sets out in considerable detail the specifications of 'one high pressure engine of 8 horse power' to be obtained from Richard Armitage & Co. of Huddersfield. This entry covers six pages of the notebook, and is very complete; every major component is noted and underlined, and its function described. It is, in short, a full working description of a Watt-type engine, and could only have been written by a skilled engineer, almost certainly English. One possibility is that it was drawn up by someone at the Leeds firm of Taylor Wordsworth & Co., who acted as agents for Wallem.[35]

Next, Wallem lists various types of information which he required: 'draw-

---

[33] *Rosendahl Papers*, Correspondence in, H. O. Rosendahl, 18 May 1846 (from Leeds); 19 May 1846 (Leeds); 23 May 1846 (Leeds); 25 May 1846; 4 June 1846 (Leeds); 30 June 1846 (Hull).

[34] *Rosendahl Papers*, Correspondence in, H. O. Rosendahl, 19 May 1846; 26 May 1846.

[35] The role of Taylor Wordsworth & Co. will be discussed in more detail in Chapter 7 below.

ings of spinning machines and machinery', 'how the heckling is done', 'get a clear drawing of every machine', 'which of the machines should be first set up – the steam engine, the boiler or the spinning machine?', 'how much will each spindle of my machinery be able to produce daily of each sort of the samples which are in the box?', 'drawings of how the rooms for the heckle, steam engine and spinning should be divided, and how the machines are all to be placed', 'where to get lamps for lighting the spinning rooms in winter – how to place them?', 'to travel to Wakefield to see how the winding machine is used', 'what each machine daily produces', and so on. Then come various items concerned with the hire of English workers: 'get the contract set up with Fothergill', 'same with the machine master', 'same with the girls'. Two notes cover the need to find out about the level of wages in Leeds, and wage rates for different types of yarn spinning. Later the notebook contains, in the same hand in which the specifications of the steam engine were described, a draft contract for Fothergill:

Mr Fothergill has promised
(1) to go into my service as soon as I want
(2) to dwell, continue and abide there one year and six months from the date I ask him to set out from Newcastle to Bergen and during the said term to serve me well diligently and faithfully as overlooker and manager of a hemp and tow spinning establishment.[36]

Fothergill's role, which will be described in more detail in a later chapter, included erecting and fitting up machinery, and instructing both Wallem and his workers in the techniques of spinning hemp and flax. While in England Wallem purchased a number of books on technical matters, including *The Practical Flax Spinner, The Steam Engine*, a book on spinning, and Ure's *Dictionary*.[37]

Wallem's reliance on skilled labour from England was shared by other Norwegian entrepreneurs, and an important aspect of visits was the opportunity they afforded to interview skilled workers for prospective employment in Norway. In 1845, for example, Adam Hjorth not only purchased machinery, but also hired skilled workers, 'to teach the Norwegian workers'.[38] Rosendahl engaged English workers during his visit in 1846.[39] In 1864 William Sharp & Sons of Cleckheaton arranged for Schou to interview a dyer and a finisher, and then arranged further interviews in 1868 and 1870.[40]

Visits to England for the inspection and purchase of equipment were not necessarily confined to the setting-up period of Norwegian enterprises, but continued to be made in order to keep up with technical developments and to

---

[36] *Wallem Papers, Notebook and Diary 1845–6, passim.*
[37] *Wallem Papers, Kopibok,* January 1845.
[38] S. Grieg, *Norsk tekstil, Vol. 1*, p. 294.
[39] *Rosendahl Papers,* Correspondence in, H. O. Rosendahl, 4 June 1846.
[40] *Hjula Papers,* Correspondence in, Sharp & Co., 4 May 1865, 13 October 1868. Correspondence out, *Kopibok,* Jan–June 1870, Richardson & Co., 23 April 1870.

purchase further equipment. Thus Fuglesang, a director of Solberg Spinnery, visited Manchester to buy machines in 1846, some twenty-eight years after the founding of the firm. And Schou, for example, wrote to Parr, Curtis & Madeley in 1858 that: 'I have notice of the new "drop box loom" that you intend to bring onto the market ... I shall have to go over on a short visit to your place next year ... to see what improvements have been made in the weaving department of late.'[41]

In 1859, presumably on the visit referred to above, Schou visited the Anderston Foundry in Glasgow, who in turn arranged for him to see one of their check looms working in the Lancefield Spinning and Weaving Company. In subsequent correspondence the possibility was raised of recruiting a skilled finisher from this mill.[42] These 'demonstration' visits were not only organized through machine makers, but also through cotton suppliers such as the Manchester firm of Hvistendahl, Holst & Co., who several times offered to arrange visits for Schou.[43] From time to time, Schou would visit England with specific technical needs. In 1863, for example, he visited Hvistendahl, Holst & Co., seeking new patterns.[44] During the same visit Schou sought and obtained from the agent George Denton technical details concerning the finishing of woollen fabrics; this was amplified in later correspondence, which included details of necessary equipment, with prices.[45] In subsequent correspondence, Denton kept Schou up to date with developments in woollen techniques, referring several times to the need for further visits. Since raw material prices had significant effect on costs and competitiveness, Schou used his visits to discuss prospective conditions in the Liverpool cotton market with those who purchased there on his behalf, so as to achieve the most effective timing of his raw material purchases.[46]

An interesting by-product of visits to England was that they sometimes kept Norwegian entrepreneurs in touch with the activities of their own domestic competitors. Thus, in 1863, the Rochdale firm of Edmund Leach wrote to Schou referring to his recent visit, and giving him details of equipment supplied to Peter Jebsen of the Arne Factory.[47] From time to time there was direct cooperation among Norwegian entrepreneurs concerning visits to Britain. I have referred above to the planned meeting between Rosendahl and Jebsen in 1846, and also to Adam Hjorth's time in Manchester in 1845. His subsequent journeys on behalf of Nydalen are difficult to trace, since only a tiny part of the Nydalen records has survived. From these sources we know that the director O. Gjerdrum visited England in

41 *Hjula Papers*, Correspondence out, *Kopibok, May 1855–December 1859*, 20 September 1858.
42 *Hjula Papers*, Correspondence in, Anderston Foundry, 2 August 1859.
43 e.g., *Hjula Papers*, Correspondence in, Hvistendahl, Holst & Co., 17 November 1864.
44 *Hjula Papers*, Correspondence in, Hvistendahl, Holst & Co., 2 July 1863.
45 *Hjula Papers*, Correspondence in, G. Denton, 2 July 1863.
46 *Hjula Papers*, Correspondence in, G. Denton, 28 January 1864.
47 *Hjula Papers*, Correspondence in, Edmund Leach & Sons, 11 August 1863.

1858 and 1859, and that Hjorth visited in April 1868.[48] However it is possible to follow some of Hjorth's other travels, because he acted occasionally for other Norwegian firms, notably the Solberg Spinnery. Here more of the records are extant, and correspondence with Nydalen refers to visits to England by Hjorth in 1852, 1853, and 1854, with repeated requests for technical assistance and advice.[49] In 1859 Halvor Schou arranged a letter of introduction for Hjorth to John Harrison & Sons, machine makers of Manchester, saying that 'he will call on you to discuss the heald knitting machine'.[50] In the late 1860s, Solberg again wrote to Hjorth in England, asking him to arrange the purchase of raw materials, machines and parts.[51] Like Hjorth, Knud Graah – who had also been in Manchester in 1845 – continued to visit England, sometimes in company with other Norwegian entrepreneurs; Hvistendahl, Holst & Co. in a letter to Schou in September 1864, remarked that 'Peter Pettersen [of Nydalen spinnery], Gjerdrum [also of Nydalen], and Graah return to Scandinavia after a two week stay here'.[52] Some years before, in 1858, Gjerdrum had chosen and purchased machinery for the Solberg director Fuglesang, who had since set up the Nøsted mill.[53]

It is important to note that some British machine builders visited Norway to see their customers direct: Curtis, of Parr, Curtis & Madeley, visited in July 1857, Thomas Broadbent sent 'a traveller' who visited Schou at about the same time, and Hetheringtons certainly planned a visit, though there is no evidence that it actually took place.[54]

CONCLUSION

It was suggested above that three broad types of technical information flow were important to the diffusion of industrial techniques. They concerned, firstly, information on the scope of developments abroad, secondly, information on the existence and availability of particular techniques, and finally on the complex technical knowledge concerned with the actual setting-up and operating of techniques. In the Norwegian case the activities of the technical societies described above are probably best seen in terms of the first of these distinctions. Technical societies appear at best to have conveyed a somewhat general sense of the scope of developments abroad, which is consistent with Svennilson's view 'that only a part, and mainly the broad lines, of technical knowledge is codified by non-personal means of intellectual com-

[48] *Nydalen Papers*, Correspondence in, Fuglesang, 7 June 1858; J. Curtis, 18 May 1859.
[49] *Solberg Papers*, Correspondence out, *Kopibok 1851–57*, 2 November 1852; 19 August 1853; 13 June 1854.
[50] *Hjula Papers*, Correspondence out, *Kopibok May 1850–Dec 1859*, 23 May 1859.
[51] *Solberg Papers*, Correspondence out, *Kopibok*, 23 April 1867; 25 March 1868; 15 June 1869.
[52] *Hjula Papers*, Correspondence in, Hvistendahl, Holst & Co., 22 September 1864.
[53] See footnote 49 above.
[54] *Hjula Papers*, Correspondence out, 11 August 1857; 12 June 1857; October 1856 n.d.

munication'.[55] The travel patterns of Norwegian textile entrepreneurs, on the other hand, appear to have been predominantly a matter of the second category of technical information flow; they suggest a widespread awareness not only of the general trend of technical development in the UK but also of the economic implications of those trends. More importantly they disclose an awareness of the commercial possibilities of the new technology, and a willingness to search out particular techniques. Visits by Norwegian entrepreneurs appear to have been focussed fairly narrowly on specific technical issues, and for that reason to have been a fruitful channel for the diffusion of innovations. But, even so, that in itself was not enough to actually set the new technology into operation; that required actual acquisition as well as considerably more detailed information flows, capabilities and skills relating to the setting up and operation of technologies. I turn now to how these specifically technological problems were solved.

[55] Quoted in N. Rosenberg, 'Economic development and the transfer of technology: some historical perspectives', in *Perspectives on Technology* (Cambridge, 1977), p. 155.

6

BRITISH TEXTILE ENGINEERING AND THE NORWEGIAN TEXTILE INDUSTRY

This chapter traces some key relationships between Norwegian textile enterprises and British suppliers of machinery and ancillary equipment who provided the technology on which the Norwegian industry was based; the objective here is to evaluate the interaction between these two industries in terms of its significance for Norwegian textile industrialization. The question asked, therefore, is what were the roles of, and the technological functions performed by British textile machinery makers in the development of the Norwegian textile industry?

Showing the importance of British machine makers for Norwegian industrialization involves two things. First, I shall demonstrate that the extent of the relationship between the two industries was large. This is of interest in itself, for it suggests that the existence of the British industry, and its active foreign role, was a necessary condition for the development of the Norwegian industry. As I showed in Chapter 4, the textile technology flow was large in relation to the size of the capital stock of the Norwegian industry, but it is also of great importance that a very large number of British firms were involved in this technology flow. At the same time, the substitution possibilities were limited or non-existent. No non-British economy had a textile machine-building capacity to compare with Britain's, and it is difficult to see how Norwegian entrepreneurs could have looked elsewhere for technology supplies on the same scale. Without the transfer of technology through British machine makers, therefore, Norwegian firms would simply not have been able to enter the business.

Secondly, there is the question of the scope or content of the relationship between Norwegian firms and British suppliers. The point at issue here can be approached in terms of a difficulty in neoclassical economic theory. In neoclassical theory the technological capabilities of firms are not in themselves a problem; firms are simply assumed to know the production set, and their problem is to select, out of all available techniques, that which maximizes profits given present and anticipated factor prices. 'Choice of technique' in the neoclassical approach is a matter of calculation, not a matter of technical capability or competence. But it can be argued that the real-world technical problem faced by firms is a great deal more complicated than this.[1] Actually being able to acquire and operate a technology requires the development of skills, capabilities and knowledges within a number of functional areas, which are moreover linked in more or less complex ways. The collection and assessment of information are central to this. For example, firms must engage in search activity in order to know something of the content and bounds of the production set. Once they have discovered the existence of new techniques they must be able to evaluate them, which involves not only strictly technical knowlege but also price and cost information, some of which may have to be developed or estimated internally. (The apparently simple matter of how much a machine should produce, for example, cannot be separated from the managerial and operative skills of the firm.) They must possess the specific technical skills required to construct and operate new equipment, which was no minor problem in early industrialization; the Arkwright technology was available in both Germany and the USA by 1780, but in neither country was it possible to construct, let alone operate, the machines with locally available workers.[2] And, since labour is no more a homogeneous commodity than capital, firms must understand, acquire and manage the types of labour required for particular machines. Furthermore, when a new enterprise is being set up, firms must acquire appropriate technological skills, not just for individual techniques, but for groups of techniques simultaneously, involving a coordinating managerial function. This suggests questions about whether the supply of machinery by British firms also involved the supply of such technological skills.

Now in all of the technical functions noted above, emerging Norwegian enterprises faced severe difficulties. Many entrepreneurs lacked technical skills and experience. Mads Wiel at Halden, the earliest 'Manchester factory', relied on imported engineering expertise; Wallem, whose notes on his visit to England in 1845 were discussed in the previous chapter, required the most elementary technical information, and his imported workers were required by contract to teach him how to run his plant.[3] In Chapter 4 it was indicated that most entrepreneurs came from backgrounds in retailing.[4] This in practice led to a heavy dependence on British machinery makers and suppliers in the various functional areas described above, and it is through this that the British mechanical engineering sector had its overwhelming influence on Norwegian textile development. The remainder of this chapter will describe first the scale of British mechanical and textile engineering activities in Norway, and

[1] For a general critique of the neoclassical approach, see R. Nelson and S. Winter, *An Evolutionary Theory of Economic Change* (Cambridge, Mass., 1982).

[2] See, e.g., D. Jeremy, *Transatlantic Industrial Revolution* (Oxford, 1981), p. 76, and J. Lee, 'Labour in German industrialization', in P. Mathias and M. Postan (eds.) *The Cambridge Economic History of Europe*, Vol. VII (Cambridge, 1978), p. 451.

[3] Wallem's contract with Fothergill (see p. 65 above) required Fothergill 'to instruct me into the full use and management of such machinery and disclose and point out to me the proper manner of conducting, working and spinning . . .'. *Wallem Papers, Notebook and Diary, 1845–6.*

[4] See pp. 40–3 above.

secondly the scope or content of these activities. The picture which is presented is essentially a disaggregated one, based on invoice records, inward and outward correspondence, works journals, and records of directors meetings. These are most complete for the Hjula Weavery, and, for a picture of how the relationship with the British textile engineering sector affected the Norwegian enterprise, I shall concentrate predominantly – but not exclusively – on that firm. As I have noted above, Hjula became an integrated enterprise, combining spinning and weaving in both cotton and wool. Prior to setting up Hjula in 1856, its owner-manager Halvor Schou had been involved in the smaller Brenneriveien weavery from 1849, and he was therefore active in the textile industry over most of the period of this study.

THE SCALE AND EXTENT OF CONTACTS

I showed in Chapter 4 – see Tables 4.5, 4.6 and 4.7 in particular – that Norway was an importer of machinery during the mid nineteenth century. Annual values of machinery imports rose from 72 thousand Kroner in 1843 to 93 thousand in 1847, and then to a mean of 368 thousand Kroner between 1850 and 1865. In Chapter 4 it was shown that a significant part of these imports consisted of textile equipment which made up approximately 50 percent of the fixed capital stock of the industry. The extent of the contacts between British and Norwegian enterprises which underlay this trade can be traced through extant correspondence, invoices, works journals and records of directors' meetings. Appendix B lists all British enterprises of all types who left some trace in the records of Norwegian textile firms before 1870; these firms included financial institutions, shipping firms, agents, suppliers of ancillary equipment and raw materials, as well as textile engineers and machinery makers. A total of 330 British firms were involved, divided among the above categories as shown in Table 6.1.

Table 6.1 *Numbers and types of British firms active in Norwegian textile industry to 1870*

Textile engineers	86
Raw material suppliers	59
Agents	28
Ancillary equipment suppliers	101
Other	55
Total	329

Source: Drawn from Appendix B

For most firms the extent of contacts with British firms was large. From invoices and correspondence sources it can be shown that between 1856 and 1870 Hjula Weavery had some kind of commercial contact with at least 162

British firms, of which forty-four were machinery makers. Arne Fabrikker in Bergen had contacts with 112 British firms, thirty-two being machine makers; the earlier Bergen firm of Wallem had twenty-five contacts, four being machine makers. Solberg dealt with twenty-eight British firms, only two or three of which made machinery (although these were important suppliers). Solberg was not alone in conducting much of its business with relatively few machine makers; Nydalen had links with eight machine makers, Halden Spinnery with three and Christiania Sailcloth with two. However two points should be emphasized about firms with apparently few British contacts. First, in each case, the surviving records are seriously incomplete; we are dealing therefore with deficient data, and it is likely that contacts were wider than indicated by existing sources. Secondly, an important aspect of the operation of the Norwegian industry – which will be described and discussed in a later chapter – was a form of interaction between Norwegian companies which involved one firm or entrepreneur dealing with foreign suppliers on behalf of others. Thus firms such as the Foss spinning mill and Akerselvens Kledefabrikk maintained contacts with the UK through Halvor Schou and Hjula Weavery. More significantly, perhaps, Adam Hjorth of Nydalen and the Jensen brothers (of the mechanical engineering firm Myrens Verksted) acted for Solberg. Finally, the importance of contacts with the UK is not given necessarily by numbers of contacts, great though these often were, but rather by their character.

Contacts between specifically machine-making firms and Norwegian textile enterprises are summarized in Appendix C. All of the Norwegian firms studied here had dealings with British textile engineering enterprises. By 1870, a total of eighty-six British engineering firms had had some contact with the Norwegian industry. It is difficult to know what proportion of the British industry was at any one time active in the Norwegian market. Kirk used a range of trade directories to establish the structure of the British cotton textile engineering industry, and for 1870 located forty-eight surviving firms making cotton spinning and weaving equipment, founded at various dates from 1790.[5] Of these nineteen, or 40 percent, appear in Appendix C, i.e. were active in Norway. A high proportion of the industry, therefore, was prepared to look to the small Norwegian market for sales. However it is important to note that some firms operating in Norway were apparently not listed in the trade directories; fourteen of the engineering firms listed in Appendix C as being active c. 1870 in Norway, do not appear in Kirk's Directory-based study. This suggests that Directories may not necessarily be an entirely reliable source for analyses of industry structure.

Appendix C suggests that firms were rarely active in the Norwegian market on a continuing basis; a characteristic pattern was for firms to be involved in

---

[5] R. Kirk, *Economic Development of the British Textile Machinery Industry, c. 1850–1939* (University of Salford, Ph. D thesis), Tables 30 and 32, pp. 115 and 121.

Table 6.2 *Timing of activity by British machine makers in Norway*

	Number of firms active
Pre-1840	1
During 1840s only	8
During 1850s only	8
During 1860s only	46
During 1870s only	3
Between 1840–60 inc.	1
Between 1840–70 inc.	2
Between 1850–70 inc.	9
Unknown	8

Source: Appendix C

the Norwegian market for a few years, and then to disappear from view. Since these periods of activity for the most part fell conveniently within decades, we can summarize the changing intensity of British machine makers' activity in Norway as shown in Table 6.2.

Since this study does not extend beyond 1870, it cannot be said whether the upsurge of activity during the 1860s was maintained. However one obvious possibility is that British textile engineering firms were reacting to the slump in the British textile industry in the 1860s by searching for markets abroad. The 1850s had been years of expansion, particularly towards the end of the decade, and Farnie argues that 'the unprecedented prosperity of the years 1858–61 brought about an inevitable reaction, since productive capacity had grown by one fifth since 1856 and had surpassed the absorptive capacity of the industry's markets ...'.[6] The problems were exacerbated by the American civil war and the blockade of Southern ports by the Northern navy. The year 1862 in particular was one of crisis, with cotton industry margins at a very low level, the gross value of output more than 40 percent below the 1860 level, exports of yarn down by 48 percent, and unemployment in the industry reaching a peak in December.[7] The effects of this on capital goods suppliers can be readily imagined, and it may be that textile engineers were forced to seek foreign markets with urgency. Certainly their prices, as I shall show below, responded to the trade cycle.

Some of the 'contacts' between British and Norwegian firms were more important than others. Some simply consisted of letters soliciting business on

[6] D. Farnie, *The English Cotton Industry and the World Market, 1815–1896* (Oxford, 1979), p. 138.
[7] *ibid.*, Ch. 4.

a more or less speculative basis, usually outlining available machinery with prices. The importance of such correspondence however should not be discounted; they are on the one hand, as noted above, an interesting indication of the eagerness with which British firms sought foreign markets even those as small as Norway, and 'on the other they presumably played some role in keeping Norwegian entrepreneurs abreast of technical developments and available equipment. This will be illustrated further below. Other contacts involved actual supply; between 1855 and 1870, for example, Hjula Weavery alone conducted business with eighteen British machine makers (i.e. 40 percent of Hjula's total machinery 'contacts'). This business gave rise to 498 extant invoices over those fifteen years, with the majority of the invoices recording multiple transactions. Apart from machinery supply the two further classes of contact concerned the supply of raw materials and the supply of ancillary equipment or complementary inputs. The latter included a very wide range of items: spindles, bobbins, belting, oil, reeds, cards, healds, leather, shuttles, soda, pipework, soap, plates, brushes, paper, machine parts, traps, pickers, rubber, wire and so on. These items have been drawn from invoices of a twenty-five year period to 1870, and are worth mentioning in detail since they indicate the continuing nature of dependence on British suppliers of inputs. Local suppliers were slow to emerge, in contrast to the experience of the United States, where, once textile production became feasible technically, local producers of ancillary equipment quickly developed.[8] The principal raw material, supplied mainly through the Liverpool market, was raw cotton, but raw materials also included a considerable quantity of spun yarn, wool, dyestuffs and rags. Important information flows frequently accompanied these transactions, both technical (e.g. operating instructions), or economic (especially on actual or prospective cotton market conditions). Again, these contacts were extensive; Hjula had contacts with thirty-nine British raw material suppliers and no less than sixty-five ancillary equipment suppliers. Arne Fabrikker dealt with twenty-seven and thirty-four respectively, Solberg with seventeen and four, Halden with twelve and two, and Nydalen with two and ten respectively. The contacts and transactions between Norwegian textile firms and their British suppliers dominated not only the physical supply of machinery and equipment into the Norwegian industry, but also the transfer of technological information. Other sources of supply were explored from time to time: Denmark and even Russia for equipment,[9] and Germany for machines and raw material (where firms in the Hamburg cotton market could be significant suppliers). However, it could be argued that only one of these transactions was important in terms of tech-

---

[8] See, e.g., J. Prude, *The Coming of Industrial Order* (Cambridge, 1983), Ch. 4.

[9] Heyerdahl, of Christiania Sailcoth, visited Russia in 1858 to buy raw material and 'a couple of smaller machines'. *Christiania Sailcloth Styreprotokoll* [Minutes of Directors' meetings], 28 August 1858.

nology transfer: that between Mads Wiel of Halden Spinnery and the Copenhagen-based engineering firm of Nordberg. Nordberg supplied equipment as well as extensive information ranging from advice on site and buildings (including drawings), to labour requirements, to types of product.[10] This however was a case of indirect technology transfer from Britain. Nordberg had acquired his expertise from the UK; he had been a state-supported spy in Britain in the late eighteenth century, making three extensive visits, and had smuggled machinery from Britain to Denmark. From such considerations Parmer has drawn the conclusion that Halden's early technology was basically British.[11] Moreover this was an early and untypical transaction which did not give rise to any continuing relationship, and after Wiel's death was supplanted by British input to Halden from the 1840s. In dealing with the British textile engineering industry, therefore, we are concentrating on the basic source of technology transfer into the Norwegian industry. The remainder of this chapter examines in detail the various facets of that transfer. That is to say, we shall be concerned not with the scope or extent of involvement by British machine makers, but with the nature of that involvement.

THE NATURE OF TECHNOLOGY TRANSFER FROM THE UK

Just as technology itself should be understood not just as tangible machines and equipment, but rather as a complex hierarchy of knowledge, information, skills and machines, so the transfer of technology is considerably more than the mere export of a machine. Central to the process is the flow of information which on the one hand makes the purchase possible, and on the other makes it possible to operate the equipment. In this section, concentrating once again on the Hjula enterprise, I shall describe flows of technological information emanating from the British textile engineering industry, making four basic distinctions between these flows. They are:

i   Information referring to, as it were, the 'Production Set'. That is,
    information on the setting up of a firm
    assessment of new machines and equipment
    availability of equipment
    technical choice
ii construction and operating information, including information on prices and costs of production.
iii Output information.
iv Labour requirements and supply.

---

[10] T. Parmer, 'Mads Wiels Bomuldsfabrik, 1813–1835. Norges første moderne industribedrift?', *Volund 1981*, Norsk Teknisk Museum, pp. 7–76.
[11] *ibid.*, p. 36.

PRODUCTION SET INFORMATION

'Setting-up' information

Early Norwegian entrepreneurs were frequently in the unenviable position of bearing, as Halvor Schou put it, 'the anxiety of entering a new business that I did not understand myself'.[12] The problem lay not so much in marketing as in production; specifically, in knowing the general disposition of equipment required to commence operations, and the costs involved. When Hjula Weavery was founded, in 1854, Schou relied heavily on his contacts with one of the oustanding engineers of the age, Sir William Fairbairn, and with Fairbairn's son George, for information on the range of equipment required and on the likely costs.[13] In March 1854 they wrote a joint letter to Schou, in two parts, with Sir William dealing with power requirements and his son with the complement of spinning equipment. Sir William estimated costs of £2,600 for power equipment: a sixty horse wheel, gearing, heating apparatus and transmission equipment. In the second part of the letter George provided equipment specifications and costs, which he had obtained from the Ancoats (Manchester) firm of John Hetherington (who had earlier been associated with Fairbairn's works).[14] The estimate included ten carding engines, a drawing frame, ten throstles of 200 spindles each, several self-acting mules, and a variety of ancillary equipment. He also specified the space required (a thousand square yards), and the projected output of this array of equipment: 2,500 pounds of water-twist, and 1,500 pounds of pin-cops per week, on an average No. 20 yarn count.

Two months later, Hetheringtons made direct contact with Schou concerning the supply of weaving equipment. They described their main product – check looms – and offered one for trial prior to purchase. They went on to discuss power requirements for their spinning equipment (300 mule and 150 throstle spindles to one nominal horsepower), and other equipment requirements, suggesting one sizing machine per hundred looms. Finally, they offered to plan the layout of the mill: 'When you come to England we shall be glad to see you & any information you require, in the meantime we shall be happy to supply you with & to make you out plans for the building.'[15] Schou went on to order through Hetherington, but remained in contact with the Fairbairn firm who acted as a kind of technical consultant. In November 1854, Fairbairn wrote offering to help, '... in our line ourselves, or to give you the full benefit of our advice in procuring it elsewhere. We will see

---

12 *Hjula Papers*, Correspondence out, *Kopibok*, 27 July 1861.
13 Fairbairn's career was of considerable importance in the development of engineering in Britain. A good account of his career is given in his autobiography: W. Fairbairn, *The Life of Sir William Fairbairn, Bart.*, edited and completed by William Pole (London, 1877).
14 *Hjula Papers*, Correspondence in, Fairbairn, 31 March 1854. Kirk, *Textile Machinery Industry*, p. 157.
15 *Hjula Papers*, Correspondence in, Hetherington, 18 May 1854; 15 June 1854; 27 July 1854; 8 November 1854; 21 December 1854.

Hetherington's designs and that they are upon the best system and arrangement.'[16]

This process was repeated, about a year later, when Schou undertook a new project – to begin sizing his own warps, which had previously been sized by the Nydalen mill. First, he requested details of equipment and prices from the Manchester firm of Parr, Curtis & Madeley.[17] Subsequently the Salford firm of Mather & Platt wrote with descriptions of necessary equipment, including drying machines and gearing; prices were included. They also discussed heating and power requirements, and indicated likely output.[18] Over the next six months correspondence continued, with letters also from Merck & Co. of Manchester on available equipment and prices. Generally, Schou sent plans of the building which would house the sizing operation, and suppliers responded with specifications. Subsequently Parr, Curtis & Madeley got the order, with Schou's letters expressing some anxiety about the size of the boiler: 'I know parties in England generally like to send boilers larger than wanted, thinking that superfluous power always will come in and be useful in time.'[19]

Assessment of new machines and equipment

Spinning and weaving were activities in which both major and minor innovations occurred throughout the nineteenth century in the UK. Machine makers frequently wrote concerning innovations or modifications in techniques. Sometimes this referred to their own equipment. Thus in July 1854 Hetherington wrote that their new check loom was 'not perfect yet'; a few years later Parr, Curtis & Madeley replied to an order saying that 'we want to perfect our three and four shuttle looms before sending them out', and predicted a two month delay.[20] On the other occasions, however, textile engineers reported on the performance of newly patented or advertised devices. For example, Parr, Curtis & Madeley reported in March 1865 on a potentially important loom innovation:

We have seen the power loom driven by compressed air and have at present only a very indifferent opinion of it, and this we believe to be shared by the whole of the loom makers in Lancashire – A few have been made by the patentees, but we have not heard of any orders being given for them by the trade ... Our advice to you is, not to have anything to do with it, until you hear of some half dozen parties having got it into work satisfactorily here, and rather think this will not be this year or next.[21]

[16] *Hjula Papers*, Correspondence in, Fairbairn, 8 November 1854.
[17] *Hjula Papers*, Correspondence out, 30 December 1856.
[18] *Hjula Papers*, Correspondence in, Mather & Platt, 8 January 1857; 21 May 1857.
[19] *Hjula Papers*, Correspondence out, Parr Curtis, 11 August 1857.
[20] *Hjula Papers*, Correspondence in, Hetherington, 27 July 1854; Parr Curtis, 15 Sept 1858.
[21] *Hjula Papers*, Correspondence in, Parr Curtis, 1 March 1865.

Two months later, the Glasgow firm Anderston Foundry wrote with an assessment of what is presumably the same machine. They suggested that it would be:

premature to offer any opinion ... of the Pneumatic loom as to whether it is practical for either single or double box looms – one idea is that it will take a considerable length of time in perfecting before they can reduce it into such a sphere as will become general for trade purposes.[22]

Both firms seem to have been clearly aware not only of the risk involved in being an early user of an untried technique, but more importantly of the role of post-innovation improvements in making a new device commercially feasible. This accords with Nathan Rosenberg's argument that 'the diffusion process is typically dependent on a stream of improvements in performance characteristics of an innovation', a matter which he argues has been neglected in modern economic analyses of diffusion.[23]

Like other Norwegian manufacturers, Schou was alert to the opportunities provided by innovation, and tended to check on new developments before ordering equipment. 'Is anything new?', he wrote to Parr, Curtis & Madeley in 1858, contemplating a new order for calico looms. In 1859, prior to the purchase of new knitting equipment, Schou wrote in similar terms to Harrison & Sons, a Blackburn firm, who replied that 'we cannot advise you of any improvement in the Heald Knitting Machine ... they are universally employed here'. They continued with a detailed description of prices, labour requirements, and output levels attained with the machine. Less than a year later Schou was in touch with them again, seeking an assessment of a Scottish innovation. Harrisons replied that, 'it has been tried here and proven a failure, we know of only *two* such machines working in Lancashire, while we can point to *hundreds* of ours'. They went on to make the pointed argument that: 'If the machines of which you speak were effective ours would have been superseded ere this, but such is not the case.'[24]

In the previous section I noted Fairbairn's offer to 'give you [Schou] the full benefit of our advice', and this they did in seeking information on innovations, looking in particular on Schou's behalf for improvements in pin-bobbin machinery.[25]

Availability of equipment

Prior to the assessment of new equipment, simple knowledge of its existence and availability is an important precondition for diffusion. Here the role of specialized capital goods producers is particularly important, since profit

22 *Hjula Papers*, Correspondence in, Anderston, 2 May 1865.
23 N. Rosenberg, 'Problems in the economist's conceptualization of technological innovation', in *Perspectives on Technology* (Cambridge, 1977), p. 75.
24 *Hjula Papers*, Correspondence in, Harrison, 12 May 1859; 6 April 1860.
25 *Hjula Papers*, Correspondence in, Fairbairn, 15 February 1852.

seeking encourages them to diffuse information as widely as possible on the available range of equipment. A persistent feature of the correspondence archives of Hjula is material from British textile engineers outlining their product ranges and prices. Even before Hjula commenced operations, English engineers such as the firm Horrocks & Son of Pilkington were writing with details of the range of their textile equipment, enclosing drawings.[26] Such firms would frequently mention the British mills for which they had supplied equipment (in Horrocks's case, the Ratcliffe Manufactory).

From time to time, British engineers would write with details of new patents they held or innovations they had developed. Thus in 1868 Sugden & Co. wrote with details of a new stop motion for milling machines, and added details of a washing machine and hydro extractor which they were promoting. Schou, who had previously bought their milling machines, purchased one of the new washing machines.[27] Similarly, Rhodes & Son wrote with details of a new patent for spinning equipment, Tomlinsons with drawings and quotes for napping machinery and other equipment, and Harrisons with information on a new powered Heald knitter.[28] During the 1860s, handwritten letters became accompanied or supplanted by printed circulars. The Rochdale cotton and woollen machinery makers John Tatham wrote with a printed circular consisting of an extract from *The Engineer* of 10 November 1865, describing machinery exhibited by Tatham at the Dublin International Exhibition: three carding engines, a self-acting mule and a loom. The mule was described in particular detail, since it involved a series of innovations and improvements.[29] By the late 1860s, printed circulars could be fairly elaborate; Tomlinsons of Huddersfield, specialists in washing, milling and finishing equipment, sent Schou a circular listing over fifty separate items, some with a range of specifications. In addition, Tomlinson himself wrote with details of special offers (lighting equipment, second-hand machines, and so on). Firms wrote not only describing equipment, but matching Hetherington's offer of a trial period. Parr, Curtis & Madeley, for example, did this, inviting direct comparison with competitors' equipment. They also supplied considerable technical detail when equipment was purchased from them; in 1855, for example, they sold Schou – among other items – three power looms which 'embody all recent improvements'. In an accompanying letter the improvements were described in considerable detail, 'as a guide to your further orders', since most were apparently applicable to existing looms as 'add-ons'.[30]

It is important to note that not all of this steady flow of correspondence was

26 *Hjula Papers*, Correspondence in, Horrocks, 21 July 1855.
27 *Hjula Papers*, Correspondence in, Sugden, 10 December 1868.
28 *Hjula Papers*, Correspondence in, Rhodes, 26 April, 1870; Tomlinson, 18 April 1868; Harrison, 31 May 1858.
29 *Hjula Papers*, Correspondence in, Tatham, 21 September 1867.
30 *Hjula Papers*, Correspondence in, Tomlinson, 2 September 1869. Correspondence in, Parr Curtis, 9 August 1855; 21 July 1855.

initiated from suppliers on the British side. In July 1863 the Brighouse textile engineer Thomas Lancaster wrote 'having seen in the *Leeds Mercury* an estimate wanted for machinery which beg leave to hand you one for the same as I am a maker ...'. He offered price quotations for carding and scribbling equipment, described where 'a sample of my make of machines' might be seen, and offered five references from his earlier customers.[31]

An interesting aspect of the flow of information on machine availability was that prices of equipment tended to reflect the state of the business cycle. I noted above that the 1860s were years of depression in the British textile industry, and that this may account for sharply increased activity by British textile engineers in the Norwegian market during that decade. The years 1862–3 were extremely difficult. In February 1863 the Blackburn firm of William Dickinson & Sons wrote with particularly low prices for 'say fifty looms', adding that 'we are induced to offer these exceedingly low prices to you through the depression in trade and our anxiety to do further business with you.'[32] Dickinson's sales effort included high quality lithographs of their patented improvements in sizing equipment. The depression continued into the late 1860s, a period which Farnie says 'proved gloomier than the years of the Cotton Famine itself.'[33] In 1869, a year of 'drastic shrinkage in margins ... almost to the low level of 1863', we find the Manchester machine maker Daniel Foxwell writing to Schou: 'If for machinery etc., you require any estimates, I shall do my best to furnish you with them at prices in accordance with the present slack state of business.'[34]

This situation stands in contrast to the expansionary years of the early 1850s, when Sir William Fairbairn wrote at one point to Schou concerning a particular item of equipment that: 'I have had some difficulty in getting the information, for all the machine making as well as spinning establishments are so busy here that we can hardly get any orders executed.'[35]

Technical choice

By 'technical choice' I do not refer here so much to the economically efficient choice of technique in terms of capital/labour ratio – which is how technical choice is usually understood in the economics literature – so much as choice among the range of available machine configurations. Although choice of machine configuration affects the capital–labour ratio, there are also strictly technical questions about how well particular machines will do the job; many textile functions could be carried out in a range of ways, with different implications for machine operation and maintenance, different implications for labour input, and questions of the compatibility of various machine types.

[31] *Hjula Papers*, Correspondence in, Lancaster, 7 July 1863.
[32] *Hjula Papers*, Correspondence in, Dickinson, 2 February 1863.
[33] Farnie, *English Cotton Industry*, p. 164.
[34] *Hjula Papers*, Correspondence in, Foxwell, 18 March 1869.
[35] *Hjula Papers*, Correspondence in, Fairbairn, 15 February 1854.

British firms frequently gave detailed advice on technical choice in this technical sense, sometimes but by no means always referring to the economics of the process. For example, Halvor Schou, when purchasing looms, showed a frequent preference – expressed in a range of letters – for underpick as opposed to overpick motions in looms. The principal reason for this was that his workers were familiar with the underpick technique. Machine makers were happy to accommodate him in this, but advised him against it on technical grounds. Thus Anderstons wrote in September 1859:

Referring to the long bands you speak of – they would not suit the looms with the underpick as at present constructed (we approve of overpick for them). As the underpick has to work in the heart of the motion it adds a deal of complication with the long bands, and on this account we strongly advise you to abandon the idea.

They went on to suggest an alternative device: 'Your better plan is rather to get another dozen of long barrel check looms (with the usual approved One pick) and we feel confident that by your doing so, you would save money in the "long run" ...'[36]

The distinction between overpick and underpick looms was not simply a technical matter however, for the looms had different labour requirements which altered the economics of their operation. Von Tunzelmann referred to this in the context of differences between British and American practice:

the English went over to the over-pick loom, invented by Dickinson at Blackburn in 1828, whereas the Americans stayed with the older underpick form. The overpick loom was generally run at 20 to 40 picks per minute faster than the underpick one, though at the cost of greater attendance and therefore lower output per labourer.[37]

This choice in the US was presumably to do with the factor price differences associated with Habbakuk's thesis. In Norway, however, it is likely to have been more a result of an absolute shortage of appropriate labour.

Parr, Curtis & Madeley offered similar definite advice to Schou on loom construction, given his projected cloth type: ' ... we cannot recommend you to have anything on the five power looms but the weft stop motion as the cloth is too heavy'.[38]

Occasionally suppliers referred, in more detail than Anderstons appear to have done, to particular cost effects of equipment they were supplying or seeking on Schou's behalf. Tomlinson wrote:

about a tentering machine about which I promised to make enquiries – I find there are two sizes, one capable of tentering 750 yards per day ... the other capable of doing 1500 yards ... the maker of these machines is Mr Whitely of this town who made a large fortune having the exclusive patent right. The saving in labour in the large

[36] *Hjula Papers*, Correspondence in, Anderston, 23 September 1859.
[37] N. Von Tunzelmann, *Steam Power and British Industrialization to 1860* (Oxford, 1978), p. 270.
[38] *Hjula Papers*, Correspondence in, Parr Curtis, 6 September 1855.

machine I am assured is about £20.0.0 per week, the smaller one correspondingly less.[39]

When acquiring equipment, Norwegian producers generally seem to have deferred to the experience of the British. Thus Solberg sought price lists and information through the Liverpool firm of Whitehead & Meyer 'in the hope of possible guidance in the choice of producer'.[40] Subsequently, presumably on the advice of Whitehead & Meyer, Solberg dealt extensively with Parr, Curtis & Madeley. Technical details were decided by the British firm. When buying carding machinery, for example, Solberg wrote saying that they would 'prefer leather to cloth ... but you choose'; subsequently they ordered further equipment, stating a preference for an earlier type, but 'since we have little experience, we leave the choice to you'.[41]

CONSTRUCTION AND OPERATING INFORMATION

Since Norwegian enterprise managers frequently lacked technical skills, they relied heavily on British workers for assembly and operating expertise. The role of British textile engineers in recruiting and supplying such labour will be referred to below and described in detail in a later chapter. Where such labour was not available, however, Norwegian firms drew directly on British suppliers for technical information and guidance. In 1845, for example, Wallem wrote to Armitage & Co. of Huddersfield, as follows:

Gentlemen,
Being from a foreign country, where the construction of that steam engine I bought of you the 3rd instant is quite unknown, I should be much at a loss for putting the engine up if I did not be in possession of a sketch of it; – and the engine being put into work, it might perhaps easily happen, that some part of it be broken, I should then likewise be at a great loss for getting it repaired without a sketch of that. I beg therefore leave to request you be so kind as to send me as well a sketch in order to set the engine up, as a sketch of *every* part of the engine in order to be able to take a copy of that part, which in the future perhaps might want repair.

In case that the sketches might be still of any use for you, I will with pleasure grant you an allowance for your trouble with sending me a copy of all the sketches of the abovenamed engine, which allowance you will be pleased to fix and I shall send it beforehand.[42]

This letter was sent via the Leeds engineering firm of Taylor, Wordsworth & Co., and may have been drafted by them. A similar request was made by Schou to his suppliers; '... I beg you to be kind enough when you send the machine to let me have a rough drawing of it with the necessary explanations

[39] *Hjula Papers*, Correspondence in, Tomlinson, 12 August 1868.
[40] *Solberg Papers*, Correspondence out, *Kopibok*, 7 December 1852.
[41] *Solberg Papers*, Correspondence out, *Kopibok*, 5 September 1853; 9 June 1854.
[42] *Wallem Papers*, Correspondence out, 11 April 1845.

how to work it and please to number the parts so that there will be no difficulty in putting it together'.[43]

These requirements were frequently repeated in subsequent years; in ordering from Hetherington in 1858, for example, Halvor Schou required numbered parts, assembly instructions with drawings, and operating instructions. On delivery, Hetherington complied, sending lithographs of the assembled machine, and despatching some parts semi-assembled. Even so, problems arose:

I have had your looms with the new drop-box motion running for several weeks but my overlooker is not master over them yet. I dare say the loom is made according to the best principles, and that the invention with the barrell is very ingenious ... but I am not yet able to form any opinion to be depended upon or satisfactory to myself before you send me further particulars about the barrell ... I shall prefer to employ these looms as soon as I understand them ... the paper you sent me did not explain sufficiently the working of the barrell and the forming of the pattern.[44]

Hetherington replied almost immediately, assuring Schou that the machines were working before delivery, and going into considerable technical detail concerning adjustment and operation.[45] The question of machine adjustment was an important one for textile equipment – as Harold Catling has emphasized drawing on his own experience as a textile operative – since it played a large part in determining output performance.[46] For this reason adjustment details, such as those supplied to Schou by the loom makers Sugden & Sons in the mid 1860s, remained of continuing importance in Norwegian mill operation.[47]

Smaller English machinery suppliers from time to time offered to come to Norway personally to help with the setting up of and operating of equipment. Thomas Baxter of Manchester, who had sold healds and ancillary materials to Schou in 1857 and 1858, wrote again in 1864 trying to sell a used heald knitter for £13, and offering to come to Norway to get it working. The price was low, since 'I have not knitted healds for 2½ years';[48] this was, as noted above, a period of general recession in the industry, which the price may have reflected, and also one in which production was concentrating.[49] Baxter's offer may well have been a by-product of the collapse of his small manufacturing and machinery-supply business. Certainly the terms on which he offered to come to Norway were barely distinguishable from those of a workman: 'If I came my terms would be my expenses both ways and £2 per week working full 10 hours per day for five days and six hours on Saturday.' In

43 *Hjula Papers*, Correspondence out, 11 October 1856.
44 *Hjula Papers*, Correspondence out, 26 November 1858.
45 *Hjula Papers*, Correspondence in, Hetherington, 9 December 1858.
46 H. Catling, *The Spinning Mule* (Newton Abbot, 1970), p. 149.
47 *Hjula Papers*, Correspondence in, Sugden & Sons, 22 September 1866.
48 *Hjula Papers*, Correspondence in, Baxter, 21 November 1864.
49 Farnie, *English Cotton Industry*, Ch. 4.

fact this was less than Schou was paying other skilled English workers in the early 1860s.[50]

Detailed information on machinery construction continued to be essential to machinery use in Norway to the end of the period studied here. By 1870, when Hjula Weavery had been in operation for fourteen years, and Schou had been a textile entrepreneur for two decades, firms such as Tathams, and Hutchinson & Hollingworth were still supplying detailed tracings, plans and drawings with equipment supplied.[51] Even so, construction skills were of great importance. Schou had originally purchased from Tathams in the 1860s; in 1870, apparently about to buy again from them, he wrote with the rueful remark that 'you advised me once to take a man from your works to put up the self-actors. *This* time I shall take your advice.'[52]

OUTPUT INFORMATION

The understanding of output levels is an important aspect of machine use. Schou often appeared to have been ignorant of appropriate rates of output from the equipment he was buying, and suppliers wrote to inform him:

We omitted in our last letter to say that the doubling frame of 100 spindles would not do the amount of work that you mention – a frame of 100 spindles doubling No 36s two fold will only produce about 85 to 90 lbs per week – or about of No 30s two fold 100 to 110 lbs per week.[53]

This letter, from Hetheringtons, incidentally goes into considerable detail about the range of technical options available. Such information was repeated over the years. Thus Leach & Co. gave details of output on hand and self-acting mules for different yarn counts:

If you take two mules of 400 spindles each we should say that one mule will produce in a day of about 10 hours about 200 lbs of the coarser sort of yarn and about 100 lbs of an average of the finer qualities ... if self-acting about a fourth more.[54]

Anderstons, after supplying a tape dressing machine and two warping machines in November 1859, wrote with British output figures; '... a similar tape dressing machine in the Lancefield Mill to the one you are getting puts through: four to five thousand yards of No 20 warp per day of ten hours'.[55] They went on, however, to make the important qualification that this was 'with practised hands', which Schou's were not; this underlines the importance of labour supply, to be discussed below.

[50] See Chapter 8 below.
[51] *Hjula Papers*, Correspondence in, Tathams, 5 May 1870; Hutchinson & Hollingworth, 28 February 1870.
[52] *Hjula Papers*, Correspondence out, 6 May 1870.
[53] *Hjula Papers*, Correspondence in, Hetherington, 9 June 1859.
[54] *Hjula Papers*, Correspondence in, Leach, 3 July 1863.
[55] *Hjula Papers*, Correspondence in, Anderston, 10 November 1859.

BRITISH TEXTILE ENGINEERS AND LABOUR SUPPLY

The problem of labour input, especially of skilled operatives, and of supervisory functions, was a particularly difficult one in early industrialization generally.[56] An extremely important question therefore concerns the relationship between labour supply, and especially labour inflow from the UK, and the acquisition of British technologies which has been described in this and the previous chapter. A separate, but closely related, question concerns the links between labour inflow and the textile engineers whose role in technology transfer to Norway was, as this chapter has shown, so very important. On the first of these questions, subsequent chapters shall show that the technological development of the Norwegian textile industry involved a significant inflow of skilled British labour, and that this labour performed a range of key technological functions. However this section is concerned not with the general inflow and functions of labour from Britain, but rather with the direct role of British engineering firms in organising and administering that inflow.

If labour supply was a pervasive problem in early industrialization in the UK, for peripheral industrializing countries such as Norway it was a frequently critical problem. Norwegian textile entrepreneurs often found that imported techniques were either, at worst, impossible to operate, or at best unprofitable with domestically available labour. British textile engineers played a key role in overcoming this blockage. What follows is simply a sketch of their role, which will be described in more detail in Chapter 8.

Running right through Halvor Schou's correspondence is evidence that he had no hesitation whatsoever in approaching his machinery suppliers for assistance whenever he had problems of labour supply, supervision or management. For example, in January 1856 he wrote to Diggles concerning the purchase of four looms, and asked them to 'find me an overlooker for weaving checks and twills'. Four months later he wrote again concerning problems with the Diggles looms, making them the following offer: 'find me a manager – then I will in a few years fill my mill with your looms'.[57] Exactly a month later the plea was repeated, and six weeks after that the prospect of further orders was once again used as bait.[58] The following month the problem of labour supply was raised in a letter to Parr, Curtis & Madeley, spelling out precisely why it was a problem. Schou asked them to find him a supervisor and warper because: 'The fact is I have never yet been able to get the same quantity out of my looms which is usual in England, and I think one of the principal causes for it is that my beaming, twisting ... etc. etc., is not managed as well as it ought to be.'[59] Parr Curtis responded by finding him a

---

[56] S. Pollard, *The Genesis of Modern Management* (London, 1865), especially Ch. 5.
[57] *Hjula Papers*, Correspondence out, 22 January 1856; 6 May 1856.
[58] *Hjula Papers*, Correspondence out, 6 June 1856; 25 July 1857.
[59] *Hjula Papers*, Correspondence out, 1 August 1856.

worker; but only four days later he was writing to them again, seeking assistance in finding a new check-loom overlooker.[60]

Having earlier used the prospect of orders to induce Diggles to seek and supply labour, Schou did the same with Parr, Curtis & Madeley, holding out the prospect of shifting from Diggles looms to those of Parr Curtis:

I have the plan instead of taking more double box looms from Squire Diggles which come very expensive and are not good ... to give you an order for a small lathe and boring machine, and to take a mechanic over who could alter Hetherington's looms into shuttle looms, which should be a very easy matter. Then I should not want to order more new double box looms and I could fill my shed with looms for regular domestic.[61]

The latter were, of course, a Parr Curtis product line. Within three months Schou was writing again seeking a mechanic 'acquainted with drop-box looms and twill motions'. Parr Curtis responded to at least the first of these requests, and the mechanic was at work at Hjula within six months.[62]

As well as requesting assistance with labour supply, Schou frequently tied machine purchases to labour acquisition. Thus in May 1859 he wrote to Harrison & Sons about the purchase of a knitting machine, requesting men both to construct it and to operate it.[63] In the same month, Anderstons of Glasgow sent twelve looms 'and a foreman'. They also sent a skilled machine fitter and engineer, who Schou poached away with higher wages. He then asked for further help recruiting a foreman, and Anderstons undertook this, arranging all details of recruitment, terms, conditions, travel, accommodation and duties; Schou played no direct role at all.[64] A month later he wrote concerning the purchase of a tape dressing machine, saying that he could not 'take a dressing machine without a man'. Anderstons recruited a worker who they also arranged to be trained, in Glasgow, specifically to operate this machine.[65]

Even where techniques were well established in Norway, Schou would tie purchase to labour supply. In 1859, a company at Bjørsheim ordered a heald knitter which it was unable to use. Schou corresponded with Hjorth about it, saying that he would buy it if Hjorth 'could get me a man'. Then he wrote to Parr, Curtis & Madeley, asking them to contact Harrison, the engineer who had made the machine, saying that 'I shall pay it when they send me such a man'.[66] Harrisons subsequently offered either to send a person who would instruct Schou's workers, or to train Schou's workers in England.[67] Examples such as these will be multiplied in Chapter 8. There I shall also

---

60 *Hjula Papers*, Correspondence in, Parr Curtis, 22 August 1856; *Hjula Papers*, Correspondence out, 26 August 1856.
61 *Hjula Papers*, Correspondence out, 30 December 1856.
62 *Hjula Papers*, Correspondence out, 19 July 1857; 20 September 1857.
63 *Hjula Papers*, Correspondence out, 6 May 1859.
64 *Hjula Papers*, Correspondence in, Anderston, 20 May 1859; 12 July 1859; 2 August 1859.
65 *Hjula Papers*, Correspondence in, Anderston, 18 January 1860.
66 *Hjula Papers*, Correspondence out, 9 November 1859.
67 *Hjula Papers*, Correspondence in, Harrison, 15 March 1860.

Table 6.3 *Workers recruited for Hjula Weavery*

Textile engineers	No. recruited
Parr, Curtis & Madeley	6
J. Tatham	1
Anderston Foundry	2
Sharpe & Sons	3
J. Richardson & Sons	4
Squire Diggles	1
Wm Fairbairn	5
Machinery-supplying agents	**No. recruited**
Hvistendahl, Holst & Co.	1
George Denton	5

deal with the other activities of firms, such as their willingness not only to recruit and supply workers, but their willingness to act as agents supplying money to the families of workers. It is also the case that this labour supply function was not necessarily restricted to labour directly linked with the operation of any particular firm's machines. The basic point here is that British textile engineers apparently saw all aspects of labour supply as part of the overall package of goods and services they supplied. The vast majority of the workers whose histories are described in Chapter 8 were recruited either by British equipment suppliers or agents active in technology supply. Twenty-eight of Schou's most important British skilled workers or managers, or just over 75 percent, were recruited by such firms. Firms and numbers of workers recruited are shown in Table 6.3.

To sum up, then, we can say that the British textile engineering industry was heavily involved in supplying the following types of labour input. First, the most straightforward form of labour input, as might be expected, was set-up or construction labour; mechanics and engineers who came for short periods to assemble equipment. But these – such as James Maiden, William Oddy,[68] plus an unknown number of others of whom we have no record – were a minority.

Secondly, in some cases the possibility of selling machines was conditional on the ability simultaneously to supply suitable labour. An example of this is the purchase of looms from the Anderston Foundry, and the recruitment of Andrew Clarke who was required to have been trained in the operation of specific techniques before Schou would place an order. Similarly the recruitment of George Murray in 1856 was linked to the acquisition of looms from Diggles.

[68] See Chapter 8 below for a full discussion of these workers.

Thirdly, a much more interesting phenomenon was that, although quite specific types of labour were supplied by British machine makers, this process was not necessarily tied to specific machine purchases. What is particularly striking, it seems to me, about the material described briefly here and in more detail below is the frequently unconditional willingness of British firms of machine makers or agents to advertise, interview, engage and advise on workers, and to deal with all of the administrative, travel and legal formalities which were entailed by the hire of foreign workers. This extended to making payments, sometimes over a long period, to the families of British workers in Norway; the families of the workers or supervisors such as Clarke, Marmont, Clegg, Roebuck, Farrington, Hunt, Kellet, Harton and Brierly were all at one time or another supported in this way.[69] In no case have I found evidence of a fee or commission being paid for this, despite the fact that the amount of work entailed was frequently large.

Why should this be? It may be that for British textile engineers the amount of work involved in labour supply was small relative to the volume of total sales. On the other hand it may be that we are seeing here a neglected but important phenomenon, namely the readiness, willingness and competence of British machine makers to supply not just machines but an overall technological 'package', that is, to include all aspects of the technology acquisition process – including labour supply – in the goods and services they offered, and moreover to do so on an international scale.

[69] See Chapter 8 below.

7

BRITISH AGENTS OF NORWEGIAN ENTERPRISES

In 1865 Hjula Weavery made a small equipment purchase from the Glasgow firm of William Hunter & Co., whose invoice heading described them as 'Machinery Merchants, Agents and Mill Furnishers'.[1] What was entailed by this agency activity, and what was its significance for the diffusion of British technology to Norway?

We have seen in the previous chapter that a large number of British textile engineers were potentially available as suppliers to the Norwegian textile industry. On the one hand this implies that the supply side of the machinery market was competitive, which would of course offer advantages to potential customers. But in order to take advantage of the competitive situation, foreign customers would require – at the very least – knowledge of the equipment alternatives, and this might entail considerable effort in seeking and evaluating information on the prices and performance of such equipment. Presumably for Norwegian entrepreneurs the time and effort involved would at worst have been impossible (since it would have meant spending an inordinate amount of time in England away from their enterprises), and at best would imply significant transactions costs. Halvor Schou, who appears to have visited Britain almost every year, pointed to the 'expense and trouble to go over'.[2] It is reasonable to assume that Schou might have felt this problem more keenly than others, seeing that he was sole owner; Heyerdahl, a partner in the Christiania Sailcloth factory, spent considerably longer periods away from the firm, a matter which generated controversy among the partners, one side claiming that this was in fact a matter of 'educating' Heyerdahl at the expense of the firm.[3] For Nydalen, Hjorth spent a great deal of time in foreign travel. But others were unable to do this and, in the face of this problem, two alternatives seemed to present themselves. One would be to deal with a relatively limited number of suppliers, accepting a certain dependence on them. One might expect that such dependence would entail higher costs, although Saxonhouse found that considerable savings in 'the costs associated

---

[1] *Hjula Papers, Faktura* [Invoices], 24 October 1865.
[2] *Hjula Papers*, Correspondence out, Richardson, 18 December 1869.
[3] Christiania Sailcloth, *Styreprotokoll* [*Minutes of Directors' Meetings*], 29 May 1868.

with acquiring information about new technologies' were made in the case of the Japanese textile industry which relied entirely on one machine supplier, Platt Brothers of Oldham.[4] An alternative to single or limited suppliers would be to employ an agent or agents in England who had specialized knowledge of the textile industry. In Norway, the latter occurred to a significant degree; most Norwegian enterprises had some kind of relationship with British agents. As an example of what Norwegian entrepreneurs sought from such arrangements, we can begin with a letter from Wallem to an agent called Whitehead in Leeds – only a sometimes indecipherable draft of the letter, in Wallem's notebook, survives.

I beg leave to ask your kindly advice about following proposal: ·
– to arrange my affairs with the engine makers Messrs Horsefield and Barras, with the tin can maker Mr [. . .], with the bobbin maker Mr Brown, with the heckle [. . .] Mr Parker, to gather the bills and finding the same reasonable and all right, to pay them their money putting the whole to my account and to care for that those goods be sent away to Newcastle in proper time.
– to take care for that every other thing I have ordered and what you think still absolut [sic] necessary for me to the machinery, may be sent in due order and proper time to Newcastle
– to make up as soon as possible an agreement with Robinson, to look for engage and make up an agreement with the manager, 2 two girls [sic] . . .
– to let me know how your firm wishes to be reimbursed for my present and future debts to the same, hoping that it will be in my power to arrange the same according to their wish. Taking in consideration I am a foreigner, not master of talking your language and notwithstanding having business of great consequence for me to perform, you will kindly excuse the trouble I cause you and meet me with forebearance . . .[5]

This chapter describes the type of business relationship which ensued, that is, the activities of a disparate group of British individuals and firms, namely agents, who acted as intermediaries between Norwegian textile firms and those who supplied their inputs, in particular machinery and labour. They acted on behalf of Norwegian enterprises in their dealings with the British textile engineering industry. But they were not an homogeneous group; the category of 'agent' cannot be precisely defined, for there was sometimes an overlap between this activity and others. While some firms had agency activity as their principal business, others were primarily raw cotton dealers, or finance houses, or even chemists, who would occasionally step outside their main activity to represent their Norwegian clients in the acquisition of technology. But agency activity was extensive, and this suggests that such activity was an important – and perhaps neglected – part of the diffusion of British technology from the 1840s.

---

[4] G. Saxonhouse, 'A tale of Japanese technological diffusion in the Meiji period', *Journal of Economic History*, 39 (1974), p. 163.
[5] *Wallem Papers, Notebook and Diary 1846.*

From Appendix B, twenty-six such firms and enterprises can be identified, and Table 7.1 lists them with details of the Norwegian firms they represented and the years during which they acted for the Norwegian firms. Where firms had a principal activity other than acting as an agent, this is indicated.

Broadly speaking, four types of agency can be identified. In the first case, there were individuals or firms, such as George Denton, who appear to have seen the opportunities created by the growth of textile engineering, and who set themselves up specifically to deal in the trade in technology. Secondly, there were firms who had been active, sometimes over many years, in general Anglo-Norwegian trade. I noted in Chapter 3, the exceptional openness of the pre-industrial Norwegian economy, which had about 30 percent of GDP entering foreign trade. Firms such as Hvistendahl, Holst & Co., or Sewell & Neck, had been active for some years in trading such goods as timber and textiles to and from Norway.

Technology transfer, in the form of machinery and ancillary equipment acquisition, fitted smoothly into this pre-existing pattern of trade. Thirdly, there were textile industry firms, engaged in the manufacture and supply of parts or equipment, who were prepared to deal as agents with other British firms on behalf of Norwegian enterprises. Finally, some agency activities were linked with the provision of finance for trade in raw materials or machinery. The typical form of business relationship between Norwegian textile firms and their British agents was that the Norwegian firm would hold an account with the agent, who would charge all transactions to the account. Since there were variable delays before settlement of the account, agents in effect provided short-term finance for trade. Often agents would allow three months interest-free credit, after which interest would be charged; this seems to have happened with the Arne Fabrikker's business with the Manchester firm of du Fay & Co.[6]

For some agents these financial activities, in turn, connected the cotton trade with the development of merchant banking, and with the rise of London as an international financial centre. Du Fay & Co., for example, which dealt with Hjula and Arne, was a branch of a Huguenot family firm which had been based in Frankfurt and had financed cloth exports, in particular textile prints, from Britain to Holland and Germany. The Manchester branch was established in 1802; it 'granted credits to some of Manchester's leading manufacturers of the day', and had a close connection with N. M. Rothschild.[7] As we shall see below, du Fay & Co. played a major role in technology supply to the Arne enterprise. Frühling & Goschen, who like du Fay dealt with Arne and Hjula, 'opened in London in 1814 as commission agents exporting colonial produce and cotton to Germany', then became significant merchant bankers, and were founder members of the Accepting Houses' Committee.[8] H. E. J.

[6] *Arne Accounts, Inngående Ullvarefabrikken, 1862–75*; Du Fay account.
[7] S. Chapman, *The Rise of Merchant Banking* (London, 1984), pp. 6, 11, 19.
[8] *ibid.*, pp. 11, 55, 61.

Table 7.1 *British agents for Norwegian firms*

Agent	Principal activity	Norwegian firm	Year(s) active
A. Andersen		Arne	1860
Benecke Souchay & Co.		Halden	1866–70
		Nydalen	
Bluhm & Co.	Raw mat.	Hjula	1858–70
G. Denton		Hjula	1863–4
J. Dockray	Machines	Rosendahl	1846–7
W. & G. Dorville		Halden	1810–18
DuFay and Co.		Hjula	1847–70
		Arne	
S. Flatow		Wallem	1846–8
		Rosendahl	
Frühling & Goschen	Finance	Hjula	1855–70
	Raw mat.	Arne	
H. E. J. Hambro		Wallem	1845
W. Hunter	Machines	Hjula	1865
Hvistendahl, Holst & Co.		Hjula	1863–8
Kington & Co.		Solberg	1854–61
		Halden	
Knoop & Co.		Halden	1858–62
		Solberg	
R. Lawton		Arne	Unknown
Lemonius & Co.	Raw mat.	Arne	1865–9
		Solberg	1873
		Halden	1870
D. Liepmann	Raw mat.	Arne	1862
	Ancil. equip.	Solberg	1860–5
		Halden	1861–5
		Nydalen	1859
Merck & Co.	Raw mat.	Solberg	1855–8
		Arne	1840s–50s
		Halden	1855
		Hjula	1849–58
John Neck		Hjula	1867–70
Oelrichs & Co.		Hjula	1863
Richardson	Ancil. equip.	Hjula	1865–70
Sewell & Neck		Hjula	1852–68
		Solberg	
Wm. Sharp & Sons	Ancil. equip.	Hjula	1863–70
		Akerselvens Kledefabrikk	
Taylor, Wordsworth & Co.	Ancil. equip.	Wallem	1845
		Rosendahl	1846
		Hjula	1864
Whitehead		Wallem	1845
H. Wingaard		Wallem	1846
		Rosendahl	1846–7
		Arne	1850s

Source: drawn from Appendix B, and firm records.

Hambro of Newcastle was presumably related to the banking family. Other agents, such as Benecke Souchay & Co., who acted for Halden and the Nydalen Spinnery, moved from the Manchester cotton trade to London and international finance.[9] Other embryonic merchant banks, such as Knoop & Co., who supplied raw material to the Solberg Spinnery, were also widely active in the cotton machinery trade.[10]

From Table 7.1 it appears that sixteen firms or individuals had their primary activity in agency representation, four were primarily raw material suppliers, three supplied ancillary equipment or raw materials, one was a finance house and two were textile engineers. The periods during which they represented Norwegian firms varied widely, as Table 7.1 indicates. But, while contacts may sometimes have been brief, they were often complex and frequent. George Denton, for example, acted as an agent for Halvor Schou for only sixteen months, between July 1863 and November 1864. But in that period he wrote Schou more than fifty letters, often of five or more pages, with a great deal of technical and financial detail, and was involved in the acquisition of a substantial volume of equipment. Denton was succeeded as a major agent by the Cleckheaton card-making firm William Sharp & Sons, who remained active in Norway to the end of the period studied here. Between 1865 and 1870 they sent over eighty often very detailed letters to Schou on all aspects of machinery and raw material purchase and labour supply. Over the same five years the Leeds chemists J. Richardson Bros. also represented Schou, writing on average about once every two weeks, a total of over 120 letters. As with Denton and Sharp, the letters were usually long and detailed. Other firms were active in trade with Norway for the whole period of this study. The firm of Sewell Hanbury & Sewell, for example, became Sewell & Neck in December 1853, then on Sewell's retirement in 1868 became known as John Neck & Sons. In announcing the latter change they noted that: 'Since 1825 our Senior has given his undivided attention to the Norwegian trade in all its branches.'[11] Each of the Sewell/Neck firms maintained an office in Christiania, headed for many years by Thomas Sewell, a senior partner of the firm. In this case, activities which were related to the growth of the Norwegian textile industry were linked to a wider participation in British-Norwegian trade. This was also the case with Hvistendahl, Holst & Co., a Norwegian firm who set up in Manchester in 1861. They had an office in Christiania, and conducted their business in Norwegian. They subsequently expanded, setting up offices in Liverpool and Leadenhall St, London, in 1864. On the latter occasion they distributed a circular, with the signature of their new branch manager, and an enclosure outlining the nature of their business:

Referring to the annexed circular, we beg to offer you our services here in either of the following branches of business:

[9] *ibid.*, pp. 139–51.   [10] *ibid.*, p. 146.
[11] *Hjula Papers*, Correspondence in, J. Neck, 30 June 1868.

1 CONSIGNMENTS, whether of timber, fish, grain or other articles.
2 PURCHASE of COLONIAL and English produce.
3 FREIGHTS remitted in drafts on Christiania at a favourable rate of exchange.
   Shipowners will find this a great convenience.
4 ORDERS for MANCHESTER GOODS placed on the most advantageous
   terms through our Manchester firm.[12]

As we shall see, the acquisition of machinery and ancillary equipment, and
the gathering of a wide range of technical and economic information, was
readily incorporated into these trading operations.

It may well be that more agents than listed above had some contact with
Norway; the point made earlier, that limitations in available sources prevent
us knowing the full scale of British involvement, applies here as it does to
machine makers. In what follows I shall describe the functions performed by
these agents in the diffusion of the new technology to Norway, under six
general headings:

The supply of general technical information
Search for, and evaluation of, new equipment and advice on acquisition
Machine purchase and despatch
Labour acquisition
Payments and finance
Raw material and ancillary equipment supply

As with the previous chapter, the primary concentration will be on Hjula
Weavery, with references to other firms where possible and appropriate.

The supply of general technical information

A wide range of technological information flowed through agents, and
Norwegian entrepreneurs frequently asked for their assistance. In 1863, for
example, Halvor Schou asked George Denton to acquire books on woollen
manufacture for him; Denton replied that everything currently available was
'twenty years old' and referred Schou to Ure's *Dictionary*, a copy of which he
promised to send on the next steamer. Three months later, perhaps referring
to the same matter, he wrote that: 'I will endeavour to get you the book you
require. I shall be up at London next week and will go over the catalogue
referring to such works in the British museum.' He subsequently reported
failure.[13]

Information included details of potential products, in particular of patterns
which were presumably a central component of non-price competition in
woven cloth. Thus Hvistendahl, Holst & Co. undertook to find a firm which
would supply Hjula with the 'newest patterns' on a regular basis, not only

---

[12] *Hjula Papers*, Correspondence in, Hvistendahl, Holst & Co., 1 July 1864.
[13] *Hjula Papers*, Correspondence in, Denton, 23 December 1863; 8 March 1864; 23 March
1864.

from England but from France.[14] Denton on a number of occasions enclosed samples of cloth, of patterns for 'winter goods', of 'the latest in check mittens', of yarn, and so on.[15] James Richardson also sent patterns.[16] Such information was sometimes difficult to obtain; Sewells & Neck wrote in 1865 that: 'Our brokers were unable to get samples of wool, such as used for Shoddy – They are promised, but parties in that trade seem very shy in affording information.'[17]

Correspondence from agents on products included information and advice on such matters as finishing. Hvistendahl, Holst & Co., for example, in discussing sales problems with Hjula, were well aware of the nature of the Norwegian market and pointed out that Hjula was not matching the finishing quality of Arne Fabrikker: 'It pains us to learn that the prospects for doing business in coloured goods is small. We do believe that when you get the right finish ... that you could deliver as good a product as Jebsen in Bergen who is drowning in orders.' They went on to argue that this was a central problem for Schou's business, and the main obstacle to increased sales. Returning to the problem a week later, they suggested that Schou needed to recruit a skilled finisher from England in order to improve 'your finish of shirtings and platillas. Only when the public has become aware that you can manage as pretty goods as Jebsen or England will you see that it will sell well.'[18] They recruited a finisher, one Wright Farrington, who will be discussed below.

Search for, and evaluation of, new equipment, and advice on acquisition

The investigation and assessment of potential machinery and equipment purchases was a vital part of agents' activities. George Denton's very first letter to Schou, for example, reported that he had 'consulted' with the loom makers J. Schofield & Sons of Huddersfield, but would delay ordering until he had recruited a tuner who could actually operate the loom. The next day he wrote again from Leeds concerning the design of a new 'dry house' for Schou. He had had discussions with people in the finishing trade:

both as regards the number of rows of tenters it will hold, and the quantity of cloth such tenters will do per diem; I find that five rows are the utmost it will hold, which will give about seventy-five yards in all, allowing sufficient space at each end for a man to pass round.[19]

He then went into outputs that could be expected with different types of cloth, and the impact of shift working. The very next day he wrote again. This time he had visited the machine-making firm of Marsden, from whom Schou

[14] *Hjula Papers*, Correspondence in, Hvistendahl, Holst & Co., 2 July 1863.
[15] *Hjula Papers*, Correspondence in, Denton, 8 March 1864; 2 July 1863; 30 June 1864; 28 January 1864.
[16] *Hjula Papers*, Correspondence in, Richardson, 5 September 1867; 17 October 1867.
[17] *Hjula Papers*, Correspondence in, Sewell & Neck, 15 April 1865.
[18] *Hjula Papers*, Correspondence in, Hvistendahl, Holst & Co, 13 and 20 October 1864.
[19] *Hjula Papers*, Correspondence in, Denton, 2 and 3 July 1863.

wished to order, saying that he had not placed an order on Schou's behalf because 'I fear there would be too much delay in getting the machines from him, orders that I gave him six months since are not yet expected'. This tells us that Denton was operating for others, of course. On his own initiative he placed orders for Schou elsewhere, with T. Nicholson of Leeds, with Thos. Firth of Huddersfield, and with Sugden & Sons. The latter supplied equipment for a new fulling mill, for which Denton not only ordered the equipment but supplied 'the details of the driving and gearing and a drawing of the stone work'.[20] Five days later he sent further plans 'of the necessary brick and masonry work', remarking that 'if there is anything about the plan not sufficiently evident pray do not hesitate to ask on any matter'. Two weeks later he wrote again with drawings of machines for possible purchase.[21] In early 1864 he reported on an improvement to the condenser of the Knowles Houghton steam engine, which was being patented, and on the situation regarding a patent feeder. The holders, Apperleys, had applied to the Privy Council for an extension of the patent, 'and until this is settled Rhodes dare do nothing'. He advised Schou to wait for a new machine being developed by Thorntons.[22] Presumably all this affected the likely price; in the event Apperley's application succeeded, and Schou purchased from them.[23] William Sharp arranged purchase of a similar machine, this time second-hand, the following year.[24]

After Schou stopped doing business with Denton in November 1864, William Sharp & Sons continued to supply a stream of information on equipment types and availability; their first letter, in late 1864, contained details of a carding machine and a billy, plus a list of machines and equipment available in a forthcoming sale in Leeds. They attended the sale but did not buy.[25] In subsequent years they frequently sent catalogues of machinery sales.[26] Later Schou asked them to find a second-hand Billy, but they advised purchasing new, and located 'a party that will make one for 12 pounds new'.[27] Subsequently they sent assessments of the Whitney machine which they examined with Schou's employee Samuel Clegg; they took the view that not enough of the machines had been made to suggest that it was useful, and that it was too dear.[28]

Information on machines included not only technical details, but aspects of operation. For example, George Denton examined a machine by Leach for possible purchase by Hjula, in August 1863, and remarked:

20 *Hjula Papers*, Correspondence in, Denton, 4 July 1863.
21 *Hjula Papers*, Correspondence in, Denton, 23 March 1863; 9 July 1863.
22 *Hjula Papers*, Correspondence in, Denton, 28 January 1864.
23 *Hjula Papers*, Correspondence in, Denton, 8 March 1864; 30 June 1864.
24 *Hjula Papers*, Correspondence in, Wm Sharp, 24 March 1864.
25 *Hjula Papers*, Correspondence in, Wm Sharp, 9 and 14 November 1864.
26 e.g., *Hjula Papers*, Correspondence in, Wm Sharp, 21 September 1865.
27 *Hjula Papers*, Correspondence in, Wm Sharp, 4 May 1865.
28 *Hjula Papers*, Correspondence in, Wm Sharp, 29 May 1865.

The only objection is this, no very great matter – the raised sides prevent the carders and scribblers being seen when at work ... for sometimes it happens the cards come loose, now with the old system the eye can detect it in a minute, but with Leach's it requires a great application, and it may not be applied in the right time to the fault ... all in all a small thing with a careful overlooker.[29]

We have seen in the previous chapter that textile engineers were often cautious in their assessments of new innovations, and this was true also of agents. Hvistendahl, Holst & Co., for example, forwarded information concerning the 'Patent ... Loom Company' who planned to demonstrate fifty new looms in Manchester: 'We will tell you of the results – but all we have talked to, including the first loom makers, say that the invention is impractical.'[30]

An important aspect of agency activity was simply advice on prices. For Schou, George Denton sent price estimates frequently: looms and finishing equipment, mules, a noiseless exhaust fan, a hydro extractor (for which drawings were included), and so on.[31] Sharp & Sons sent a price for a washing machine from Sugden & Sons,[32] and Richardson & Sons frequently forwarded price lists for machinery and ancillary equipment, either to Schou or to his English manager.[33]

Machine purchase and despatch

Equipment acquisition was from the point of view of this study the most important activity of agents, and a substantial volume of machinery was purchased through them. For example, details of purchases made by George Denton on behalf of Halvor Schou are shown in Table 7.2

Denton kept up a similar pace of activity through most of 1864, and was thus involved in a substantial programme of equipment acquisition. (On Schou's behalf Denton also frequently purchased raw materials and items of ancillary equipment: yarn, oil, soap, and so on.)[34]

In late 1864 Schou quarrelled with Denton, and wrote to William Sharp & Sons of Leeds, reminding them that they had met in Leeds the previous autumn, and asking them to buy him some second-hand machinery. In subsequent years they acquired equipment for Hjula in volume similar to Denton. They also negotiated prices on Schou's behalf: 'We have seen the party from whom you got the Doffing plates and told him he was charging too

---

[29] *Hjula Papers*, Correspondence in, Denton, 15 August 1863.

[30] *Hjula Papers*, Correspondence in, Hvistendahl, Holst & Co., 27 March 1864.

[31] *Hjula Papers*, Correspondence in, Denton, 30 July 1863; 26 March 1864; 18 June 1864; 29 June 1864.

[32] *Hjula Papers*, Correspondence in, Wm Sharp, 8 June 1865.

[33] e.g., *Hjula Papers*, Correspondence in, Richardson, 12 June 1865; 2 August 1866; 13 December 1866.

[34] *Hjula Papers*, Correspondence in, Denton, 27 August 1863; 26 September 1863; 1 October 1863.

Table 7.2 *Equipment purchases by George Denton for Hjula Weavery,
1 July 1863 – 31 December 1863.*

Date	Equipment
2 July 1863	1 steaming globe; 6 copper rollers; 1 winding frame; 1 boiling cistern
4 July 1863	1 66' Perpetual; 1 raising gig; 1 brusher; 1 fulling mill; 2 stocks
9 July 1863	6 power looms
14 July 1863	4 packs French and English teazles
15 July 1863	2 power looms plus gearing, belting, 40 shuttles. 2 gross bobbins
17 July 1863	9 gross bobbins
23 July 1863	1 drawing frame and roller
30 July 1863	1 hydraulic press
25 August 1863	1 drying oven
26 August 1863	2 Jacquard power looms, plus gears, shuttles, straps, pickers etc.
27 August 1863	Shuttles
? September 1863	Reeds
31 September 1863	Laces and machine cloth
5 October 1863	1 patent Mungo machine; 1 sewing machine
19 October 1863	1 120 spindle spinning machine; 1 36' teazer
22 October 1863	1 60' scribbler
30 October 1863	1 Broad Perpetual
31 October 1863	1 pair 'machines' (Mules?); 1 grinding frame
3 November 1863	1 pair mules (552 spindles); 1 condenser; 1 billy; 1 bobbin making machine with tools; 2 woollen power looms; 2 power Jacquard looms
11 November 1863	1 raising gig

Sources: Correspondence and invoices of dates indicated.

much for them and agreed to take off 7½ [indecipherable] from each instead of 2½ as we wrote you last.'[35] In succeeding years they negotiated prices and purchases of Witney machines, washing machines (from Sugden & Sons), feeding machines, a second-hand billy of 100 spindles, a roller, looms, a milling machine, as well as frequent shipments of ancillary equipment such as cards, bobbins, gearing, and so on. They appeared to hold some equipment in stock:

The scribbler you write for we have not one in just now but probaly [sic] we shall have before long as such machines are for sale frequently but if we hear nothing in the course of a few days we shall advertize in the Leeds Mercury for such.[36]

[35] *Hjula Papers*, Correspondence in, Wm Sharp, 8 December 1864.
[36] *Hjula Papers*, Correspondence in, Wm Sharp, 1 October 1868.

This letter suggests that Sharps were quite active in the machinery trade, buying equipment speculatively, as it were, and waiting for orders. Richardsons were similarly active with a different range of products; apart from their own products (chloride, soap, dye, fuller's earth, bichrome etc.) Richardsons sent sugar, belting, bobbins, leather, oil, a boiling cistern, pressing paper, rollers, 'machinery', and so on. They usually took the detailed decisions on purchase; thus, with the boiling cistern, they had been instructed to seek out a second-hand one, but instead 'ordered a new one which we think is very cheap'.[37] Similarly high levels of activity occurred with other agents and other Norwegian firms; for Arne Fabrikker, for example, du Fay & Co. purchased, between mid 1855 and the end of 1856, eighteen power looms, a picking machine, two slubbing frames, two roving frames, seven self-acting mules, six carding machines, and a very substantial volume of ancillary equipment and materials (warps, bobbins, pulleys and so on) – altogether at least 155 invoices over the period 1855–68 went to the Arne Fabrikker from du Fay, all of them involving multiple transactions. This volume of activity was maintained right through to the end of the period studied here, i.e. 1870, and no doubt beyond. (Hjula Weavery, incidentally, also used du Fay & Co., but, probably because Schou had a number of agents involved in equipment supply, du Fay supplied only raw material.) Arne Fabrikker also had a number of minor agents such as the Norwegian A. Andersen, based in Leeds, who purchased a Whitney machine, feeding machines, warps, a cylindrical brushing machine, and so on.[38] Frühling & Goschen also purchased machinery for Arne, from the Manchester textile engineer Asa Lees.[39]

In Hjula's case, assistance in machinery purchase extended to helping Schou's British workers when they were in England. The important Hjula manager Stephen Marmont, for example, visited Richardson & Sons, and they wrote to Schou that, '... we also informed him that we should be very glad to hand him money on your a/c, and he has promised to give us another call, we also promised to obtain the prices of different articles for him'.[40] Subsequently they gave him £8 5s 0d to pay the equipment supplier G. W. Tomlinson, and Marmont also ordered belting for Schou for which Richardsons undertook to pay.[41]

Other agents were less active but nevertheless dealt frequently with equipment acquisition; Bluhm & Co., of Manchester, for example, dealt on behalf of Hjula Weavery with the textile engineers Edwin Moorhouse and Jos. Hetherington, whom they paid for equipment in August 1859,[42] and with Dickinson & Sons of Blackburn, from whom they transmitted details of

---

[37] *Hjula Papers*, Correspondence in, Richardson, 21 February 1868.
[38] *Arne Fabrikker Papers, Faktura*, [Invoices], 27 March 1867; 13 May 1867.
[39] *Arne Fabrikker Papers, Faktura*, 28 March 1857.
[40] *Hjula Papers*, Correspondence in, Richardson, 20 June 1867.
[41] *Hjula Papers*, Correspondence in, Richardson, 27 June 1867.
[42] *Hjula Papers*, Correspondence in, Bluhm, 18 August 1859.

equipment which had been ordered.[43] Sometimes, people engaged in agent-like activity would make only one appearance in firm records, and then disappear from view; in 1862, for example, the Arne accounts record a purchase of a raising machine from Robert Kershaw of Rochdale for £30; the next entry in the account is commission of fifteen shillings (i.e. of 2.5 percent) to one Robert Lawton of Rochdale on this purchase. (He was also paid 3s 6d for 'one day's work'.)[44]

A frequent problem in acquisition was delay in the supply of machines which had been ordered; Sharp & Sons wrote, for example, concerning delays in the despatch of a self feeder, saying that the maker was taking 'longer by a month than expected'. They frequently passed on Schou's complaints concerning delay to machine makers, who usually sought other scapegoats ('they say the fault is with the Great Northern Railway').[45]

In some cases, Norwegian firms appear to have conducted business with agents through other agents. The Rosendahl enterprise, for example, had what they termed 'our commissionaire in Leeds' who purchased machinery and equipment for them. But they dealt with him through the Leeds agent Solomon Flatow:

Under the time I was in Leeds [sic] having bought of Mr Jacob Dockray the different Machines I wanted, with the exception of a twisting frame, single side with 34 spindles, with 5' traverse, so you will be so kind as to see Dockray and give him order to get one made as soon as possible and sent to me.[46]

Subsequently they had Flatow acquire, through Dockray, a range of other equipment – strapping, spinning machines, a roving frame and so on. For Hjula, James Richardson and William Sharp & Sons sometimes collaborated, particularly on labour recruitment. In terms of machinery shipping also, British agents themselves often had agents in Hull with whom they arranged transport of equipment.[47]

Labour acquisition

The role of British labour in the Norwegian textile industry has already been mentioned with respect to British textile engineers, and will be discussed in detail in a subsequent chapter. But a central point concerning the flow of labour from the UK to Norway is that it was frequently tied to specific purchases of machinery. In the previous chapter I noted that British textile engineers were often responsible for the recruitment of skilled workers or managers, and that this frequently occurred as a condition of making a machinery sale in Norway. But agents also played an important role in

[43] *Hjula Papers*, Correspondence in, Bluhm, 7 August 1962.
[44] *Arne Fabrikker Papers*, Account Book, 11 October 1862.
[45] *Hjula Papers*, Correspondence in, Wm Sharp, 4 and 27 May 1865.
[46] *Rosendahl Papers*, Correspondence out, 21 July 1846.
[47] See, e.g., *Hjula Papers*, Correspondence in, Richardson, 5 September 1867.

advertising for workers, in interviewing, in recruitment, in arranging travel to Norway, and in maintaining the families of workers while they were away. In George Denton's correspondence with Halvor Schou, for example, labour recruitment is a persistent theme. In his very first letter to Schou, in early July 1863, he referred to a purchase of looms and said that he would not place a definite order before he had recruited a loom tuner to operate it. A week later, referring to another purchase, he wrote that 'I am in touch with a first class man who is used to every kind of cloth both linen and wool', who would operate the equipment. Just over a week later he was interviewing an overlooker, one Emmanuel Brown, who would work for £3 per week.[48] Another week passed, and he was writing that he would not engage a miller 'until I hear whether you have chosen a finisher who understands milling from the names I submitted to you'. After another week he wrote again concerning a new type of finishing machine he had purchased; this was apparently different from the fulling machine he had been commissioned to buy, and he went into some detail of its operation, concluding however that 'the finisher I have engaged will show its use'. At the same time he recruited a power loom overlooker, Benjamin Haigh. Two days later he wrote enclosing a testimonial from a previous employer for George Richardson, a power loom weaver who subsequently worked at Hjula for several years. Two weeks after that he wrote enclosing a formal agreement with Richardson, and referred to seeing another possible employee, Hicks, who was accompanied by a lawyer; 'he has given up his situation and is ready at any time to come'. Another two days and he had signed one Stocks, a finisher, to whom he advanced £18, and he had also advanced £21 to Richardson.[49] Over the next few weeks he dealt with a matter of great importance for Hjula Weavery, namely the recruitment of a factory manager. Denton interviewed five men, and in a long letter described in detail the background of each and his impressions of them. Of the eventual appointee, Stephen Marmont, he wrote:

Aged 36 years – is now manager of a mill at Eccleshall making principally low mungo yarns – was ten years with Walker & Co of Chenwell (?) makers of good cloth principally plain – then with Clapham of Leeds who says of him as follows 'I have known Marmont for seven or eight years part of which time he has been manager of my place – I have no hesitation in saying that he is a practical scribbler and spinner and manager of woollen machinery' – Marmont says if shown a piece of cloth he can select the raw material, he has been a manufacturer himself but compelled to give up on account of the want of means – Richard Marston of Watby, manufacturer – says Marmont has been in my employ has 'thorough knowledge of carding and scribbling and spinning of fine and low goods and with shoddy and wool, he has a good knowledge of woollen machinery and is able to both to get it up and get it to work – shall be glad at any time to furnish samples of his work – from what I learn he is a respectable man but I have my suspicions he likes his glass'.[50]

[48] *Hjula Papers*, Correspondence in, Denton, 2, 9 and 17 July 1863.
[49] *Hjula Papers*, Correspondence in, Denton, 23 and 30 July 1863; 1, 13 and 15 August 1863.
[50] *Hjula Papers*, Correspondence in, Denton, 5 September 1863.

Marmont got the job, and Denton subsequently dealt with contractual arrangements, made provision for the upkeep of Marmont's wife and child, and arranged for the further recruitment of a carder on Marmont's advice. As the next chapter will show, Marmont's years with Schou were on the whole successful, and he subsequently set up his own enterprise in Norway. When Marmont left Hjula in 1868, William Sharp & Sons commiserated with Schou and helped seek a replacement, in company with Richardson & Co., who advertised in the Leeds *Mercury* on Schou's behalf.[51]

The problem of labour acquisition was a major theme in the correspondence between William Sharp & Sons and Schou. In May 1865, for example, they advertised in the Leeds *Mercury* and in the Dewsbury newspapers for a dyer and finisher for Schou, though they advised Schou that the wage on offer, £2 per week, was unlikely to be enough. But they suggested that Schou should visit England and personally interview applicants: 'Meantime we will get each persons caracters [sic] and certificate from their former employers and interview with them if you will please write us a few days prior to your coming.'[52]

The man who was hired, Harrison, was not an immediate success, and this gave rise to correspondence concerning a possible replacement, with Sharps advising patience.[53] A few months later Schou decided to replace him, which led to a convoluted argument with Sharp & Sons concerning the wage Schou was prepared to offer:

As you have put the matter in our hands to find you a good Man we will try our best but very possibly we may be deceived for there are many men who do not at all understand the business out of employment and wishful to be engaged & could soon be so employed if they understood the business for Manufacturers here are always ready to give good wages when they meet with good men. We are rather afraid £3 per week will not command a first class man as they can get more money here & not disposed to go abroad for same money.[54]

Schou was not prepared to offer more than £3 per week, which led to continued problems in the carding room, and continued suggestions from Sharps that he pay more.[55]

Sharp & Sons also passed on problems concerning English employees. The following example was alas not unique:

and we have had a letter from Mrs J. E. Kellett, respecting the allowance from her husband, and she states that he had made arrangements with us to pay her 1£ per week, which he has done nothing of the kind, and she states that she has nothing to support herself and three children but what he allows her, please look into the matter and say what we are to do in your next letter.[56]

---

51 *Hjula Papers*, Correspondence in, Wm Sharp, 13 October 1868.
52 *Hjula Papers*, Correspondence in, Wm Sharp, 4 May 1865.
53 *Hjula Papers*, Correspondence in, Wm Sharp, 11 March 1869.
54 *Hjula Papers*, Correspondence in, Wm Sharp, 10 July 1869.
55 *Hjula Papers*, Correspondence in, Wm Sharp, 11 March 1870.
56 *Hjula Papers*, Correspondence in, Wm Sharp, 22 June 1865.

Schou asked them to pay her ten pounds, which they did. Other agents also made payments to relatives; Hvistendahl, Holst, for example, paid £5 per month to the wife of the dyer and finisher Wright Farrington.[57] Farrington's employment arose out of Hvistendahl, Holst's advice concerning defects in the finish of Hjula cloth. They recruited him, negotiated wages, took up references, sent full reports to Schou, and so on.[58] Subsequently they forwarded dyestuffs to Farrington which had been collected by Farrington's wife.[59] Dyeing and finishing remained a problem for Schou. In 1870 he wrote to the Leeds agent James Richardson, who had previously recruited a number of workers for Hjula, saying that he had a German dyer and a Norwegian finishing foreman and that the results were poor; he asked Richardsons to recruit him an experienced English dyer. Three weeks later he asked them to recruit a skilled carder for him.[60] Richardsons did so, and maintained the families of the workers while they were in Norway. For the Rosendahl enterprise at Bergen, Solomon Flatow recruited workers, and also made payments to their wives.[61]

Agents were in fact prepared to seek out labour over a range of trades. Sewell & Neck reported, for instance, that: 'It is not so easy a matter as you suppose to get an A1 Malster to leave his employment for a year, especially to visit a country respecting which, as you know, we are most remarkably ignorant in Britain.'[62] This was for a brewer to work in the Schou family brewery, an enterprise which preceded Hjula and which still exists.

Payments and finance

Some agents performed a quasi-banking role, holding accounts for customers, making payments on their behalf, and generally facilitating transactions. In the previous chapter I outlined the way in which Hjula Weavery was set up, with advice and equipment coming through the engineer Sir William Fairbairn, and the Manchester textile engineer J. Hetherington. Both Fairbairn and Hetheringtons were paid through the agents Sewell & Neck; Fairbairn received payments of £300 and £61 in early 1854.[63] The same agents from time to time advised on conditions in financial markets: 'People think that financial matters look better but many firms have been frightful losers. We are glad to say that our wool trade is sound.'[64] In January 1865 they wrote saying that they had charged the Hjula account 'the lowest Bank rate of interest', and continued: 'Now things look better and give hope it will be many years ere

---

57 *Hjula Papers*, Correspondence in, Hvistendahl, Holst & Co., 2 November 1864.
58 *Hjula Papers*, Correspondence in, Hvistendahl, Holst & Co., 11, 12 and 15 August 1864; 8 and 22 September 1864.
59 *Hjula Papers*, Correspondence in, Hvistendahl, Holst & Co., 10 November 1864.
60 *Hjula Papers*, Correspondence in, Richardson, 3 and 24 February 1870.
61 E.g., to Booth's wife: *Rosendahl Papers*, Correspondence in, 21 July 1846.
62 *Hjula Papers*, Correspondence in, Sewell & Neck, 8 March 1859.
63 *Hjula Papers*, Correspondence in, Sewell & Neck, 14 March 1854; 29 April 1854.
64 *Hjula Papers*, Correspondence in, Sewell & Neck, 4 November 1854.

money is at such an extraordinary quotation as during 1864.' But a year later money market conditions had apparently not improved: 'You will have noticed how very high the value of money continues in London: there must be a lot of bad paper still afloat.' A month later they remarked that 'we have a panic here among Joint Stock companies ... money market most unsettled'.[65] Sewell & Neck commented also on financial conditions and the development of the textile industry, asking Schou whether the activities of the Scandinavian Credit Association and the English and Swedish Bank would 'Cause too many fabrikker [i.e. factories] to be started?'.[66] Hvistendahl, Holst & Co. also kept up a running commentary on money market conditions, referring to such matters as the effects of the continuing civil war in the USA and Lincoln's reelection, to Grant's military success, to the bankruptcy of banking firms in Leeds, to rumours of the fall of 'an Indian House' in London, to 'large exports of gold to Alexandria', to the closure of banks and possible financial crisis in Bombay.[67]

The most usual financial service was simply to organize payment for Norwegian firms. Thus, for example, Richardsons paid Bottomley, the machinery supplier, in August 1867, and two months later, presumably concerning another purchase, 'sent a letter to Mr Bottomley advising him to call here for the amount of his bill'; they paid Cornock and Wade in November 1867, on behalf of Hjula. They paid 'Sugden's bill for machinery' in April 1868 and E. Hey and Wm Harrison £200, in November 1868.[68] Such transactions were extremely frequent. Rather than settle the account at regular intervals, Schou frequently simply sent a draft for £100, for example in November 1867, twice in April 1868, then in August, September and October 1868, then £200 in November 1868 and £400 in December 1868 and so on. A similar relationship occurred between Rosendahl and Solomon Flatow, who took care of the Rosendahl accounts with their main machinery supplier, Taylor Wordsworth & Co.[69] One major advantage of this system was that it made it possible for Norwegian purchasers to bargain for discounts with machinery suppliers for cash payment. For Arne Fabrikker, the agents du Fay & Co. normally obtained discounts of between 1½ and 3 percent for cash (which compares with their own normal commission of 2 percent). For Hjula, Schou normally received 2½ percent discount,[70] although on one occasion he suggested to Sharp & Sons of Leeds that he should receive 15 percent discount for cash.[71] A dispute over the amount of cash discount was in fact one of the reasons for the break-up of the relationship between Halvor

[65] *Hjula Papers*, Correspondence in, Sewell & Neck, 11 January 1865.
[66] *Hjula Papers*, Correspondence in, Sewell & Neck, 7 April 1866; 11 May 1866.
[67] *Hjula Papers*, Correspondence in, Sewell & Neck, 7 November 1863.
[68] *Hjula Papers*, Correspondence in, Hvistendahl, Holst & Co., 23 December 1863; 12 August 1864; 22 September 1864; 10 and 22 November 1864; 6 December 1864; 1 January 1865.
[69] *Hjula Papers*, Correspondence in, Richardson, 8 August 1867; 10 October 1867; 14 November 1867; 9 April 1868; 5 and 19 November 1868.
[70] *Rosendahl Papers*, Correspondence out, 28 December 1846.
[71] *Hjula Papers*, Correspondence out, 18 February 1869.

Schou and George Denton, with Schou claiming to have received an insufficient discount, and Denton insisting that he had fully credited Schou with the
available discount.[72]

RAW MATERIAL AND ANCILLARY EQUIPMENT SUPPLY

The organization of raw material purchase, and the purchase of ancillary
equipment, were a key activity of agents; this very frequently included
arranging payment and shipping, and was accompanied by much correspondence concerning conditions in the markets for these inputs. Thus Sewell &
Neck, over a twenty year period, purchased and shipped wool for Hjula
Weavery, as well as such products as indigo; sperm oil; olive oil and so on.
They were not themselves wool brokers, but simply acted as purchasing
agents; their correspondence with Hjula frequently enclosed reports or
circulars on the state of the wool market, and offered their thoughts on likely
price movements: 'Cotton has advanced on rumours of peace in Germany & if
this should be the case wool is pretty sure to follow.'[73] A frequent problem in
ordering was that Schou's orders were relatively small, and they found
difficulty in purchasing small quantities of six or so bales.[74] John Neck & Sons
continued this flow of wool market information into the late 1860s and
presumably beyond, sending circulars, reports from *The Times* and so on.[75]
And a similar flow of raw material information and purchase came through
Hvistendahl, Holst & Co., who frequently referred to the effects of the
American civil war, and monitored incoming shipments from Calcutta and
Bombay, and from China. They also sent a detailed account of how the
Liverpool market worked, particularly in terms of speculation.[76] Where
necessary they communicated by telegram: 'Lincoln reelected cotton market
wild yarns fourpence higher bought only what advised shall we buy more?'.[77]

Most Norwegian enterprises had definite and continuing arrangements
with such suppliers. Thus Arne Fabrikker dealt with the Manchester house of
Frühling & Goschen over many years, buying raw cotton, indigo, dyestuffs
and so on. Arne dealt also with Merck & Co., a firm which had branches in
several countries, and thus from time to time received shipments of wool
through the Hamburg market rather than from England.[78] Halden and
Nydalen dealt with Benecke Souchay & Co., which subsequently became a
significant merchant bank, but which purchased raw cotton and supplied a

---

[72] *Hjula Papers*, Correspondence out, 4 November 1864.
[73] *Hjula Papers*, Correspondence out, 18 November 1864.
[74] *Hjula Papers*, Correspondence in, Sewell & Neck, 27 February 1866; 7 July 1866; 7 January 1868.
[75] *Hjula Papers*, Correspondence in, Sewell & Neck, 20 April 1866.
[76] *Hjula Papers*, Correspondence in, John Neck, 20 February 1869.
[77] *Hjula Papers*, Correspondence in, Hvistendahl, Holst & Co., 6 October 1864; 6 December 1864.
[78] *Hjula Papers*, Correspondence in, Hvistendahl, Holst & Co. (Telegram), 22 November 1864.

large volume of market information. Solberg dealt with Whitehead & Meyer, from whom they frequently requested information on market conditions and prospects.[79]

REPRESENTATIVES IN OSLO

An important aspect of the agency business was dual representation, that is, offices in each of the countries engaged in trade. This worked in two ways, with some British-based firms having offices or representatives in Oslo or Bergen, and some Norwegian-based firms operating in Britain. Examples of the former include the equipment suppliers Parry & Co., of Birmingham who were represented in Christiania by one Henrik Dons, who sold leather bands and other items to Hjula Weavery. The latter included S. H. Lund, 'Ingeniör og Maskineri Agent' (Engineer and machinery agent), who had an office at New Broad St. in London, and who also dealt with Hjula.

CONCLUSION

The material discussed in this chapter suggests that British based agents were a very important component of the technology transfer process. Why should this have been? There seems to have been essentially two reasons. First, there is the problem of transactions and information costs as the British textile engineering industry grew and diversified. As the division of labour was extended within the industry, so the number of techniques and types of equipment grew, and this presumably complicated the task of acquiring information about available products, as well as that of evaluating their technical and economic suitability. A further complication would have been 'inter-relatedness' among these products, for groups of products were required in order to operate the overall textile process. For foreign firms, the use of agents was no doubt a way of simplifying the problem of information gathering and assessment associated with the purchase of equipment. Secondly, there is the question of assessing the reliability of information emanating from British machine makers. Norwegian entrepreneurs were often hesitant here, and thus used the experience and expertise of agents. Solberg Spinnery put this explicitly to their agents Whitehead & Meyer, the Liverpool cotton traders:

The purpose of this letter is to ask you, through your acquaintances in Manchester, to send us a price list for the enclosed machines with which we propose to extend our mill. Forgive us for making use of you in this matter, when we could get the information direct from the makers. But through you we hope to get more reliable information, just as we hope for advice in the choice of manufacturer, in particular putting us in touch with respectable firms.[80]

[79] *Arne Papers*, Correspondence in, 20 May 1857.
[80] E.g., *Solberg Papers, Kopibok 1851–57*, Correspondence out, 17 February 1854; 3 August 1854.

The list which Solberg enclosed included a willow, four carding machines, six throstles, and a grinding machine.

It is important to note that not all agents were British, Hvistendahl, Holst & Co., for example, were Norwegian and corresponded in Norwegian with the textile firms discussed here; A. Andersen, who was based in Leeds, was also Norwegian. Agents such as Merck & Co. typically corresponded in German. It may have been that the non-British influence was strongest in those agencies whose activities overlapped with those of merchant banking and the general finance of trade with continental Europe. The extent of this European influence can be gauged, perhaps, by the circular with which one agent, Gustav Oelrichs, sought business:

I beg leave to inform that I have this day established an agency business under the firm of

Gustav Oelrichs & Co.

and that I have been kindly permitted to refer to the houses below.

References

Messrs Frühling and Goschen, London
D. H. Wätjen & Co, Bremen
Gebrüder Schiller & Co, Hamburg
Wunderly & Co, Amsterdam
Johann Liebig & Co, Vienna
Kapherr & Co, St Petersburg
Charles Lüling & Co, New York[81]

This suggests not only a strong continental influence in agency activities, but also a very widespread network of such activities. The composition of the group of agents was very heterogeneous, and apparently barely formalized. Certainly the picture which has emerged here, of agency activities from the 1840s, contrasts with the much more formal and organized agency picture shown by Kirk for the later nineteenth century.[82] By 1880, Kirk suggests, the major textile engineers were represented by a single agent in each of the major textile producing countries. But the picture I have presented above suggests something rather more complex, with British-based agents representing not textile engineers, but rather their foreign customers, and facilitating the flow of technology to them. If the Norwegian experience was in any way typical in the period following the repeal of the prohibitions on the export of machinery, then the influence of British-based agents on the general spread of the new technology may have been very great.

[81] *Hjula Papers*, Correspondence in, Oelrichs, 15 August 1863.
[82] Kirk, *British Textile Machinery Industry*, Vol. II, pp. 425–8.

8

BRITISH WORKERS AND THE TRANSFER OF TECHNOLOGY TO NORWAY

INTRODUCTION

A 'technology' is a complex amalgam of knowledge, skills and devices. Even where technology is defined in terms of information or knowledge, this knowledge resides, to some extent, in people and the skills they possess. Both the definition and the role of a skill pose difficulties for economic and historical writing, where the notion of skill is frequently used in ad hoc ways. While this is not the place for a full discussion of the concept of skill, some points should be made about it since the focus of this chapter is on the problem of skilled labour supply and its role in the technological development of the Norwegian textile industry.

Skills have a number of characteristics. The most important for our purposes here have been described by Nelson and Winter as follows:

In the first place skills are programmatic, in that they involve a sequence of steps with each successive step triggered by and following closely on the completion of the preceding one. Second, the knowledge that underlies a skilful performance is in large measure tacit knowledge, in the sense that the performer is not fully aware of the details of the performance and finds it difficult or impossible to articulate a full account of those details. Third, the exercise of a skill often involves the making of numerous 'choices' – but to a considerable extent the options are selected automatically and without awareness that a choice is being made.[1]

The key point here is that the knowledge involved in skills cannot be readily codified and transmitted independently of the people who hold these skills. If this is the case, then the international transfer of technology is likely to involve the international movement of labour as well (although this could presumably be in either direction). This suggests that the availability of appropriate quantities and qualities of skilled labour could form an important constraint on the possibility of technology acquisition from abroad.

This point needs some emphasis, it seems to me, because it is frequently assumed that the general advance of technology has led to a simplification of

[1] R. Nelson and S. Winter, *An Evolutionary Theory of Economic Change* (Cambridge, Mass., 1982), p. 73.

operative skills required. It is believed that, as processes become more capital intensive, then technology replaces skilled labour and it becomes progressively easier to transfer technologies internationally since the skilled labour constraint is being removed by technical means. In this type of 'deskilling' approach to technological diffusion, the availability of labour skills is sometimes seen as a constraint on early industrialization (that is, prior to about 1820), but is not subsequently seen as a major problem. Kenwood and Lougheed, for example, remark that:

Even where there was a local shortage of particular types of skilled labour, it could be overcome in a number of ways ... The use of mechanical methods, particularly the development of automatic 'special purpose' machines designed for a single operation, and dispensing largely with skilled labour, was [one].[2]

But is it the case that technological advance facilitated technology transfer by embodying skills in machines? This problem is too complex for a detailed treatment here, although the following general points are relevant:

1 It does not seem, as an empirical matter, that labour was readily transferable between processes, even within particular industries, throughout the nineteenth century, or even that it is so today. Yet this would presumably be the case if techniques required progressively less 'skill'.

2 In general, the long-run development of technology does not seem to have led to a diminution of skill requirements. For example, much of the contemporary development economics literature sees skill requirements as a continuing obstacle to technology transfer. Thus Frances Stewart writes, in an extended analysis of technological problems of underdevelopment, that:

techniques designed in [developed] countries have been able to assume high levels of worker skills and literacy at all levels ... the need for associated skills imposed by the use of advanced-country technology often leads to an apparently chronic shortage of skilled manpower.[3]

3 Even where technological change has modified the nature of required skill inputs, practical skills may still be required at a level beyond the capacity of recipient countries to provide.

It is also important to remember that the skills necessary for production are not simply direct operative skills, but also include a range of ancillary skills in maintenance, repair, adoption and development of equipment. Beyond this, there are questions of capabilities in supervision, coordination and management. Pollard has emphasized the very great importance of management

[2] A. Kenwood and A. Lougheed, *Technological Diffusion and Industrialization Before 1914* (London, 1982), p. 104.
[3] F. Stewart, *Technology and Underdevelopment* (London, 1978), pp. 74–5.

capabilities in early British industrialization,[4] and Kenwood and Lougheed have reiterated their importance in the context of technological diffusion: 'In some countries these supervisory and managerial skills were in even shorter supply than technical skills.'[5]

On the basis of such considerations it is reasonable to argue that the transfer of operative and managerial skills were a crucial part of the diffusion of industrialization from Britain. Now there are essentially three ways in which such skills can be acquired within an industrializing country. First, workers can travel to the originating country of the technology for training; this occurs fairly frequently at the present time. Secondly, workers can, by a process of trial and error, learn but doing without formal training. This is rare, but it does happen.[6] Then skill transfer can be institutionalized, through the establishment of technical schools. Finally, workers with appropriate skills can travel from the originating to the host (importing) country either to operate technology, or to instruct, or both. This chapter will discuss the last of these mechanisms in the Norwegian context. In an account concentrating again on the Hjula enterprise I shall show that an influx of foreign skilled labour, almost entirely British, was an important concomitant of the development of the Norwegian textile industry. This labour inflow was linked, in a general sense, to the acquisition of British machines and equipment, but I shall also be concerned with an extremely specific link between labour inflow and the textile engineers and machinery-supplying agents who provided the new technology.

The role of foreign, and especially British, labour has been widely acknowledged in the literature on the diffusion of industrialization. Landes argues that the prohibitions on the emigration of artisans, and on the export of machinery prior to 1842, were ineffective and that 'by 1825 there must have been two thousand – and perhaps more – skilled British workers on the continent'.[7] However his suggestion is that this flow was important in early European industrialization, but diminished in importance from the 1840s. Similarly, Crisp confines discussion of foreign labour in nineteenth-century Russian industrialization to the 'proto-industrial' period, though elsewhere she shows that foreign technicians remained of considerable importance until into the twentieth century.[8] This emphasis runs through much of the literature; as Lee remarks in his discussion of labour in German industrialization: 'If imported labour played an important role in the early stages of

[4] S. Pollard, *The Genesis of Modern Management* (London, 1965), Ch. 5.
[5] Kenwood and Lougheed, *Technological Diffusion*, p. 104.
[6] See O. Crisp, 'Labour and industrialization in Russia', in P. Mathias and M. Postan (eds.) *The Cambridge Economic History of Europe*, Vol. VII, Part 2 (Cambridge, 1978), pp. 315–16.
[7] D. Landes, *The Unbound Prometheus* (Cambridge, 1969), p. 148.
[8] O. Crisp, 'Labour and industrialization', p. 315; O. Crisp, 'French investment and influence in Russian industry, 1894–1914', in *Studies in the Russian Economy Before 1914* (London, 1976), p. 168.

industrialization, the natives proved apt apprentices.'[9] Nevertheless Lee stresses the importance of British labour, particularly with respect to textile industries:

Difficulties experienced with the new machines were mainly due to the want of the necessary skill on the part of the workers. English workers proved as indispensable as English materials in breaking the crucial bottlenecks. Brugelmann had to hire an English mechanic to construct a spinning machine at his Cromford works in 1780 when none of the locals could persuade the machine which he had smuggled from Arkwright's factory to function. The Harthau cotton manufacturer, Karl Friedrich Bernard, wisely secured the services of the mechanic Watson, the spinner Evan, and the iron-worker Moult not only to install but to supervise the functioning of the first mule in Saxony in 1799.[10]

A similar emphasis, and similar problems, emerge in Jeremy's study of American textile development:

The crucial importance of the manager and machine builder in the Arkwright system and of the operative in the Crompton system ... could not be surmounted by importing machines without men. At Philadelphia, a disassembled spinning mule confounded interested parties for four years, and was eventually shipped back to Britain in 1787, leaving Philadelphians none the wiser but angrier.[11]

As I shall show, these kinds of problems existed in the emergent Norwegian textile industry, and were associated with an inflow of British labour. However, British workers and managers remained important beyond the early stages of industrialization, and their presence in Norway is associated with indications that they were important elsewhere in Europe later than is generally acknowledged in the literature.

In what follows I shall first give a general picture of the aggregate numbers and lengths of stay of British workers in the Norwegian textile industry. I shall then give a detailed, year-by-year description of the recruitment and careers of British workers and managers employed by Halvor Schou at Hjula Weavery. On the basis of this I shall describe the technological functions performed by British workers, and outline the problems associated with their employment. Finally, I shall consider the relationship between this inflow and the process of technology acquisition; the key point here is the role of British textile engineers and agents in labour recruitment and management, which has already been discussed in Chapters 6 and 7. I shall argue that the activities of these agents gave a distinctly new perspective on British labour in Western Europe, and that this emphasizes the importance which I have suggested should be ascribed to British engineers and capital goods producers in European industrialization.

Any comprehensive discussion of the role and functions of British workers

---

[9] J. J. Lee, 'Labour in German Industrialization', in P. Mathias and M. Postan (eds.) *Cambridge Economic History of Europe*, Vol. VII, Part 1 (Cambridge, 1978), p. 453.
[10] *ibid.*, p. 451.   [11] D. Jeremy, *Transatlantic Industrial Revolution* (Oxford, 1981), p. 76.

should, it seems to me, be based on firms' records, in particular correspondence files. But as with previous chapters variability in surviving records forms a constraint on discussion; for this reason I concentrate detailed analysis on the Hjula enterprise where extant materials are most complete. However, in the case of workers, we are in the position of finding a number of sources other than correspondence and contract records referring to their presence, occupations, wage levels and so on. These are:

1 Firms' accounts books recording workers' names and wages.
2 Norwegian communal (i.e. local government) taxation archives, where workers earning over a particular level (99 Specie Daler per annum) were recorded and assessed for tax.
3 The censuses of 1865 and 1875 which recorded birthplaces and occupations; this provides a means of tracing British workers living in textile districts.

The coverage of these sources is far from complete. For example, short-stay workers (who were, as I shall show, the majority) might not appear by name in firms' wage books, or might have left no trace at all since they may have been paid by British machine suppliers. The taxation records list only those earning above a threshold income, and, more importantly, only those staying over a full tax year. Thus those staying less than one year are excluded. So even where workers are traceable, they may not appear in the tax records; in Oslo, for example, out of seventy-seven traceable workers, only forty-seven appear in the tax listings. The implication of this, since most workers were short-term, is that the number of British workers is understated, perhaps very significantly understated, by surviving sources. The best source appears to be correspondence archives, and it is, I think, no accident that the firm with the best surviving correspondence records is the one for whom most workers can be traced.

All traceable British workers are listed by name, with relevant information summarized, in Appendix D. The firms covered in this study employed a total of ninety-six British workers over the period to 1870, of whom twenty were women. The distribution among firms is shown in Table 8.1 (year of establishment of the firm is given in brackets).

Table 8.1 *Numbers of British workers employed by Norwegian textile firms*

Foss (1856)	Br.v/Hjula (1849/56)	Nydalen (1845)	Wallem (1845)	Arne (1846)	Christiania Sailcloth (1856)
4	39	3	7	7	11

Halden (1813)	Vøien (1845)	Rosendahl (1845)	Solberg (1818)	Grorud (1870)
1	3	3	0	3

Source: Drawn from Appendix D.

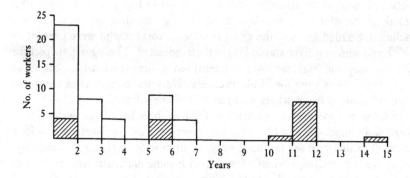

Figure 8.1
All British workers: average length of stay
Source: State tax records

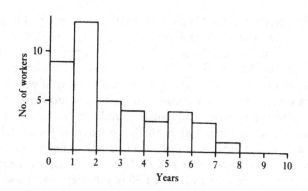

Figure 8.2
British workers at Hjula: average length of stay
Source: Hjula Papers: correspondence, invoices, account books. State tax records.
Census 1865 and 1875

With only one exception every Norwegian textile firm used British labour at some point. Clearly there were differences in the extent of use, though these may be more apparent than real because of the data problems noted above; other reasons for differences in dependence on British labour will be discussed below. In general, lengths of stay were short. The aggregate picture, based on tax records only, is as shown in Figure 8.1. It should be noted, as mentioned above, that those staying less than one year are not included. Shaded areas in the chart represent workers who were present in 1870, and who may have stayed longer than indicated. This aggregate picture of short-stay and high turnover is confirmed at firm level, where the most complete records exist for Hjula Weavery. Here the picture is as shown in Figure 8.2, for those workers who can be definitely traced.

In terms of functions, these workers fell into three broad categories. First, there were mechanics, who came for short periods (perhaps two to four months) in order to set up machinery, or to modify or repair it. Secondly, there were operatives, normally familiar with some particular process: check loom weaving, for example, or finishing or dyeing. Thirdly, came the most important – numerically and otherwise – namely supervisors of various types. These categories were not always clearly distinguishable; the skills possessed by operatives frequently conferred some kind of supervisory authority, sometimes implicitly, often explicitly. Mechanical skills were a basic qualification for a managerial post.

In the following section I shall describe in detail, year by year, the inflow of British workers to one enterprise, namely the Hjula works; following sections will draw some conclusions concerning technological functions from this data, and will discuss other firms.

BRITISH WORKERS IN THE HJULA ENTERPRISE

The Hjula enterprise did not begin until 1856, but prior to that its proprietor Halvor Schou ran a smaller establishment, something of a 'pilot' to Hjula. His association with British employees seems to have begun in March 1850, with payments to one Joseph Oddy. These are associated with payments to William Fairbairn, and Oddy subsequently wrote asking 'if your engine and all is going well', so he was presumably an engineer or mechanic.[12] Brenneriveien was powered by steam, and possibly Oddy was employed to set it up.

At about the same time, March 1850, the name of Joseph Kingston, a weaving master, first appears in the account books of the Schou enterprise; his wages, varying between four and six Specie daler (approximately £1 to £1 10s 0d) were entered on a weekly basis. In July they almost doubled to 11 Specie daler per week. Kingston's son Jonathan was also employed, at about half his father's wage rate. In October 1850 they were, it seems, joined by

---

[12] *Schou Papers*, Correspondence in, 19 July 1851.

Kingston's daughter Emma, whose travel expenses were charged to the weavery account – she stayed for approximately two years it seems – an amount of £4, presumably for return travel expenses, was paid to her by the Manchester firm of Merck & Co. in October 1852. Joseph Kingston stayed for several years; he appears in the tax records for the three years 1851–3, and Jonathan appears in 1851 and 1852. Kingston returned to England in May 1853 – travel expenses and a gift totalling £44 were paid by Merck & Co.[13] It may be that Kingston was recruited for Schou by William Fairbairn, since in November 1850 Schou paid an account of £12 to Fairbairn for the support of Kingston's wife. There is no correspondence relating to this, but in other cases those who pay dependants are usually those who have done the recruiting. Joseph Kingston's brother William acted on Schou's account in England, for in October 1852 the supplier Thomas Hitchings wrote to say that he had despatched pickers 'that was ordered by William Kingston when he was at my place'.[14] Further light is thrown on Kingston and his travels in a letter dated February 1854, from the Manchester supplier James Townson; he mentioned that he had had an order for healds, reeds and bobbins from Kingston, who was in the USA. He went on, with slightly idiosyncratic grammar:

Mr Barnes[15] told me that you was doing very bad indeed and would have to part with your present manager. I mention it to John Kingston that his Joseph brother he said he would have no objection to coming to Norway for 6 9 or 12 months to superintend your weaving and put you in the same way has Joseph had you when he left ... the wages he would want would be £2 10s 0d per week to start with.[16]

Schou did not take up this offer. A foreman named Jackson was working for Schou during 1855. In August and September Schou wrote with orders to three British equipment suppliers (Diggles; William Smith; Parr, Curtis & Madeley) with enclosures describing in detail the equipment required; these were drawn up by Jackson.[17] He was gone a year later, since a letter to Parr, Curtis & Madeley in late August 1856 referred to equipment ordered and delivered 'in Jackson's time'.[18] In January 1856 Schou wrote to Squire Diggles in Manchester seeking 'a clever overlooker for weaving checks, twills and trousers'. Getting no response, he wrote again in May, saying, '... if I had somebody to manage gingham and tweed weaving with knowledge and energy, I should be able in the course of a few years to fill my mill with several hundred of your looms'.[19] Diggles eventually engaged one George Murray,

13 *Schou Papers, Cassa Bok [Account Book], 1850–52*, Various entries.
14 *Schou Papers*, Correspondence in, Hitchings, 12 October 1852.
15 This was Samuel Barnes, an Oldham textile engineer.
16 *Schou Papers*, Correspondence in, Townson, 27 February 1854.
17 *Hjula Papers*, Correspondence in, Parr, Curtis & Madeley, 9 August 1855; *Hjula Papers*, Correspondence out, Diggles, 24 August 1855; Parr, Curtis & Madeley, 7 September 1855; Wm Smith, 14 September 1855.
18 *Hjula Papers*, Correspondence out, 23 August 1856.
19 *Hjula Papers*, Correspondence out, 6 May 1866.

who arrived in August 1856 and quickly proved unsuitable: 'I am afraid that Murray is not the man that I wanted. At all counts I do not think that he is worth his wages. He might be a fair overlooker but as a foreman and a manager he is only half a man.'[20] Murray turned out to be 'an incorrigible drunkard', and was dismissed, returning to England after a stay of fourteen weeks. He was replaced by the 'steady and respectable' John Hunt, who was recruited through Parr, Curtis & Madeley. Hunt stayed for at least six years, appearing in the tax records in 1857, 1858 and 1861. In January 1862 he was given three months notice, with no reason being recorded. But this appears to have been rescinded, for Schou's *Kopibok* contains a record of three months notice being given to him again in June 1862.[21]

In June 1856 Parr, Curtis & Madeley also recruited a foreman weaver called Pollit, who was initially a success, starting up looms which had been idle for some time.[22] At the same time Schou asked Parr, Curtis & Madeley to recruit a four-loom weaver for him. On Pollit's recommendation they engaged Thomas Barrat, who arrived in late August or early September. The Pollit-Barrat combination was not a happy one for Schou; they drank heavily, and Schou wrote a series of letters to Parr, Curtis & Madeley, saying that Barrat was 'a rough fellow and unsettled', who 'will have to go the same way as Murray if not steady', and asking Parr, Curtis & Madeley to write personally to Barrat and Pollit warning them that 'their behaviour will spoil their future in England'.[23] Barrat left when his contract expired in July 1857. Pollit left at about the same time, with Schou writing that:

You will perhaps have heard by now that Pollit has behaved so badly here that I was obliged to send him home. Every one of his countrymen here says that I have treated him far better than he deserves.

I shall be glad to see the new overlooker here the sooner the better.[24]

This was Frederick Holt, whose career in Norway will be described below.

In September 1856, Parr, Curtis & Madeley recruited another skilled worker, John Waddington, who 'understands beaming, sizing healds, twisting or drawing and setting out of healds, and will bring out a correct receipt for sizing healds'.[25] Waddington appears in the tax records for 1857 and 1858, with earnings of 350 Specie daler per year (just under £2 per week). After he left Schou's employment, in 1858, he returned to England where he subsequently purchased materials for Schou.[26] Waddington retained some connection with Schou and his employees, because Waddington's son Arthur, who was born in 1864, later came to live in Oslo as a foster child of Alfred Hudson, who was Schou's foreman in 1874.

[20] *Hjula Papers*, Correspondence out, 18 August 1856.
[21] *Hjula Papers*, Correspondence out, 29 January 1862; June 1862.
[22] *Hjula Papers*, Correspondence out, 23 August 1856.
[23] *Hjula Papers*, Correspondence out, 29 September 1856.
[24] *Hjula Papers*, Correspondence out, 12 June 1857.
[25] *Hjula Papers*, Correspondence out, 4 September 1856.
[26] *Hjula Papers*, Correspondence out, 18 June 1858.

Despite employing Waddington, Schou wrote again to Parr, Curtis & Madeley in March 1857 asking them to 'engage a new overlooker in place of Pollit'. He 'must understand plain loom and twills' and would receive £2 per week. The request was repeated insistently in April, May and June. In July Parr, Curtis & Madeley engaged Frederick Holt who, they said in a letter of introduction, 'we have no doubt you will find . . . steady industrious and sober, with a perfect knowledge of his business'.[27] By August Schou was writing that although Holt seemed 'a steady and sensible young man' he was 'not as acquainted with twills as I could have wished'.[28] By May the following year he was 'given to drink', and Parr, Curtis & Madeley were lamenting: 'We are truly sorry you think Holt is not likely to be steady, we had great confidence in him when he *left*, but they strangely forget themselves when away from home. Perhaps your lecture to him may be of service to him, I hope it will.'[29] But within a month Holt was to leave. Schou was not 'totally displeased with him and had no wish to harm him'.[30]

At about the same time, in May 1857, Parr, Curtis & Madeley recruited a 'loom mechanic' called James Brierly, who arrived with various parts for Schou's machines. Brierly was employed for a year, and until June 1858 Parr, Curtis & Madeley made regular payments on his behalf to his wife. Brierly must subsequently have returned to Oslo, since he appears again in the tax records in 1861 and 1862. There is only one reference to him in the correspondence in these later years, namely a letter to Schou from Brierly's vicar, writing on behalf of 'one of my parishioners – Marianne Brierly, a poor needy woman with three helpless children, the wife of one James Brierly'. Brierly had ceased to send her money and she was destitute; the vicar asked Schou to assist, which he did, sending money to her through Bluhm & Co. of Manchester in April 1862.[31]

The year 1859 saw the recruitment of three British workers: Andrew Clarke, Thomas Horrebin and John Orme, all weavers. Clarke was engaged by the Anderston Foundry of Glasgow, who were supplying Schou with looms. A condition of Clarke's employment was that he learnt how to operate a tape-dressing machine, 'so that he could start that machine here'.[32] This he did, spending some time training in a British mill, at Schou's expense. Clarke was not, however, a success; he did not seem particularly skilled with the machine, and was frequently ill. He was back in Glasgow by April 1860. There is more to this episode than meets the eye, however; it will be discussed in more detail below, in relation to the employment of David Rorison.

27 *Hjula Papers*, Correspondence out, 24 April 1857; 10 May 1857; 19 June 1857. *Hjula Papers*, Correspondence in, Parr Curtis, 9 July 1867.
28 *Hjula Papers*, Correspondence out, 11 August 1857.
29 *Hjula Papers*, Correspondence out, 18 May 1858. *Hjula Papers*, Correspondence in, Parr Curtis, 26 May 1858.
30 *Hjula Papers*, Correspondence out, 18 June 1858.
31 *Hjula Papers*, Correspondence in, Parr Curtis, 27 May 1857; Rev. J. Edwards, 5 February 1862.
32 *Hjula Papers*, Correspondence out, 5 September 1859.

At the same time Thomas Horrebin was recruited by Parr, Curtis & Madeley, his wife being supported through the Manchester firm of Bluhm & Co. He worked for Schou for nearly four years, appearing in the tax records until 1862, ånd earning 400 Specie daler per year, or approximately £2 per week. In June 1865 he wrote a long letter to Schou from Küchen in Germany, from a large spinning and weaving establishment where his contract was coming to an end; he hoped to work once again for Schou. Another worker at Hjula in 1858, John Orme, also wrote several times after his departure, on each occasion with a request to be re-employed by Schou.[33]

I referred above to a purchase of looms from the Anderston Foundry in Glasgow; this gave rise to an episode which deserves more detailed treatment. Schou sought two types of labour input with respect to this loom purchase, and indeed the supply of appropriate labour was a condition of the purchase. He needed a fitter, to set up the looms, and a tenter or overlooker to operate them. Anderstons had some difficulty engaging an overlooker at the wage Schou was prepared to pay; most wanted 'no less than £3 to £3 10s 0d', so '... we have fixed upon sending our own Tenter for such a length of time as will enable one of your own hands to get so initiated with the work of these looms that you will have no difficulty'. However they added the proviso that: 'We would like our man to be as short with you as possible as we require him to go to several other places on the Continent to put our Patent Check loom to work.'[34] Schou agreed to this, 'if I can keep him as long as I need him'.[35] The man concerned, David Rorison, was essentially a fitter and a mechanic rather than an operative, but he could operate the loom. He presumably left Glasgow in early July 1859, since he bore a letter of introduction dated 9 July which remains in the Hjula archives; however he had other machinery to set up first in St Petersburg. In late July the machinery arrived in Christiania, Schou deciding not to unpack it before Rorison's arrival.[36] At this point Schou wrote again to Anderston's saying of Rorison that 'I understand that you will only let me keep him for putting the looms together', and asking that:

you let him stay here in my service until he has instructed my overlookers in the management of your looms so far, that they are thoroughly acquainted with the fittings of them in every respect with all the twill motions and the drop-box motion in particular.[37]

Schou wrote again in early August, pointing out that 'I have engaged new hands', and emphasizing the need for them to be instructed. However this applied not only to his Norwegian workers but also to English weavers in his mill: 'I am afraid that my English overlookers ... shall not be very willing to

33 *Hjula Papers*, Correspondence in, Horrebin, 4 June 1865; Orme, 15 January 1860; 20 February 1860; 14 March 1860; 16 April 1860.
34 *Hjula Papers*, Correspondence in, Anderston, 14 June 1859.
35 *Hjula Papers*, Correspondence out, 21 June 1859.
36 *Hjula Papers*, Correspondence out, 12 July 1859; 22 July 1859.
37 *Hjula Papers*, Correspondence out, 22 July 1859.

acknowledge the superiority of your machine unless it is proved to them in such a manner that it would be quite impossible to anybody to deny it.'[38]

Perhaps this was more a matter of Scots-English rivalry than of the technical competence of the English overlookers. However Schou pointed out that as a result of this problem it might be mutually advantageous for him to keep the fitter through the winter, 'or if you could get another clever man sent off as an overlooker for one year'. This was coupled with a thinly veiled commercial threat; Schou claimed to be worried that: '... my English foremen would not be impartial with your looms, they would try to persuade me, if I saw your looms not working as well as the English, to go back to our old friends in Manchester and Radcliffe'.[39] This galvanized Anderstons into action. Two weeks later they responded in detail:

In noticing your remarks in regard to a permanent tenter being sent out we think it very advisable that it should be so – from long experience we have observed that when anything like a prejudice exists that however good the article may be there is nothing but fault finding – On our man leaving we gave him instructions that he was not to leave your place until you were quite satisfied that all was right – We have however in the meantime thought it better that we should set ourselves the task of looking out for a good Tenter, that will engage with you for twelve months, and we are glad to say that we have got an offer from a first rate man ...

This was Andrew Clarke, referred to above. He was to tend 'all the looms ... teach your workers, act as overlooker'.[40] In the meantime, Anderstons cabled Rorison in St Petersburg, and wrote to Schou on 4 August that he would soon arrive. After two weeks quibbling about Clarke's wages ('how shall I manage to pay a foreman £3 without raising the wages of my other hands?') Schou agreed to employ him, but with an important qualification: that Clarke should also be able to operate a tape dressing machine which Schou wished to order from Anderston. Once again Schou tied the purchase to labour input.

As I should not like to take a man from Scotland solely to manage the tape dressing machine, I cannot give you an order for this machine unless you can manage to hire a tenter who would undertake to make himself acquainted with it, but if such be the case you may, as soon as you have signed the agreement with the man in question ... set in work for me a *tape dressing machine* ... which I suppose will suit the looms you sent me.

Schou offered to pay the wages of this man while he learnt to operate the machine in the UK; he would then have to teach its use to Schou's Norwegian workers. Acquisition of this skill was made a definite condition of the purchase of the tape-dresser, and also of the hire of the weaving overlooker (on which, in turn, future loom purchases depended): 'If you cannot find a man, who will comply with my wishes, here expressed, you will send me

[38] *Hjula Papers*, Correspondence out, 22 July 1859; 2 August 1859.
[39] *Hjula Papers*, Correspondence out, 22 July 1859.
[40] *Hjula Papers*, Correspondence in, Anderston, 2 August 1859.

neither a tenter nor a tape dressing frame.'[41] Anderston's and Andrew Clarke, agreed to this, so Clarke left his present employers and went to work in a factory to learn 'tape dressings and warping'.[42]

Clarke eventually arrived on 25 November 1859; he had been asked to bring examples of 'pretty tartans' and 'nice patterns in cotton checks and stripes' with him.[43] Rorison had arrived in the meantime from St Petersburg, on 19 August, and was at work setting up the looms. Schou was clearly impressed by him, and was already suggesting that his stay should not be a brief one:

> your man, who is a sensible fellow, that I like very much, says that he must do the greatest part alone, when putting the various machines together, and I know that neither he nor you should like him to leave the looms before they are in good working condition.[44]

The work proceeded. Then, in early November – prior to the arrival of Andrew Clarke – came something of a bombshell – Schou offered Rorison a permanent post, 'to take the management of the mechanical part of my factory', and Rorison accepted. The news was broken to Anderstons in a letter in which Schou assumed, surely hypocritically, that Anderston would be glad that Rorison had been seduced away by higher wages. The pill was sweetened with the prospect of new orders. It was true that Rorison had no 'experience in managing'; however:

> I consider him to be such a thorough, experienced mechanic and weaver, and knowing him as a quiet respectable and industrious man, I did not hesitate to secure his services by offering him a permanent situation, my only consideration being the fear of doing anything that would displease you by taking from you such a fine old hand.
>
> You have employed the new tenter for 3 guineas a week and I could not offer Rorison less than £3 10s 0d, a salary that will satisfy him and you also, so that you will see his position considerably mended ...
>
> I must confess, that the superiority of your looms to any other I have got in the factory has been the great cause of my wish to engage Rorison. I will extend the fancy weaving as fast as I can, and I shall suppose that I shall be obliged to break up or sell some of my old looms. I shall give you new orders ... to be effected in the spring.[45]

Anderston accepted the *fait acompli* with reasonably good grace, although 'it certainly is what we didn't anticipate'. Despite the 'considerable inconvenience' they praised the 'honest and liberal way in which you have referred it to our decision' (which, unless there is missing correspondence, Schou had not) and trusted 'it will benefit all parties concerned'.[46]

In fact this episode does not seem to have benefited Anderstons, since no

[41] *Hjula Papers*, Correspondence out, 5 September 1859.
[42] *Hjula Papers*, Correspondence in, Anderston, 23 September 1859.
[43] *Hjula Papers*, Correspondence out, 4 and 29 October 1859.
[44] *Hjula Papers*, Correspondence out, 20 August 1859.
[45] *Hjula Papers*, Correspondence out, 11 November 1859.
[46] *Hjula Papers*, Correspondence in, Anderston, 18 November 1859.

major orders actually ensued. Not surprisingly, Clarke's employment did not endure. He was ill, and Schou claimed that he was incompetent with the tape dressing machine. After six months he returned to Glasgow.[47]

Rorison, on the other hand, stayed in Schou's employment for some years. He appeared in the tax records between 1861 and 1865 inclusive, with earnings rising from 600 to 900 Specie daler per year. In 1865 and 1866 Rorison visited Scotland, ordering equipment on Schou's behalf from the firm of Landell, Gibson & Sons of Glasgow. It may be that relations with the Anderston foundry had deteriorated, since Rorison had Landell, Gibson & Sons order equipment for Schou from Anderstons – there seems no obvious reason why it could not have been ordered direct.[48] However, Anderstons wrote to Schou, after years without any communication, in 1870 following a major fire at the Hjula Weavery, which somehow Anderstons had heard about, offering their services in equipping him with new looms (this Schou declined, on the grounds that he would use this opportunity to extend his woollen production, thus wanting no cotton looms).[49]

At about this time Rorison was suffering from ill-health, and it may be that after ordering equipment for Schou he did not return to Norway. There is one further reference to him in the correspondence; in late 1869, in a letter to Schou, Landell, Gibson & Sons refer to seeing Rorison, and getting an order from him (though on whose behalf is unclear).[50]

In mid 1863 Schou made efforts through the agent George Denton to recruit a 'finisher and loom tuner' (i.e. two separate posts). Denton interviewed a number of workers and subsequently engaged one, who then backed out in a dispute over pay. In August Denton engaged George Richardson of Birstal, 'a young man of first class abilities ... teetotal and most steady'. Although primarily a weaver, he was '... also a good mechanic and can take down and set up any looms that you will require. He can warp, size and do all the duties of a power-loom overlooker.'[51] He was to be paid £2 10s 0d per week. Richardson stayed for some years, appearing in the tax records between 1864 and 1869 inclusive, with earnings of 700 Specie daler (approximately £3 per week). A receipt for tax paid, of 28 Specie daler, was issued in 1868. Since it was in the Hjula archives, this may mean that Schou paid his taxes.

At the same time Schou was seeking a mill manager, and Denton undertook to 'obtain the names of proper men'. In a long letter to Schou in September 1863 Denton listed five possible managers he had contacted, going into considerable detail about their previous careers, and including references from their previous employers. One, Stephen Marmont, 'is now a manager of a mill at Eccleshill', aged thirty-six, he apparently had a 'good

[47] *Hjula Papers*, Correspondence in, Anderston, 14 January 1860.
[48] *Hjula Papers*, Correspondence in, Anderston, 18 October 1865; 11 November 1865; 11 November 1865.
[49] *Hjula Papers*, Correspondence in, Anderston, 18 May 1870.
[50] *Hjula Papers*, Correspondence in, Landell Gibson, 14 November 1869.
[51] *Hjula Papers*, Correspondence in, Denton, 3 August 1863.

knowledge of woollen machinery and is able both to set it up and get it to work'.[52]

Marmont was hired, at £200 per annum, and subsequently became a very important component of the Hjula weavery. Schou relied heavily on him for technical advice in dealing with British suppliers, and he made a number of trips to England to purchase equipment on Schou's behalf; these technical functions will be discussed in more detail below.

Marmont remained with Schou for five years, leaving in early 1869. In his first letter to Schou concerning Marmont, Denton pointed out that 'he had been a manufacturer himself but was compelled to give up for the want of means'.[53] In 1869, on leaving Schou's employment, Marmont set up on his own again, this time in Oslo, and in company with Schou's other employee George Richardson. In collaboration with Peter Pettersen they set up as partners in the Leerfossen mill at Grorud, on the outskirts of Oslo. The parting was evidently an amicable one since Schou gave some equipment to Marmont:

In consideration of the good services of Mr Stephen Marmont during the years he has worked as a foreman spinner and carder in my factory, I hereby give him permission to bring with him and put up in Leerfossen Woollen factory the following belonging to Hjula, viz:

2 spinning mules
1 spinning billy
1 piecing machine

which machinery I hereby give him the right to keep and to use as long as he continues to be the owner of or partner in Leerfossen Factory. When he intends to give up this business he shall inform me of such intentions and give me the necessary assistance in removing the above mentioned machinery from the premises of Leerfossen and back to Hjula.[54]

Marmont signed a similarly phrased statement. His association with Schou continued; Schou continued to take technical advice from Marmont, and during 1870 referred to Marmont's views in five letters to Sharp & Sons, and to the Leeds supplier J. Richardson.[55]

The Leerfossen partnership between Marmont, Richardson and Petterson lasted until 1879. During his time with Schou, Marmont brought his family to Oslo. His son John, born in Leeds in 1850, married a Norwegian woman, had three children in the early 1870s, and subsequently worked himself as a foreman at Hjula.

Wright Farrington, a finisher, was engaged on a short-term basis through the Manchester firm Hvistendahl, Holst & Co. He had been ten years with the weaving firm of Redgrave, and had been offered a post with the English

52 *Hjula Papers*, Correspondence in, Denton, 5 September 1862.
53 *Hjula Papers*, Correspondence in, Denton, 5 September 1863.
54 *Hjula Papers*, *Kopibok*, 8 January 1869.
55 *Hjula Papers*, Correspondence out, 15 and 25 March 1870; 15 April 1870; 27 May 1870.

weaver John Lancaster, beginning in March 1865. In the meantime 'it suits him to take a temporary post', and he stayed for about six months.

A fulling miller named William Stead was recruited by Sharp & Sons, through advertisements in the Dewsbury newspapers; his wage was £1 10s 0d per week. He was chosen on the advice of another of Schou's employees, Samuel Clegg, who was at that time in Manchester. Clegg appears to have been a mechanic – Sharp & Sons showed him models of a new machine, of which he had a low opinion.[56] No other references to Clegg have been found, although four years later the machine maker G. W. Tomlinson wrote to Schou that: 'I had a visit yesterday from Mr Clegg formerly in your employment – I showed him two narrow perpetual shearing machines I bought at a sale ... he said he thought they would do very well for you.'[57]

In 1868 the imminent departure of Marmont and Richardson faced Schou with the necessity of recruiting more managers. On Marmont's recommendation he hired Alfred Hudson of Leeds, who was engaged through the machine makers James Richardson & Co. Hudson arrived in November 1868, and in turn recommended that one William Harrison be engaged as a foreman carder and spinner. Harrison also was engaged through Richardson. But, by the end of January 1869, Schou was writing to Sharp & Son that:

It was certainly a mistake of mine when I gave way to Hudson's wish and engaged Harrison as a foreman spinner. He is a very quiet and respectable man, but he is certainly not a competent foreman. He is too sleepy and there is no energy about him. We have agreed that he shall go home by one of the first steamers.[58]

He then asked Sharp & Son to find him a new foreman. Four more letters followed over the next month, but Harrison gradually improved and Schou decided to let him 'see the year out'. However, Harrison was still at Hjula in May 1870 despite another half-dozen letters to Sharps and to Richardson. Harrison's improvement must have been limited, since in May 1870 Schou wrote that 'I have new cards to nail, and I do not let Harrison do this work, which he has proved not to understand'.[59] Hudson was slightly more successful, though Schou had repeated reservations concerning his advocacy of Harrison. Certainly Hudson was active in purchasing for and advising Schou. However by May 1870 Schou was writing to Richardson that:

I engaged Hudson as a manufacturer chiefly in consequence of Marmont's recommendation. I had at that time so much confidence in Marmont's judgements that I omitted to take the usual and necessary investigations about Hudson, and I soon found out that I would have got a better man, but I hate changing foremen, and I always hoped, that he should improve and get more experience by degrees. I feel now the necessity of trying another man.[60]

[56] *Hjula Papers*, Correspondence in, Wm Sharp, 4 and 29 May 1865.
[57] *Hjula Papers*, Correspondence in, Tomlinson, 15 June 1869.
[58] *Hjula Papers*, Correspondence out, 28 June 1869.
[59] *Hjula Papers*, Correspondence out, 6 May 1870.
[60] *Hjula Papers*, Correspondence in, Richardson, 27 May 1870.

The essential problem with Hudson was that he had 'very little knowledge of power looms which has been very much against him in the manufacturing of reversibles'. Schou went on to specify in detail the skills he wanted his foreman to possess, and asked Richardson to advertise and engage someone on his behalf. Hudson attempted subsequently to set up manufacturing for himself in Oslo, with little success.

In February 1869 Schou wrote to James Richardson saying that he needed a 'foreman finisher' to replace his present finisher (who cannot be identified). Schou wanted a 'Leeds finisher' (implying that he was going to make fine cloth) who must know boiling and cutting and understand cylinder grinding: not, he emphasized, a 'Batley or Dewsbury man'.[61] After some delays and hesitations Richardson engaged James Pollard, who came to Oslo with his young family (though Schou stressed he was 'not to bring sons', presumably because Schou could not employ them). Pollard was selected from twelve applicants, most of whom were asking £3 10s 0d rather than the £3 per week Schou was willing to pay. Pollard arrived in May 1869. He stayed at Hjula for some years, since he and his family appear in the 1875 Norwegian census.

When Schou came to replace Hudson he set out the desired qualifications of the new foreman in considerable detail:

You will have to look out for a person who has been in the Batley and Morley trade, accustomed to *make cheap goods*. The principal articles whose make he must thoroughly understand is
union reversible (Presidents) and all woollen reversibles
Union pilot and Devons (very cheap)
Waterproof tweeds
and lastly all woollen cloth like the enclosed samples.[62]

He emphasized that he would like to keep this foreman for some years, and that he 'should certainly not repent to have come into my service if he really could make himself useful to me'. The desired qualifications of this foreman were spelled out over several pages, and repeated in very considerable detail in another letter only a week later.[63]

Richardson advertised on Schou's behalf and recruited William Roebuck in August 1870, praising him fulsomely to Schou.

We think we have got the right man for you his late employers give him the very best of character, in fact they told us they did not think a better manufacturer could be found in Yorkshire, but he is not a power loom tuner in fact we could not find a good manufacturer that would tune they consider tuning too menial ... we know that you have a tuner so that what you require is a man to make good and cheap cloth & we believe you will have the right man.[64]

---

61 *Hjula Papers*, Correspondence in, Richardson, 26 February 1869.
62 *Hjula Papers*, Correspondence in, Richardson, 27 May 1870.
63 *Hjula Papers*, Correspondence in, Richardson, 3 June 1870.
64 *Hjula Papers*, Correspondence in, Richardson, 18 August 1870.

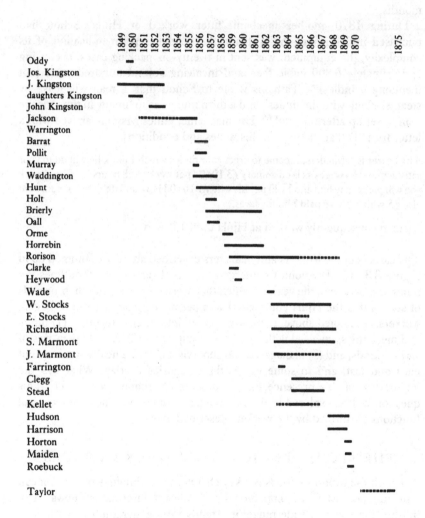

Figure 8.3
British workers in the Hjula enterprise, 1849–1870
Key: Solid lines indicate period of stay. Broken lines indicate probable extension of stay
beyond the period given by the solid line.
Sources: Hjula Papers: correspondence, account books, invoices. State Tax Records.
Census 1865 and 1875

Schou appeared satisfied with Roebuck, but retained reservations about his qualifications ('He brings no certificates with him') and his steadiness ('Are you quite sure that he is a sober man?').[65] Richardsons thought it worthwhile to reply immediately in reassuring tones and at considerable length.[66]

In March 1870 Richardson also recruited a specialist dyer, James Horton. He turned out to drink excessively, and returned to England within six months.

During 1870 another mechanic/fitter worked at Hjula. Schou had puchased mules from John Tatham of Rochdale. As an indication of its complexity, the equipment was sent in twenty-six packing cases, occupying approximately 6,800 cubic feet, and involving several hundred parts (not including spindles).[67] Tathams wrote to Schou that 'a man will leave by steamer along with the mules', and a third mule was to 'follow in time for the man to set up after the two'.[68] The mechanic, James Maiden, arrived with a letter from Tatham setting out his wages and conditions:

> The bearer is J. Maiden ... come to erect your mules which I think he will do to your satisfaction. His wages as is customary £3 10s 0d per week of 58 hours ... £2 per week you will please pay him and I will pay his wife £1 10s 0d here and debit to your account also £5 which I have paid him for fares.

Maiden subsequently worked at Hjula until 15 August.

The careers of the workers and managers described above are summed up in Figure 8.3. The key point to emerge from the diagram, which outlines the number of workers, the years in which they were recruited, and their periods of stay, is that the Hjula enterprise had a permanent complement of British workers. As I noted above, these workers fall into three categories: (1) fitters and mechanics, involved with setting up equipment, (2) skilled operatives of various kinds, and (3) managerial and supervisory staff. The divisions are not hard and fast, and to some extent the categories overlap. What was the importance of this presence for the process of technology transfer? This question will be explored in the next section, which examines the technical functions performed by the workers described above.

THE TECHNOLOGICAL ROLE OF UK WORKERS

Although the export of goods is a key channel for technology transfer, it can only function when accompanied by significant information flows. The information covers a wide range; it extends from general information concerning production possibilities, to knowledge of the capabilities of particular devices and machines, to construction and operating knowledges, and to

[65] *Hjula Papers*, Correspondence out, 13 September 1870.
[66] *Hjula Papers*, Correspondence in, Richardson, 22 September 1870.
[67] *Hjula Papers*, *Faktura* [Invoices], J. Tatham, 24 May 1870.
[68] *Hjula Papers*, Correspondence in, Tatham, 16 May 1870.

methods of coordination and supervision. Such capacities must not only be transferred but also diffused within the receptor economy, which implies that there must be a process of instruction and skill transmission. Within the Hjula enterprise, British workers were active in all of these areas, and were thus a central component of the overall process of technology transfer. In this section I shall draw on the descriptive material above to analyze the activities of British workers, under the following headings:

Specific skill inputs
Technical information and advice
Contacts with British firms
Skill transmission
Supervision and management

Specific skill inputs
Some aspects of technology transfer require quite localized and specific skills. An example would be the construction of equipment, which was shipped disassembled. In previous chapters I have noted Hjula's need for technical plans and drawings of imported equipment, but skilled fitters and mechanics were also required: David Rorison, for example, who was scheduled to spend some three months setting up looms purchased from the Anderston foundry. James Maiden came in order to assemble the myriad of parts shipped by James Tatham to make up two mules. Other workers were hired with regard to their ability to 'set up and get going' looms from England: George Richardson, for example, who worked at Hjula for at least six years. Likewise the 'loom mechanic' James Brierly, who brought spart parts for machines with him from England, and presumably fitted them. Thomas Pollit, recruited by Parr, Curtis & Madeley, would they said 'alter all your looms so they work well'.[69] This he apparently did, and to Schou's delight he got a machine going which had stood idle 'since Jackson's time', i.e. at least three and possibly as much as five years. This is not only an indicator of the importance of skilled labour input, it also shows the degree to which machine purchases depended on the availability of mechanical skills, since Schou immediately ordered more machines of the same type, writing to the manufacturers that: 'I am very pleased with it now and beg you to send five twill motions of this pattern, which I will put to your five heavy looms.'[70]

Other workers were hired with specific operating skills: the four-loom weaver Thomas Barrat, for example, John Waddington, who 'understands Beaming, Sizing Healds, Twisting' and so on, and who brought with him correct formulae for sizes. There were weavers such as Clarke, Horrebin and Orme, finishers such as Farrington, and the fulling miller William Stead. Andrew Clarke, as I noted above, acquired a particular skill, tape dressing, as a condition of employment.

[69] *Hjula Papers*, Correspondence in, Parr Curtis, 1 August 1856.
[70] *Hjula Papers*, Correspondence out, Parr Curtis, n.d.

This skilled labour input was clearly an important element of productivity, and Schou saw the remedy to low output per machine in the hire of British labour.

Technical information and advice

British workers provided a great deal of technical information, either directly or in correspondence from England. This was of considerable importance to the Hjula operation. 'As I am not a practical man myself', Schou once wrote, 'I cannot do without one',[71] and he relied heavily on 'practical men' particularly in dealings with British textile engineers. Even before leaving England, a British worker might examine or obtain information on some machine being considered for purchase. Samuel Clegg, for example, reported on the Whitney machine, about which he was dubious; Sharp & Co wrote to Schou that 'Clegg thinks that if the machine was anything first class there would have been more made and cheaper'.[72] Similarly, before his departure in 1864, Wright Farrington reported on new chemicals for dyeing, this information being transmitted through one of Schou's contacts and agents in England, the Manchester firm of Hvistendahl, Holst.[73] They then ordered, 'on Farrington's advice', various ancillary inputs.[74] Schou frequently cited his employees' advice in orders and correspondence with British firms. James Horton, for example, a dyer, advised Schou on substitute materials, and was referred to in orders to the Leeds firm James Richardson: 'Horton says this will do just as well and will be 50% cheaper.'[75] Frequently, rather than consulting his employees, Schou would simply enclose details drawn up by them. Thus he wrote to Squire Diggles in August 1855: 'My foreman Jackson thinks you have got a pattern that will be easy for the yarn, in the enclosed note he writes something about this matter ...'[76] And two weeks later, to Parr, Curtis & Madeley:

This day I have only the intention to send you the enclosed note from my foreman from which you will see that he wants some alterations about the shedding tappets and ... wheels. I hope you will understand what he means and make your looms accordingly.[77]

This note seems to suggest that Schou did not know what his foreman meant. Two weeks later Schou was writing to William Smith: 'My foreman Jackson's note enclosed in this letter will give you further information ...'[78]

From time to time British suppliers, when corresponding with Schou on technical matters, would refer him to his own employees for enlightenment.

[71] *Hjula Papers*, Correspondence out, 11 November 1859.
[72] *Hjula Papers*, Correspondence in, Wm Sharp, 28 May 1865.
[73] *Hjula Papers*, Correspondence in, Hvistendahl, Holst & Co., 25 August 1864.
[74] *Hjula Papers*, Correspondence in, Hvistendahl, Holst & Co., 15 September 1864.
[75] *Hjula Papers*, Correspondence out, 3 February 1870; 1 April 1870.
[76] *Hjula Papers*, Correspondence out, 24 August 1855.
[77] *Hjula Papers*, Correspondence out, 7 September 1855.
[78] *Hjula Papers*, Correspondence out, 14 September 1859.

Thus in 1868 G. W. Tomlinson wrote about a napping machine and various accessories, and concluded by referring Schou to his dyer: 'I suppose Mr Stocks understands this branch of finishing perfectly and will be able to explain the matter thoroughly.'[79]

As an example of the range of technical activities undertaken by Schou's employees, we shall examine the foreman Stephen Marmont. Marmont in fact travelled to England on Schou's behalf on several occasions. Over the five years of his employment we have a reasonable picture of his activities since he frequently reported back to Schou via the agent George Denton, or was mentioned in correspondence by British suppliers. During the years 1863–8 he engaged in the following activities:

1 Advising on the employment of British workers ('a professional nailer of cards ... will expedite matters a month' ... Marmont 'knows a man that will come for 5s a day and expenses and will guarantee to finish the affair in 18 days').
2 Advising on the quality of yarn purchases ('Marmont says the second lot of yarns from Hollins you will find satisfactory').
3 Advising on ancillary equipment purchases, such as belting ('It was at [Marmont's] wish particularly they were ordered, he knows how well they are adapted for the machines').
4 Inspecting machines before shipment from England (Thornton Brothers 'Assert Marmont had the fullest opportunity of examining the machines before they were packed').
5 Advising on likely prices of second-hand equipment ('My manager Mr Marmont presumes that you could buy a good 32 inch carder for 10 or 15£, a piecing machine for 6 or 8£, a 60 spindle billy for 5 or £7').
6 Advising on specifications and dimensions of new equipment ('Marmont begs me to tell you that the back doffer wants ⅞' space and that the carder is to do fine work. Let the cards be 135–11').
7 Having new equipment investigated ('When your Mr Marmont was over here he mentioned to me about a tentering machine about which I promised to make enquiries. I find there are two sizes ...').
8 Generally dealing with British suppliers ('Thank you for the £100 your Mr Marmont handed to us, we also informed him that we should be very glad to hand him money on your account and he had promised to give us another call, we also promised to obtain the prices of different articles for him').[80]

The conclusion which emerges from this is that Marmont was a kind of technological 'man of affairs' for Schou, and it may well be that Schou depended at least as much on this side of Marmont's activities as on his role as foreman of the factory.

Some forms of technical information flow from British workers covered the whole gamut of mill operation. An extraordinary example of this is the

[79] *Hjula Papers*, Correspondence in, Tomlinson, 18 April 1868.
[80] *Hjula Papers*, Correspondence in, Denton, 1 and 10 October 1863; 28 January 1864. Richardsons, 20 and 26 June 1867. Tomlinson, 12 August 1868. Tatham, 11 December 1868. Correspondence out, 7 and 29 October 1864; 24 November 1864.

correspondence between J. Wallem and his former employee William Yearley.[81] Yearley's letter of 1 March 1848 to Wallem is nothing less than a
full-scale description of mill management practice in Preston; it covers such
topics as (1) power sources and power use, (2) amount and types of machinery
used, (3) product range, (4) manning levels, output per worker hour, the
timing of operative tasks (which could be said to be pre-Taylorite in some
respects), systems of payment, (5) factory hours, breaks, etc. Whether
Wallem had specifically requested such information is unclear, but it seems
unlikely that such a letter would have been written otherwise. Wallem was in
fact eager for information; the contract with his employee Fothergill, which
has been referred to in Chapter 5, contained specific details not only on the
provision of information but also on secrecy. He was required to work
'without disclosing the secret of his employment, business or dealings';
moreover 'after the time is expired he must not act as overlooker, manager,
assistant or journeyman to any person or persons in Bergen stift [area], but go
back again to Newcastle ...'.[82]

Contacts with British firms

A not insignificant problem for a European textile entrepreneur must have
been knowing which British firms to contact for technical purchases. Schou
depended on his British workers as a source of such information, and
frequently referred to them in ordering. For example: 'Your firm has been
recommended by my overlooker, as an experiment, for a small order'; 'I have
your address from the manager of the finishing department in my factory, and
hereby give you an order for one improved perpetual cutting machine to cut
64 inches'; 'I have your address and a list of prices for your hydro extractors
through my English foreman'; 'The manager of my woollen factory Mr Alfred
Hudson has given me your address ... send samples of your cheap oil for
coarse as well as for finer woollen goods'.[83] This kind of thing is a continuous
refrain in Schou's correspondence.

Skill transmission

Not surprisingly, Schou required his foreign workers to be 'knowledgeable',
and one of their important functions was to pass on their skills to Norwegian
workers. Sometimes this was not so much a matter of formal teaching as of
showing what could be done. In 1856, for example, Schou considered
engaging two female weavers through Parr, Curtis & Madeley; they appear to
have possessed no particular skill which Schou's workers did not already
possess. He wrote of them '... if you send me weavers, do not let me have any
who is not very sharp. I have plenty of middling good double-box weavers

---

81 *Wallem Papers*, Correspondence in, Yearley, 1 March 1848.
82 *Wallem Papers*, Notebook and Diary.
83 *Hjula Papers*, Correspondence out, Moorhouse, 18 August 1856; Nicholson, 24 April 1870;
Ramsden, 8 September 1864; Wilkinson, 9 August 1869.

here and some very good, therefore should the English serve as an example for the others by their ability.'[84]

More frequently, however, Schou required his British workers to teach his Norwegian employees: 'I want a working man that I can turn to either of these branches (i.e. Beaming and warping). He should not only instruct my hands but do likewise work himself.'[85]

In a number of cases the teaching role was a specific requirement of employment with Schou. It appears to have been usually the case that when Schou engaged a British worker a formal contract was drawn up between them. Only two such contracts survive, but it is a noteworthy feature of each that they contain provision for the worker to instruct the skills which were being purchased. Wright Farrington's contract, for example, spells out quite explicitly his role as a bearer of technical knowledge and his duty to pass it on:

I promise during my stay to further Mr Schou's interests by paying proper attention to the different finishes required and also by giving Mr Schou and his people every information in my possession respecting stiffening and finishing generally.[86]

A similar provision occurs in the contract of the fulling miller William Stead:

The said William Stead shall and will faithfully serve the said Halvor Schou as a miller of woollen cloths and as a foreman over the fulling stocks and scouring machines in the manufactories of the said Halvor Schou and also to instruct the workmen of the said Halvor Schou in the various details of the milling and scouring.'[87]

In some cases such duties were set out not in a contract with the worker but rather in an exchange of letters with those who recruited him. Thus, when the overlooker Andrew Clarke was engaged by the Anderston Foundry, they wrote to Schou setting out his wages and conditions, and continuing, 'These being agreed he binds himself to serve you faithfully and diligently – tenting all the looms either by us or any other you may have in your mill – he is to teach your workers, act as overlooker ...'.[88]

This requirement for teaching and instruction remained for many years. In 1870, when Schou had been in the textile industry for twenty-one years, he wrote to the Leeds textile engineer, James Richardson & Co., seeking a dyer who would 'honestly undertake to instruct my men and teach them everything he knows himself about dyeing'.[89] Richardsons engaged James Horton for this.

It is interesting to note that Schou seemed to rely entirely for the training of his Norwegian workers on British workers visiting Norway rather than sending Norwegian workers to England. However this seems to have been at

---

[84] *Hjula Papers*, Correspondence out, 16 May 1856.
[85] *Hjula Papers*, Correspondence out, 1 August 1856.
[86] *Hjula Papers*, Contract 24 August 1864.   [87] *Hjula Papers*, Contract 27 May 1865.
[88] *Hjula Papers*, Correspondence in, Anderston, 2 August 1859.
[89] *Hjula Papers*, Correspondence out, 3 February 1870.

least a possibility. In 1860, for example, Schou ordered a heald knitting machine from the Blackburn firm of J. Harrison & Sons. They wrote that they would be 'very glad to send you a person to teach your people how to manage the Heald Knitting Machine', but went on: 'We think your best plan would be to send a person over here to learn how to manage the machine, he could learn everything in connexion with it in a month and we should be glad to receive him into our mill for that purpose.'[90]

Schou did not take up this offer. There are a number of possible reasons for this. First, it may have been easier to retain skilled English workers, since they were bound to him on relatively long-term contracts. There were occasions when Norwegian workers, trained at Hjula, left leaving Schou rather annoyed.[91] Secondly, English workers, though formally engaged to teach one particular process, frequently possessed a wider range of skills which Schou may have wanted to exploit. This point will be discussed further below.

Supervision and management

The skills associated with production management are a central component of any process of technical change, particularly where technical change involves an increasingly complex division of labour. At Hjula the quality of production management definitely affected output, and Schou was very much concerned with it. In 1856, for example, he wrote to Parr, Curtis & Madeley that:

The fact is that I have never yet been able to get the same quantity out of my looms which is usual in England, and I think one of the principal causes for it is that the beaming, twisting . . . etc. etc. is not managed as well as it ought to be. I think therefore it would be advisable to take over a man, who could superintend all these things here mentioned.[92]

In February 1870 he wrote to James Richardson in similar terms: 'I am sorry to say I am not doing so well as I could wish. I am inclined to think, that the fault lies chiefly in bad management in the carding room, and I must try another carder.'[93]

It is significant that the majority of British workers employed by Schou were in managerial and supervisory roles. Appendix D shows that at least eighteen of Schou's employees from Britain were managers of one kind or another. In the material above on such managers as Marmont and Rorison we have seen the extent to which Schou depended on them for a wide range of activities related to technology acquisition.

Even where workers were not hired specifically as foremen or managers, they frequently carried out a supervisory role. The possession of some

---

90 *Hjula Papers*, Correspondence in, Harrison, 15 March 1870.   91 See Chapter 9 below.
92 *Hjula Papers*, Correspondence out, 1 August 1856.
93 *Hjula Papers*, Correspondence out, 24 February 1870.

particular skill was usually associated with a position of authority, and the distinction between operatives and supervisors is consequently a difficult one to draw. William Harrison was a 'foreman carder and spinner', James Pollard was a 'foreman finisher', and William Stead was a 'fulling miller foreman'. The implication to be drawn from Figure 8.1 therefore is that this British managerial role was a permanent and continuous feature of the Hjula enterprise.

PROBLEMS IN THE EMPLOYMENT OF BRITISH WORKERS

This section discusses some of the key problems faced at Hjula in the employment of British workers. For convenience these may be divided into three types: economic, technical and what might be called social.

The economic problems revolved around the scale of the Hjula operation. Although Hjula was a relatively large enterprise, it became an integrated one, combining spinning and weaving in both cotton and wool, with a full range of preparatory and finishing processes as well. This implies that particular processes within the plant were conducted on a relatively small scale. Output appears to have been sometimes insufficient to support a skilled British worker in one process alone, and Schou frequently attempted to find workers with capabilities in more than one process. But this problem of skill-fit was a difficult one to solve. As we have seen above, Andrew Clarke was required to acquire a further skill, tape dressing, in addition to weaving, as a condition of his employment. Schou also raised this problem in relation to the employment of the finisher, Stocks, by George Denton in 1863.[94] In 1856, in correspondence with Parr Curtis, he discussed the necessity of employing a beamer, to remedy a problem of low output with Parr, Curtis & Madeley looms, and continued:

I think therefore it would be advisable to take over a man who could superintend all these things here mentioned, but I would not take him this autumn if you could not find one who was at the same time a warper, because I have not exactly use for, or work for another beamer before I am going to take more looms in the spring.[95]

At about the same time Schou wanted a man who would 'make himself acquainted with the mechanical part of a printing machine ... further with a doubling machine for making ... yarn'.[96] His English correspondent, Squire Diggles, advised him of the difficulty of this, and Schou remarked that 'if that is so I must give it up', continuing rather plaintively that if the man 'would take the trouble before he leaves Radcliffe just to have a look at these machines he would be able to assist me in putting them together'.[97]

[94] *Hjula Papers*, Correspondence in, Denton, 4 March 1863.
[95] *Hjula Papers*, Correspondence out, 1 August 1856.
[96] *Hjula Papers*, Correspondence out, 16 May 1856.
[97] *Hjula Papers*, Correspondence out, 6 June 1856.

The principal technical problem faced in the employment of British workers was straightforward incompetence. Schou expressed dissatisfaction with five of his workers, for example with Murray, 'as a foreman and manager he is only half a man', with William Harrison 'he is certainly not a competent foreman' and with Hunt who was 'too soft' and was twice given notice.[98]

Under the heading of 'social' problems in employing British workers one difficulty stands out above all others – drunkenness. This is, of course, a familiar problem with expatriate British workers in the late eighteenth and nineteenth centuries. Landes, for example, refers to the problem of drunken English workmen in France;[99] Jeremy quotes an early American mill manager whose English carders and spinners made him 'a little apprehensive from their frequent state of intoxication'.[100] At Hjula this problem was a very serious one; Schou expressed concern at one point or another about the drinking habits of Barrat, Holt, Pollit, Marmont, Roebuck, Richardson, Harton, Brierly and Kellet. In his correspondence he frequently expressed the view that sobriety was the key attribute he required. To take from one of many examples:

Mr Sharp has written a letter to me the contents of which fully convinces me, that he is quite unfit for giving me any valuable assistance in selecting people for me. I must mention one instance to you which plainly shows his peculiarity of reasoning. He says that he is sure he can recommend Walsh because his former master told him that Walsh could do his work well *as long as he kept sober*. Now I should think it would be a much better recommendation to Walsh if he *always* kept sober.[101] [emphases in original]

The problem was such a pervasive one that English recruiters of labour tended to blame Schou himself for excessive leniency, or simply foreign climes where 'they simply let themselves go'. Schou himself tended to blame the low price of spirits in Norway.

The Wallem enterprise also had persistent problems with drunken English employees. The firm's *Kopibok* records that on one occasion Andrew Yardley was drunk, and 'as a consequence forgot to fill the boiler with the required water and probably there has never before been as little water in the boiler while the engine was running'. On the following day, Wallem himself recorded that 'Andrew was absent all morning in consequence of being drunk yesterday ... and I had to take his place'.[102] Yardley does not appear to have been particularly diligent, but neither does Wallem seem to have been able to exert much authority:

---

[98] *Hjula Papers*, Correspondence out, 18 August 1856; 28 January 1869; 29 January 1862.
[99] Landes, *Unbound Prometheus*, p. 149.
[100] Jeremy, *Transatlantic Industrial Revolution*, p. 113.
[101] *Hjula Papers*, Correspondence out, 6 May 1870.
[102] *Wallem Papers*, Kopibok, 17 and 18 September 1846.

Yardley went home at 11.00 to write letters home and remained there till 6 – thereafter he went out and stayed out all night – till 9 next morning – said he couldn't get back because of the bad weather – stayed at home all that day till 6.[103]

It is difficult to assess the overall significance of such problems. Do they indicate, for instance, that those British workers who were prepared to go abroad were particularly shiftless and unruly? This seems unlikely, for first we should remember that drunkenness among British workers was not a problem confined to those who went abroad. Secondly, these workers were not emigrants, but were recruited within England, frequently – as the above chapter has indicated – by textile engineering firms or agents. Many of them were in effect hand-picked. It should also be remembered that most were apparently fairly solid types; thirty of Schou's workers were married, and many had families. However twenty of those who were married left their wives and families in the UK, and it may be that separation and the difficulties of living in a foreign country led to increased drinking by men who, in the eyes of those who had recruited them in the UK, were 'steady'. It is also the case, as one might expect, that Schou's Norwegian workers were not necessarily angels. We know little of the details of their lives, but the Hjula correspondence files do contain references to various social problems: a letter from a former employee, who had been sentenced to twelve years in prison, seeking money from Schou to enable him to emigrate to America on his release; a letter from a doctor concerning a pregnant mill girl; a letter seeking employment from a former Hjula mill girl now in prison for theft and about to be released; a letter from the Poor Law Commissioners to one of the girls at Hjula whose child had been fostered, and so on.[104]

Wage rates

What kind of wage differential was necessary to attract British workers? Normally, British workers in Norway commanded a differential both over rates for similar employment in the UK, and over rates for similar work by Norwegian employees in Norway. As an example of the first differential, Schou wrote to Sharp & Sons in early 1869 that:

Hudson [one of Schou's employees] says that there are many good overlookers in and about Leeds, quite competent for the situation here who have got only £2 per week in salary and he thinks that if a man for some reason or other is willing to go abroad he will go for £3. You remember I saw several who commenced by asking £4 but at length said they were willing to go for £3.[105]

Throughout the 1860s this was the wage paid by Schou to Clarke, Clegg, Harrison, Horton, Kellet, Pollard, Roebuck and Stocks. The margin

[103] *Wallem Papers, Kopibok*, 6 October 1846.
[104] *Hjula Papers*, Correspondence in, Johan Olsen, 21 February 1864; also 4 May 1861 and 28 August 1864, unidentifiable correspondents; Poor Law Commission, 4 September 1869.
[105] *Hjula Papers*, Correspondence out, 17 February 1869.

involved, that is 50 percent, seems large, but it is important to remember that Schou frequently had difficulty recruiting at the wages he was prepared to pay; this has been a persistent theme in the above pages.

Differentials for British workers over local workers were marked. Ramstad has shown, for example, that, at the Christiania Sailcloth Factory, Norwegian female spinners average daily wage in 1861 was 34.2 Norwegian shillings; British female spinners earned 49 shillings.[106] This can be confirmed by wage-book entries over a period of years. In the last week of March 1859, for example, Norwegian spinners were paid on average 36 shillings per day, while the British spinner Ann Duff was paid 54 shillings per day. In the first week of December 1870, Norwegian spinners were paid between 28 and 34 shillings per day, whereas Kate Cunningham an English spinner was paid 49½ shillings per day.[107]

CONCLUSION

British workers never formed more than a small minority of those employed by the firms studied here, although there is good reason for believing that their numbers were greater than the surviving evidence suggests. But the Hjula material suggests that their importance in the diffusion of British technology was a function of their skills, not of their numbers. I have mentioned in previous chapters what I regard as the key points about the labour inflow described here. They are first, that this inflow is associated with the acquisition of British technology, and secondly, that the inflow was to a large degree directly organized by those from whom equipment and machinery was purchased. It is also the case that much of the literature on European industrialization regards the flow of British labour as important for early industrialization, but not so significant from the 1840s. Yet the other main conclusion to emerge from this chapter is that British labour may well have remained important in European industrialization beyond the early period of industrial development. Lee's remark that 'the natives proved apt apprentices' does not, from the Norwegian case at least, imply that there was no place for British workers in the second half of the nineteenth century.

---

106 J. Ramstad, *Kvinnelønn og Pengeøkonomi* (Hovedfagthesis, Norges Handelshøyskole, Bergen 1981), Vol. II, Appendix 4.
107 *Christiania Sailcloth Factory papers*, Wage Book I, May 1858–August 1859, Week 31 March–7 April; Wage Book VIII, November 1870–June 1872, Week 24 November–7 December.

9

INTERRELATIONS AMONG
NORWEGIAN FIRMS

This chapter discusses interactions between Norwegian firms in the diffusion
of British textile technologies within Norway. I have suggested that this
technology consisted of three main elements: flows of technical information at
various levels, the acquisition of equipment, and a range of managerial and
operative skills. Thus far I have dealt with the process by which this
technology was transferred in terms of direct international relations between
Norwegian firms on the one hand and firms and workers from the originating
country, Britain, on the other. But, once a technology is implanted in a host
economy, it may begin to spread of its own accord. In the United States skilled
workers brought the new technology from Britain, becoming entrepreneurs
in the process; Samuel Slater, for example, set up plants first on Rhode Island
and then in southern Massachusetts, training many workers and managers in
the process. His contribution to internal diffusion in the USA lay in these
workers and managers, as David Jeremy has pointed out: 'Slater's business
operations formed the single most fruitful node of technology diffusion in
American cotton manufacturing before 1812.' Subsequently independent
machine makers became the primary vehicle of the internal diffusion of new
technology in the American textile industry.[1] Pollard has argued that it was
the ability to generate internal diffusion, the successful adoption of the new
technology on a wide enough basis, which was at the heart of the industrialization process as such.[2] In Norway the mechanisms of the internal diffusion
of new technology were sometimes different from those of the USA, but an
important question concerns whether internal diffusion was as important. In
this chapter I shall discuss the main indigenous channels of the internal
diffusion of British technology under the following headings:

Technical societies
Sales and loans of machinery and equipment
Inter-firm cooperation in machine acquisition
Inter-firm flows of labour and management
Interlocking directorships

[1] D. Jeremy, *Transatlantic Industrial Revolution* (Oxford, 1981), pp. 89–90.
[2] S. Pollard, *Peaceful Conquest* (Oxford, 1981), p. 142.

TECHNICAL SOCIETIES

In Chapter 5 I argued that the overall contribution of technical societies in the transfer of technology from Britain lay primarily in the creation of a general awareness of the importance of industrial culture, and the importance of foreign industrial developments. But this does not mean that specific forms of technical information were not disseminated through the societies. Apart from the general spread of information through publications and libraries, the societies were places of direct contact among entrepreneurs. It was common, for example, for entrepreneurs returning from Britain to address one or more of the societies on their experiences. Society meetings often involved the exhibition of machines and models, and new technologies were frequently discussed with reference to the local environment. As I pointed out in Chapter 5, the heterogeneous nature of the societies' activities did not preclude lectures on very specialized topics; between 1855 and 1870 there were a number of lectures and lecture courses on spinning and weaving, on cotton and woollen mill organization, on aspects of steam power, and on technical training. Most of the textile entrepreneurs belonged to one or more of the societies, and several played important roles within them; contacts here presumably overlapped with general business contacts and facilitated the spread of technical information on textiles. The inner circle of the societies not only numbered a high proportion of Norwegian entrepreneurs, business and professional people, but also included British managers working in Norway; in 1868, for example, a factory master called Forderman, and an engineer called Harris, both became members of the Polytechnic Society.[3]

SALES AND LOANS OF MACHINERY AND EQUIPMENT

Intra-Norwegian transfers of machinery by sale or loan occurred in various forms, and the effects, as we shall see, went beyond the straightforward extension of the use of techniques; these effects also involved bargaining over markets and types of output, flows of technical advice and information, and flows of skilled labour.

Changes in the ownership of machinery are not a simple redistribution of an existing capital stock; changes also involve an extension of technical capacities, and as such are vehicles of diffusion. Second hand markets in machinery arose in various ways. Sometimes firms divested themselves of machinery and equipment when closing down a mill completely or in part, or when ownership changed. The Bergen firm of Wallem, for example, which started as a steam-powered rope manufactory in 1845, closed down in 1848 and sold its British machinery to the firm of Arne Fabrikker. This technological opportunity was the basis of diversification for Arne, which added rope to

---

[3] *Polyteknisk Tidsskrift*, 2nd Vol. 1868, 7 January 1868, 14 January 1868.

cotton goods production. In 1856 the owner of the Nøsted cotton weaving mill (also steam powered incidentally) was forced to close down and sold up to a group of seven partners. This sale was preceded by an offer to sell the entire machine park to Hjula Weavery. Halvor Schou considered this very carefully, making an offer based on English machine prices plus transport costs, customs duty, etc. Despite his disavowals ('no Norwegian weaving mill could bother me with competition for the first five years') he must have had in mind, to some extent, the idea of preempting competitors. Even so he drove a very hard bargain, asking for a loan of the purchase price (5,500 Specie daler) for a year, interest free, and a further 2,000 Specie daler at 6 percent for five years as working capital.[4]

More significant, from the diffusion point of view, was a transaction made by Schou in 1864, when Hjula was well established. Cotton output at Hjula had fallen sharply during the American Civil War, and Schou arranged to sell over 100 looms to the Nydalen enterprise. This purchase represented a departure towards full integration of Nydalen. With some looms bought from England, some from the Bjørsheim mill and the looms from Hjula, Nydalen added an extensive weaving department to their spinning department. The transaction was a complex one, since it involved questions of competition as well as problems of transfer. With these looms, Nydalen intended to weave coarse cloth ('stout'), and attempted to extract from Schou an undertaking not to compete with them in this field. Schou riposted with a demand of his own, and the negotiations on respective product lines were apparently unsuccessful: 'I am willing to sell you my 100 looms ... Nydalen will not tie itself to a promise as regards production of patterned goods, however I do at the same time claim similar freedom ... so will not promise never to weave stout.'[5]

A constraint in this bargaining, for Nydalen, was that Schou was their most important customer for thread. In a subsequent letter Schou reassured Nydalen, saying that he intended to reduce the production of coarse cloth, and in fact this transaction reflects Hjula's shift towards woollen products from the mid 1860s.[6]

Since these looms represented a new type of equipment and product for Nydalen, they relied heavily on technical expertise and information from Hjula. Information covered output rates, types of labour input, and general mill management problems associated with this type of equipment. Expertise involved the use of Hjula engineers to set up the equipment, and there is some evidence of Hjula workers being transferred as part of the transaction; these aspects of the sale will be covered below.

At the beginning of November 1864 Schou wrote to Nydalen with details of the loom types: sixty-eight were by Hetheringtons, four were by Hetheringtons but of a different type, six were by Mark Smith, four by Lees

[4] *Hjula Papers*, Correspondence out, 9 November 1856.
[5] *Hjula Papers*, Correspondence out, 7 October 1864.
[6] *Hjula Papers*, Correspondence out, 12 October 1864.

Barnes, eight by Harrisons, twelve by Dickinsons, and six by Parr, Curtis and Madeley. Types of output were described.[7] Schou had earlier remarked that it was not possible to run the Blackburn looms as fast as they were run in England if unpractised (uøvede) workers were used.[8] In November he elaborated on this: 'Dickinson's and Harrison's looms can be run with much higher speeds than the others, and produce much more with *good* weavers, who must be taught especially for these looms. Hetherington's looms are best for apprentices.'[9]

On the question of precise machine speeds he deferred to his English engineer, whose importance has been emphasized in previous chapters: 'Take my advice: leave it to my factory master Rorison to give each loom the speed which after long experience has proved the most profitable at Hjula (which factory master Rorison has done at Hjula).'[10]

Schou suggested that in general workers had machine-specific competences; generally workers should not be moved between machines, and in particular 'the weavers used to the heavy looms from Mark Smith or Parr Curtis ought not to be moved to lighter looms'. He then offered specific advice, drawn from his own experience, concerning supervision. His remarks here deserve more extended quotation for the insight they give into this important topic. Where words are unclear, or indecipherable, I have used empty round brackets, or round brackets containing the likely word:

The engagement of a literate married man as overlooker is of utmost importance. His function is to 'go through' the finished product and penalise the weavers for mistakes. The manager [bestyrer] should at least once a week (payday) walk around and talk with each worker in the weavery personally to find out ( ) activities during the week. If too little or bad products are produced he must investigate

1 if it is the weaver's fault – caused by incompetence [ukyndighet] or laziness
2 whether the overlooker has got his loom ( ) or if it breaks the yarn
3 in the case of snarls whether they are caused by the cotton or by the weavers themselves
4 whether the yarn is too strong or too weak.

The importance of all this is very strongly emphasized by Schou:

I am sure Gjerdrum knows all this, I only mention it because I have never during my long practice found a manager who thoroughly, neutrally and conscientiously has investigated all these things, and because I know that had I not myself (learnt) and controlled each such detail in the weaving, and thus personally known each workers ( ) then things would have been bad for me.[11]

---

[7] *Hjula Papers*, Correspondence out, 1 November 1864.
[8] *Hjula Papers*, Correspondence out, 7 October 1864.
[9] *Hjula Papers*, Correspondence out, 1 November 1864.
[10] *Hjula Papers*, Correspondence out, 7 October 1864.
[11] *Hjula Papers*, Correspondence out, 1 November 1864.

These are of course managerial rather than technical activities which Schou is discussing; they do not presuppose any particular technical skill on his part. But these problems of supervision were deeply characteristic of early factory production and were to a considerable extent independent of the problem of keeping equipment maintained and running.

A further aspect of this transaction was the use of skilled workers from Hjula. The agreement provided for Schou to get the machines to Nydalen, to set them up and help place them. Schou was clearly anxious that Nydalen might poach his workers, just as he had enticed David Rorison away from Anderston's of Glasgow: 'Nydalen now has one of my overlookers in their service; he has also been taught as a mechanic and I do not want him to leave my service. It would be bad for me if more of my trained people followed him . . .'12

There were various disputes over workers; Nydalen engaged one of Hjula's loom mechanics, and Schou was threatening to take on several workers from Nydalen. One of these had trained at Hjula some years before, and Schou justified engaging her by saying that 'I regard her skill as capital, to which I have more right than anyone else'. Including herself, presumably.13

By March 1865 this sale to Nydalen had been more or less completed. What is interesting about it from the point of view of the diffusion process is that Schou played a role *vis-à-vis* Nydalen almost exactly similar to that played towards him by British machine-making firms, in terms of provision of information, equipment and, to a lesser extent, skilled labour. Even the problems of the transaction bear a marked similarity to those faced by Schou himself in his dealings with British suppliers; in particular Nydalen experienced unforeseen problems in getting the looms running properly, caused by the fact that Schou, unlike his British machine suppliers, was unwilling to supply Nydalen with workers to run and manage the machines:

I see . . . that [Nydalen] have problems with getting the looms from Hjula running . . . it is a misunderstanding of my contract with Nydalen [to] . . . believe that I have the duty to get the sold looms going . . . as soon as the looms have been started up with pickers and shuttles by my own people, then I have done more than I am bound to. The weaving is no concern of mine . . .14

The transaction with Nydalen is the best documented but not the only one Schou had with other Norwegian firms. Between August 1863 and August 1864 he issued seven invoices to the Vøien enterprise mainly for cards and spare parts. He advertised a cutting machine for sale in 1857 and a couple of mules for sale in 1868, '550 spindles and 800 spindles, English made, 2–3 years old'.15 A letter from a dyer, Mikkelsen of Haugesund (on the south-

12 *Hjula Papers*, Correspondence out, 1 November 1864.
13 *Hjula Papers*, Correspondence out, 5 December 1864.
14 *Hjula Papers*, Correspondence out, 26 November 1864.
15 *Hjula Papers*, *Faktura* [Invoices], 31 August 1863; 31 December 1864; 31 January 1864; 31 March 1864; 2 July 1864; 1 August 1864.

west coast of Norway), suggests many more transactions may have been completed; he appears to regard Schou as an agent 'for a factory supplying spinning and carding machines' and asks for information, prices, etc. Schou also supplied equipment to Stephen Marmont when he and George Richardson bought Leerfossen and set up on their own in 1869 (this later became the Grorud Klædefabrikk): two mules, a spinning billy and a piecing machine.[16]

Christiania Sailcloth factory would also borrow parts and equipment from Schou; several letters during the years 1859 and 1860 requested temporary loans of pullies, tools, pickers and so on.[17]

INTERFIRM COOPERATION IN EQUIPMENT ACQUISITION

The Norwegian textile industry appears to have been characterized by a complex mixture of competition and interdependence between firms. Where textile firms were interdependent, perhaps because one was supplying inputs to another, there appears to have been a readiness to pool information regarding equipment supply from Britain, and a mutual willingness to act as intermediaries with British firms. As we shall see this extended to ordering equipment on behalf of each other. This pattern of cooperation was an important aspect of the diffusion of British technology within Norway. This section is concerned with examples of this process.

This pattern of cooperation runs right through the extant correspondence of these firms. In 1853 and 1854, for example, Solberg Spinnery wrote three letters to Adam Hjorth of Nydalen concerning preparatory equipment: 'I will be very grateful if you would tell me the best card maker in Manchester, and which [frame?] you think best, either leather or cloth.'[18]

Subsequent letters indicate first, that Hjorth had in fact previously ordered on behalf of Solberg, and secondly, that Solberg were technically rather cautious, in the sense of being unwilling to use equipment other than devices they were familiar with. They wrote, for example, concerning a willow (a preparatory device), saying 'if you could be bothered please to inform us about the name and address of the willow maker who has made the one we now have',[19] having previously turned down an offer of a willow from Hjorth: 'Thank you very much for the offer of the willow but it is difficult for us to buy as we prefer one which is similar to [indecipherable] for the reason that it works mechanically and seems to us to be less dangerous to the workers.'[20]

In the conclusion to this letter they refer to an order from England, asking Hjorth to 'see to it for us that it would be sent off' and seeking an indication of

16 *Hjula Papers, Kopibok*, 8 January 1869.
17 *Hjula Papers*, Correspondence in, Christiania Sailcloth Factory, 21 October 1859; 26 April 1860; 17 January 1861.
18 *Solberg Papers*, Correspondence out, 19 August 1853.
19 *Solberg Papers*, Correspondence out, 13 June 1854.
20 *Solberg Papers*, Correspondence out, 4 February 1854.

a delivery date. Here Hjorth has clearly been acting as an agent in the purchase of British equipment, and his travels in England thus had a wider technological impact than on just his own firm. In general Nydalen appear to have had similar contacts in the UK to Schou; a letter to Schou from Parr, Curtis & Madeley in August 1855 refers to orders from Pettersen of Nydalen and appears to be very well informed about Pettersen's business plans and problems. The tone of the letter certainly suggests that they regarded Schou as a conduit to Pettersen:

We regret to find nothing is to be done in the autumn in Mr Pettersen's Spinning Mill but sincerely hope that during the winter he will be enabled to make such arrangements in finding a new partner as will induce him to proceed with filling the plant early in the spring, and hope, if he does, he will be good enough to try to treat with us, when every attention will be paid to his enquiries.[21]

This common use of machine suppliers appears to have been widespread. In 1852, for example, Solberg wrote to the Liverpool dealers Whitehead & Meyer, asking for help in obtaining prices of machinery from 'respectable' machine suppliers, including as examples the names of machine makers, such as Parr, Curtis & Madeley, who had done business with other Norwegian firms.[22]

Sometimes cooperation among Norwegian firms took the form of very direct advice on technical change and technology acquisition. In 1859, for example, Halden Spinnery wrote to Schou exploring the possibility of selling yarn to him. He replied that their quality of warp was too low, and suggested ways of improving it (going as far as offering to train one of Halden's key workers at Hjula). He went on to say that they needed better equipment, and told them how to acquire it:

One only has to write to England, to Parr, Curtis & Madeley, or to Jno Hetherington & Sons in Manchester, or to any other cotton machinery maker, and order a '*14 yard warping mill* together with creel and hack and the necessary gearing to drive the mill by [hand or] power ... [indecipherable] *a big bobbin winding frame* to wind from throstle bobbins to big bobbins for warps'.[23]

The passage in quotes here is in English in the original. Halden appears to have taken Schou's advice on the matter, but did not contact British suppliers direct. Rather, Schou wrote to Hetherington in May and July 1859, ordering equipment on behalf of the Halden works. The machinery itself was made by Parr, Curtis & Madeley, while Hetherington made various parts for which Schou sent drawings.[24]

This kind of arrangement appears to have happened on a number of occasions with different firms. For example in 1856 and 1857 Schou recom-

---

21 *Hjula Papers*, Correspondence in, Parr Curtis, 9 August 1855.
22 *Solberg Papers*, Correspondence out, 7 December 1852.
23 *Hjula Papers*, Correspondence out, Halden, 22 February 1859.
24 *Hjula Papers*, Correspondence out, 6 May 1859 and 8 July 1859.

mended the heald and reed maker Baxter to Christiania Sailcloth factory, and wrote three letters to Baxter concerning the precise equipment needed.[25] In 1856 he dealt with Squire Diggles for Akerselven Klædefabrikk, and in late 1857 he ordered woollen looms for them from Parr, Curtis & Madeley and temples for looms which had previously been ordered by the Christiania Sailcloth factory.[26] In 1855 and 1857 he dealt with Parr, Curtis & Madeley on behalf of the Foss enterprise. In 1865 he corresponded with Dickinson & Sons concerning drying machines for unnamed 'friends'. They replied with lithographs of the equipment, technical details and prices, 'hoping your friends will give this matter their consideration'.[27] Olav Gjerdrum, of the Nydalen enterprise, visited Manchester in mid 1858, and bought machinery for both the Nøsted mill and for Solberg Spinnery; in the latter case he chose the machinery, and therefore does not seem to have been acting simply as a messenger.[28] Six years later he corresponded with Hjula Weavery about machine oil: 'I have at the moment no oil I can recommend for wool spinning machines, but I am awaiting reports from England ...'[29] Adam Hjorth, of Nydalen, was active in acquiring British machinery for other Norwegian firms; in 1867 he visited England and while there purchased bobbins and oil for Halden and looms, grinding machines, brushes and preparatory machinery (at least some of it from Parr, Curtis & Madeley) for Solberg. He also forwarded samples of dye-extracts to Hjula, 'which have been sent to me from Manchester'.[30] Throughout these years Halvor Schou purchased on a regular basis for Akerselven Klædefabrikk, from Sharp & Sons and through his agent George Denton. All of this seems to indicate that a network of connections between Norwegian firms facilitated the pooling of information and acquisition, and thus promoted the internal diffusion of the new technology.

INTERFIRM FLOWS OF LABOUR AND MANAGEMENT

In previous chapters I have emphasized the importance of labour inputs, since the operation of new techniques depended on workers and supervisors who could operate them. Flows of workers and supervisors between firms in Norway were therefore one vehicle among others of the spread of technological capacities. In general, firms appear to have been protective of their skilled labour and alert to opportunities to acquire new workers with appropriate skills. The Bergen firm Wallem, for example, employed an English worker called Booth from mid 1845, but a year later he appears in the correspon-

---

[25] *Hjula Papers*, Correspondence out, 21 October 1856; 2 February 1857; 1 April 1857.
[26] *Hjula Papers*, Correspondence out, 22 October 1857.
[27] *Nydalen Papers*, Correspondence out, 7 June 1858.
[28] *Solberg Papers*, Correspondence out, 7 August 1858.
[29] *Hjula Papers*, Correspondence in, Hjorth, 20 July 1864.
[30] *Hjula Papers*, Correspondence in, Hjorth, n.d.

dence and account books of the Rosendahl enterprise. One partner wrote that he 'is very useful to us'; in October 1845 the accounts record a gift of three bottles of cognac to him. His son was subsequently employed and money was still being sent to his wife in England in 1848.[31] Firms were quick to complain if workers left to a competitor; Guttler of the Ellendalen firm, for example, complained to Christiania Sailcloth factory, to Graah of Vøien Spinnery and to Nydalen in 1856 that workers were leaving, without being dismissed, to take up work with them. The implication was that this was unfair.[32] Nydalen complained about the same thing to Halvor Schou, who suggested that wage rates at Nydalen were too low.[33] Where there were technical issues to resolve among firms, skilled workers were normally involved; Rorison, for example, left Hjula briefly to set up the looms which Schou had sold to Nydalen, and when Schou complained to Vøien about the quality of the yarn he was buying from them, they 'took your Master over the factory to examine the matter'.[34] Interfirm movement of labour was of great importance in new enterprises; when Pettersen (previously of Nydalen) became a partner in the Grorud enterprise it was surely the participation of Schou's factory manager Stephen Marmont, who Schou was loath to lose, as technical manager which made the operation viable.

INTERLOCKING DIRECTORSHIPS ETC.

From time to time formal links were made between Norwegian textile sector firms which appear to have been related to the technical cooperation outlined above. Adam Hjorth, for example, was a director not only of Nydalen but also held shares in the Bjørsheim enterprise; Knud Graah, the sole owner of Vøien, held shares in the Christiania mechanical weaving mill. There were connections also between Nøsted, Vestfossen and Solberg via the director Fuglesang, who at various times held shares in all three firms. The most important link appears to have been that between Hjula and Akerselven Klædefabrikk via Halvor Schou. As noted above, Schou had played an important role for some years in acquiring machinery for Akerselven Klæde-fabrikk. In 1861, this led to Schou entering into negotiations to take over what he referred to as 'the management' of the firm. Whether this meant that he would own the firm, or play some role in running it is unclear. At first this transaction seems to have been conditional on the appointment of an English manager, called Gray. This however fell through; the following year Schou lent Akerselven Klædefabrikk 3,000 SD, at 6 percent. He declined a partner-ship, on the grounds of the 'factory's state'.

---

31 *Rosendahl Papers*, Correspondence in, 26 May 1846.
32 S. Grieg, *Norsk Tekstil*, Vol. I (Oslo, 1946), p. 309.
33 *Hjula Papers*, Correspondence in, 1 November 1864.
34 *Hjula Papers*, Correspondence in, Vøien, 24 November 1864.

CONCLUSION

It is difficult to be precise about the extent to which commercial and cooperative relationships between Norwegian firms facilitated the internal diffusion of British technology. But it is important to note that direct relations with British machine makers were not strictly necessary in order to be able to use British machines. Schou, of Hjula, and Hjorth, of Nydalen, in particular were important conduits of British technology, both in terms of information and more directly of acquisition. The material presented in this chapter suggests therefore that the diffusion process was even wider, perhaps considerably wider, than indicated even by the large scale of direct contacts between British and Norwegian firms.

10

THE EUROPEAN DIMENSION

To what extent were the technological diffusion processes, which have been described in the above chapters, typical of other firms and other countries in the nineteenth century? In focussing on the technological, rather than the economic or commercial bases of Norwegian textile development, this study has concentrated – in terms both of sources and treatment – on the *recipients* of technology, and on the technological problems which British suppliers solved for them. The central theme has been the importance of active, expansionary market-seeking by the British textile engineering industry, and by the specialized agencies which sold its products. The existence of this industry, and its readiness to supply a complex array of information, equipment and labour, seems to have been a primary condition for the rapidity with which a modern, mechanized textile industry was constructed in Norway from the mid 1840s. What might have been a major bottleneck in the diffusion process, namely the engineering inexperience and relative lack of technical expertise among Norwegian textile entrepreneurs and workers, was overcome through the willingness of British machinery makers and suppliers to provide not only equipment but, in effect, technological packages comprising a wide range of technical services. These 'packages' included:

> basic information on the technical requirements of new enterprises and on the availability of techniques,
> the evaluation and assessment of innovations,
> help with choice of technique,
> the supply of drawings and blueprints,
> provision of cost and output projections,
> the supply of machinery and all ancillary equipment.

British textile engineers also supplied labour to operate or supervise particular processes or entire plants. This full-scale process of technology transfer began in the mid 1840s, after the removal of the prohibitions on the export of machinery, and continued unabated until 1870, the end of the period studied here. The primary function of this study has been to expand our knowledge both of the fact that this occurred, and of how it occurred, by a detailed analysis of hitherto unused source material.

The central conclusion which emerges must be that the Norwegian textile enterprises studied here were heavily dependent on the technological expertise, services and products supplied by British textile engineers and machinery-supplying agents. This conclusion prompts a number of further questions. The first is whether, in the absence of the technology transfer process initiated by British machinery suppliers, the formation of a modern textile industry would have been possible at all in Norway. The answer to this depends in large part on the extent to which the firms studied here, especially Hjula Weavery, were representative of the Norwegian industry as a whole. Here one cannot be categorical, but it is my belief that, within the Norwegian industry, Hjula was not anomalous in terms of the quantity of transactions or the character of its relationships with the British textile engineering sector. The main reason for our ability to trace the technological experience of Hjula in such detail is the existence of complete incoming and outgoing correspondence records over many years. These provide a fascinating insight into the practicalities of technological diffusion; there are few really comparable sources for other Norwegian textile firms. But I have shown that all of the Norwegian textile enterprises examined here dealt with British textile engineers, that they all acquired techniques on a similar scale to Hjula, that they used British workers (the numbers of which are probably understated by surviving sources), that their owners and directors trained or travelled frequently in Britain and so on. The general quantitative outlines of the development of these firms are entirely similar to those of Hjula, and therefore it seems reasonable to infer that, had their correspondence archives survived with completeness similar to that of Hjula, we would be able to trace qualitative relationships with British suppliers which also were similar to those of Hjula. This implies that Norwegian textile industrialization was predicated on the development of a British capital goods industry, in particular a mechanical engineering industry producing textile techniques. Norwegian textile development was, therefore, not just an imitation of the British experience, in which domestic resources were used to replicate the British 'model', it was a diffusion from Britain, more precisely an extension of British industrialization once a specialized machine-making sector had emerged there and become free to export. What made it possible was a process of interaction between British technology suppliers and a Norwegian entrepreneurial class which was technologically aware – that is, alive to the scope and commercial implications of the new technology – although not necessarily technologically skilled.

The second, and perhaps much more significant question raised by this study concerns its implications for European economic history. Is the picture presented here, of large-scale interaction between domestic entrepreneurs and British machinery suppliers, representative of continental Europe as a whole? There are, in my view, *prima facie* grounds for believing that it is. One obvious point is that, since Norway was such an extremely small market, it

Table 10.1 *British machinery and millwork exports, 1841–50*
(declared value, £000)

Country	1841	1842	1843	1844	1845	1846	1847	1848	1849	1850
Russia	29.7	36.0	13.8	158.1	116.1	108.0	226.6	212.7	205.9	204.0
Sweden	4.8	6.5	1.8	2.4	5.2	10.1	30.2	10.5	29.6	22.0
Norway	0.8	4.2	1.4	2.5	9.4	15.5	5.3	5.7	4.2	12.2
Denmark	2.8	3.0	9.1	5.9	6.6	11.0	11.6	2.5	8.5	30.6
Germany	60.0	69.9	115.1	107.0	124.5	176.3	173.5	61.0	51.0	93.9
Holland	34.3	29.2	47.0	34.1	50.0	38.4	59.0	27.6	14.0	18.7
Belgium	20.5	11.4	19.4	27.8	36.6	20.2	20.0	5.0	16.4	22.6
France	96.6	106.4	90.6	84.3	103.1	167.2	78.8	35.2	26.9	59.1
Italy	58.8	64.0	96.0	96.3	60.8	60.3	108.9	83.6	45.1	117.4
Spain	13.5	27.8	36.2	54.6	65.3	109.2	97.5	97.7	35.8	73.2
Total	321.8	358.4	430.4	573.0	577.6	716.2	811.4	541.5	437.4	653.7

Source: *Parliamentary Papers*, 1854–55, LII, 226.

seems hardly credible that the eighty-six British textile engineers and twenty-eight machinery-supplying agents I have identified as active there between 1845 and 1870 would have confined their attentions merely to Norway. Indeed it is easy to demonstrate that, as a component of the European market for British machinery exports, Norway was very small beer. Table 10.1 shows British machinery exports of all types through the 1840s; the upsurge after 1843 is clearly visible in all markets, with sales between 1842 and 1847 increasing at an average of over 18 percent per year. By 1847 worldwide machinery exports from Britain totalled over £1.25 million; the level of trade fell, presumably because of the political events of the late 1840s, to recover from 1850.

Machinery exports were certainly only a small part of British commodity exports as a whole, indeed less than 1 percent in 1850;[1] but this is simply because Britain was such a massive exporter of cotton and wool textiles and (non-machine) iron and steel manufactures. The small proportion belies the importance of this trade, whose absolute size, as Table 10.1 shows, increased sharply in the 1840s. But what about the textile machinery component of this overall machinery trade? Trade statistics for the period after the liberalization of machinery exports do not distinguish between textile and other machinery, with textile equipment not being recorded separately until 1893.[2] But continental cotton spindleage increased sharply from 1845, almost doubling from 1860 to 1875, as Farnie shows (see Table 10.2).

It is reasonable to suppose that a large part of this European spindleage increase derived from British exports:

[1] See P. Deane and W. A. Cole, *British Economic Growth*, Table 9, p. 31.
[2] D. A. Farnie, *English Cotton Industry*, p. 57.

Table 10.2 *Factory cotton spindleage, 1845–75*
(millions of spindles)

	Britain	Continent
1845	17.5	7.5
1850	21.0	9.6
1861	30.3	10.0
1875	37.5	19.5

Source: D. A. Farnie, *The English Cotton Industry and the World Market 1815–1896*, Table 8, p. 180.

With the final removal of export controls in 1843, British machine-making firms greatly expanded overseas sales, in Europe, India and the USA, as well as having a vastly growing home market. The foundations for this growth ... had already been firmly laid by mid-century, and old-established firms continued to expand remarkably. Platt's of Oldham were employing 7,000 men in two works by 1875 – John Platt, indeed, could justifiably claim to be 'the largest mechanical engineer in the world' – while Dobson & Barlow of Bolton had about 2,000 and Curtis & Madeley of Manchester, 1,400.[3]

For textile engineering firms such as Platt Bros., we know that foreign sales expanded sharply after 1843. John Foster examined card indices listing orders to Platts from individual customers, and showed (Table 10.3) that foreign orders were consistently a high percentage of sales.

Kirk suggests that these estimates 'appear far too high' without saying why, other than suggesting that the home boom of the early 1850s would have led to a reduction in the share of exports.[4] In fact Foster's estimates show precisely this in each case, and in any event the effect on exports of a home boom would depend also on how simultaneous changes in the level of foreign activity were affecting export demand. In general, continental as well as British growth accelerated in the 1850s. Kirk himself produced estimates of Platt's foreign sales, which can be combined with their own 'Abstract of Yearly Returns' to show the division between foreign and domestic sales up to 1875. The results, shown in Table 10.4, accord well with Foster's corresponding estimates; by far the most important element of foreign sales were spinning mules, and Foster's estimate of 56 percent going to foreign sales during 1860–4 appears to be compatible with Kirk's estimates which imply an average of 54 percent of total sales going to foreign buyers during the identical period.

In any event, we have a substantial proportion of sales deriving from export

[3] A. E. Musson, 'The engineering industry', in R. A. Church, *The Dynamics of Victorian Business. Problems and Perspectives to the 1870s* (London, 1980), p. 103.
[4] R. M. Kirk, *Textile Machinery Industry*, p. 422.

Table 10.3 *Platt Bros. of Oldham: foreign orders, 1845–69*
(Foreign orders as % of total orders)

	Roving machines (% of machines)	Rings and throstles (% of spindles)	Mules (% of spindles)
1845–9	82	95	95
1850–4	34	16	82
1855–9	48	17	85
1860–4	59	62	56
1865–9	59	45	60

Source: J. Foster, *Class Struggle and the Industrial Revolution: early industrial capitalism in three English towns* (London, 1974), p. 329.

Table 10.4 *Domestic and foreign sales by Platt Bros. of Oldham (£000)*

Year	Home sales	% of total	Foreign sales	% of total
1860	340.0	52.2	311.7	47.8
1861	333.8	47.4	370.8	52.6
1862	156.7	35.2	288.6	64.8
1863	247.6	51.9	229.6	48.1
1864	257.0	42.8	344.1	57.2
1865	358.7	53.1	322.7	52.5
1870	279.1	54.4	233.6	45.6
1871	392.9	52.5	355.0	47.5
1872	409.8	44.0	521.2	56.0
1873	469.5	41.4	665.2	58.6
1874	617.2	51.2	589.3	48.8
1875	705.3	60.2	465.8	39.8

Sources: 1860–5, Kirk, *Textile Machinery Industry*, Table 16, p. 423; 1870–5, Platt Bros., *Abstract of Yearly Returns, Sales etc.*, DDPSL/1/75/8, Lancashire Record Office.

demand. What were the principal destinations of these exports? For Platt Bros., these are readily ascertainable from the 1870s; Table 10.5 shows the proportion of export sales to each area by Platts for 1873.

The sales to Norway by Platts were in the main handled through the agent, D. Foxwell. The central point about Table 10.5 is not the particular distribution, for clearly there were differences between textile engineering firms in the areas to which they sold, as well as differences in emphasis within firms over time, but rather the general dispersion over a wide range of markets. This export effort was maintained into the late nineteenth and early twentieth

Table 10.5 *Geographical distribution of export sales, Platt Bros.,*
1873 (%)

Russia	36.6
Poland	3.6
Denmark, Norway, Sweden	0.3
Switzerland	0.9
Australia	0.7
Germany	9.5
Holland	0.3
Belgium	5.6
France	4.1
Italy	4.8
Spain and Portugal	5.5
United States	8.1
Canada	3.4
Mexico and South America	1.9
India	12.0
Australia and New Zealand	0.6
Egypt, Turkey and the Levant	1.8
Others	0.3
	100.0

Source: Platt Bros., *Compendium of Overseas Sales and Agents*,
December 1873–December 1913, DDPSL 1/75/8, LRO.

centuries; Kirk in particular has shown the detailed dimensions of this for a
range of countries, machine types and firms.[5] Milward and Saul point out
that, 'even in Alsace where there was a distinguished tradition of machine
making, four fifths of the spinning machinery was English in 1912'.[6]

None of the details of this machinery trade should be particularly surprising; the extent of the trade, particularly by such large firms as Platt Bros. or
Dobson & Barlow, is well-known, as is the reliance of the British textile
machinery industry on exports, and the continuing role of British workers and
managers in continental Europe. Pollard, in arguing that industrialization
should be seen as a Europe-wide rather than as a national phenomenon,
pointed out that:

in the post-1815 period it can be shown that every major iron and engineering works
of the modern kind in Belgium and France and every major railway, beside many
textile mills and other enterprises, operated with British help. Similarly every new

[5] See Kirk, *Textile Machinery Industry*, Appendix B.
[6] A. Milward and S. Saul, *Economic Development of Continental Europe*, p. 196.

German industry used British technology and many used French capital and entrepreneurship.[7]

For the textile industry, Milward and Saul rightly point out that 'if the production of textiles was widely spread, output of the necessary machinery was highly concentrated. All but the most specialised of spinning machinery was the monopoly of a few British makers.'[8] The only hesitation one might have with Milward and Saul's remark is whether the term 'few' is appropriate; as I have shown, very many enterprises were involved (although, of course, often with very uneven market shares). But, if we know a great deal about the general trade in textile machinery exports from Britain to continental Europe, it still remains to tie the trade to the process of technology transfer, to ask whether this trade involved similar transfer and diffusion functions in other countries as it did in Norway. Is it plausible that the British firms which operated in Norway treated Norway as a special case, offering services in that country which they were not prepared to offer elsewhere? Or did they, on the contrary, perform technological tasks elsewhere in Europe similar to those they performed in Norway? If this is the case, then the implications are of some significance for our understanding of European industrialization. In particular, the export figures depicted above would indicate something considerably more than a process of arms-length trade; rather, they cover complex inter-firm relationships involving a technological diffusion process which underlay industrialization itself.

In fact, some of the continental technological activities of British firms and workers can be traced simply from the Hjula archives in Norway. We know, for example, that the Anderston Foundry sold machinery in St Petersburg, since in Oslo Halvor Schou faced delays in equipment being set up while their engineer David Rorison completed the delivery and setting up of equipment in Russia. We know that Parr, Curtis & Madeley had 'many friends' abroad, with whom they could arrange employment for British emigré workers. The agents Knoop & Co., who dealt with Hjula, were linked with the banking firm De Jersey which was run by Ludwig Knoop. He had sole agency for Platt Bros. machinery in Russia, and between 1840 and Knoop's death in 1894 the firm was responsible for building over 120 cotton mills in Russia.[9] We know also that as late as the mid-1860s German textile firms were buying British machinery and using British labour on a large scale. The latter point emerges from an interesting letter within the Hjula papers; in 1865 one of Halvor Schou's former employees, the weaving master Thomas Horrebin, wrote to Schou from Kuchen in Germany. He was working at that time for a large spinning and weaving establishment; from the lithograph at the head of the firm's writing paper which he was using it appears to have had two steam

[7] S. Pollard, 'Industrialization and the European Economy', in J. Mokyr (ed.) *The Economics of the Industrial Revolution* (London, 1985), p. 173.

[8] A. Milward and S. Saul, *Economic Development of Continental Europe*, p. 196.

[9] S. Chapman, *The Rise of Merchant Banking* (London, 1984), p. 145.

engine houses, very extensive mill buildings, and a range of other buildings including workers' housing. In the course of asking Schou whether he might return to Oslo Horrebin remarked that:

Me and my family is at present in Germany. I have been here a few years, and I have started a whole shed of looms and there is also about forty weavers from England that the master has hired for two years ... I have two daughters weaving and a son a Mechanic here ... all the looms that we have here is Dickinsons from Blackburn ... [10]

Horrebin's German employer wished him to stay on, but Horrebin felt that the mill was too far from a town. The machinery supplier, Dickinsons, also supplied Hjula Weavery in Oslo; Schou purchased twelve looms and a variety of other equipment from them in 1862. Schou's British employees seem to have treated this kind of international movement as a matter of course. In 1852 Schou's former employee Oddy was in Germany and in 1854 his employee Kingston was in the United States. When his employees Waddington and Brierly were laid off in 1858, Schou wrote to Parr, Curtis & Madeley (who had recruited them) expressing satisfaction with them and saying that: 'As I have no more work for them I shall be very glad if you could get a place abroad with some of your friends, which I think they wish both.'[11] Parr, Curtis & Madeley readily undertook to help, 'because of the good character you have given them'.[12]

The impression which emerges from this is that the Norwegian experience was not atypical, and that the technology transfer process offered to Norway by British firms was a routine business procedure for British firms. Could it be, therefore, that the Hjula experience was representative not only of Norwegian textile development, but of European textile industrialization in mid century? If this is the case then we would have, in my view, a rather new perspective on European industrialization. This perspective would view continental industrialization as a natural outgrowth of earlier British developments, with the transmission mechanism between Britain and the continent being the British capital goods industry. Certainly this was true for the Norwegian textile industry. Its development rested on trade in machinery, but behind the export statistics we have seen a complex process of interaction, of international diffusion, of adaptation, and of learning; this process was driven by international market-seeking, and an international outlook, on the part of British mechanical engineering firms. If the same is true of other economies and other industries, then the differentiation of the British economy in the early nineteenth century, which produced the world's first comprehensive capital goods industry, produced at the same time the instrument which made European industrialization a practical reality.

[10] *Hjula Papers*, Correspondence in, Horrebin, 4 June 1865.
[11] *Hjula Papers*, Correspondence out, 18 May 1858
[12] *Hjula Papers*, Correspondence in, Parr Curtis, 26 May 1858.

Appendix A

INSURED MACHINE AND EQUIPMENT STOCKS

This Appendix shows the entries in the fire insurance records on which the estimates of fixed capital formation in Chapter 4 are based. The records consist of individual entries listing either complete stocks of machines and equipment for any particular date, or additions to stocks since the last entry. Where the entry is an addition, this is indicated; otherwise entries represent total stocks at a particular date. Types of equipment are indicated: 'prep&fin' indicates preparatory and finishing equipment; other entries are self-explanatory. The Solberg enterprise was divided into two parts for insurance purposes, 'Upper' and 'Lower'; entries for these two halves are noted separately. All entries are in Specie daler. They are consistent with Tables 4.3 and 4.4 in the text, at an exchange rate of 16 Specie daler = £1.

Date/firm	Machines insured	Values	Total insured
Arne Fabrikker			
30 July 1846	5 prep&fin	1360	7780
	36 looms	4000	
	1 water wheel	940	
1 March 1847	7 prep&fin	1470	11220
	54 looms	6100	
	1 water wheel	940	
29 November 1849 (added)	40 looms	3600	16090
16 December 1850 (added)	19 prep&fin		35480
	10 spin.mch.		
	1 water wheel		
10 November 1851 (added)	5 prep&fin	670	
	14 spin.mch.	2100	
14 June 1853	2 water wheels	1500	11400
20 July 1853 (added)	32 prep&fin	7650	31140
	14 spin.mch.	5660	
14 November 1853 (added)	105 looms	8500	41190
11 July 1854 (added)	20 looms	1800	45740

Date/firm	Machines insured	Values	Total insured
21 July 1854	8 prep&fin	1850	51930
(added)	4 spin.mch.	1800	
29 February 1856	47 prep&fin	10120	51950
	18 spin.mch.	6400	
	141 looms	10960	
1 July 1857	29 prep&fin	10400	56090
(added)	19 spin.mch.		
18 September 1863	22 prep&fin	6500	48160
	10 spin.mch.	2876	
29 May 1867	30 prep&fin	9100	47260
	9 spin.mch.	3000	
	192 looms	14630	
Arne Wool			
18 September 1863	25 prep&fin	12345	48750
	4 spin.mch.	840	
	22 looms	12760	
28 May 1867	48 prep&fin	19990	50820
	5 spin.mch.	1560	
	73 looms	8580	
Brenneriveien			
2 May 1850	6 prep&fin	1900	13030
	24 looms	2000	
	1 steam engine	3000	
12 December 1850	6 prep&fin	1900	15640
	60 looms	3800	
	1 steam engine	3000	
6 June 1851	9 prep&fin		18960
	60 looms	3800	
	4 spin.mch.		
	1 steam engine	3000	
28 July 1853	6 prep&fin	1990	26960
	107 looms		
	4 spin.mch.		
	1 steam engine	3000	
7 August 1854	12 prep&fin		28990
	107 looms		
	4 spin.mch.		
Christiania Sailcloth factory			
14 July 1859	4 prep&fin	3600	150290
(added)	1 spin.mch.	1350	
4 August 1859	6 prep&fin	1690	162760
	44 looms	8240	
9 February 1860	10 prep&fin	5110	174370
(added)	1 spin.mch.	1600	
	14 looms	3000	

Date/firm	Machines insured	Values	Total insured
15–21 Apr. 1861	61 prep&fin	41171	147340
	18 spin.mch.	1185	
	67 looms	12935	
	1 turbine	3200	
	1 steam engine	2000	
27 June 1861	10 looms	1680	151070
(added)	2 spin.mch.	2000	
6 November 1861	4 prep&fin	640	153500
(added)	14 looms	2030	
16 July 1862	8 prep&fin	2700	158520
(added)			
2 December 1862	6 prep&fin	5265	167030
(added)	2 spin.mch.	3150	
14 January 1863	1 spin.mch.	1575	169325
(added)			
9 February 1864	14 prep&fin	5500	184494
(added)	4 spin.mch.	4940	
	6 looms	900	
22 December 1865	1 prep&fin	1250	195570
(added)	1 steam engine	4500	
September 1868	116 prep&fin	56685	198710
	39 spin.mch.	19780	
	96 looms	17655	
	1 turbine	1025	
	1 steam engine	4600	
2 April 1870	4 prep&fin		203780
Halden			
1815	6 prep&fin	1450	8520
	4 spin.mch.	2750	
	9 looms	1819	
15/16 December	15 prep&fin	8130	15760
1846	6 spin.mch.	3000	
	1 water wheel	1000	
12 September 1867	39 prep&fin	10490	33960
	12 spin.mch.	5000	
	1 water wheel	4000	
	1 steam boiler	1600	
Hansen & Co			
30 September 1852	11 prep&fin	2860	7780
	2 spin.mch.	600	
	8 looms	1200	
19 July 1853	2 prep&fin	1550	6990
	2 spin.mch.	480	
	1 water wheel	500	
15 October 1853	6 prep&fin	848	10800
(added)	6 looms	790	

Date/firm	Machines insured	Values	Total insured
24 March 1854	2 prep&fin	440	12720
(added)	7 looms	930	
6 December 1854	1 prep&fin	250	14720
(added)			
22 September 1855	6 prep&fin	2020	19810
(added)	2 spin.mch.	720	
	8 looms	1120	
1 March 1856	18 prep&fin	5320	20240
	4 spin.mch.	1200	
	20 looms	2750	
25 August 1860	9 prep&fin	3710	36720
(added)	2 spin.mch.	720	
	5 looms	650	
Hjula			
16 March 1850	1 water wheel	1190	2500
17 April 1856	20 prep&fin	3500	83380
	220 looms	16050	
	1 turbine	1800	
	1 steam engine 20HP	900	
17 November 1857	2 prep&fin	1900	86870
(added)	23 looms	2000	
12 January 1860	32 prep&fin	7735	104360
	324 looms	25995	
	1 turbine	1800	
	1 steam engine 20HP	900	
18 January 1864	18 prep&fin	7095	122882
(added)	2 spin.mch.	882	
	10 looms	2365	
10 March 1850	6 prep&fin	7000	126600
(added)	2 spin.mch.	1300	
	5 looms	1100	
10 July 1866	5 prep&fin	3430	135920
(added)	1 spin.mch.	600	
	2 looms	600	
6 March 1867	1 prep&fin	200	141058
(added)	9 looms	1640	
14/16 January 1868	86 prep&fin	34204	147930
	5 spin.mch.	2494	
	257 looms	27708	
	1 turbine	2400	
	1 steam engine	250	
Nydalen			
31 July 1846	21 prep&fin	8785	28145
	10 spin.mch.	4500	
	1 water wheel	3500	
	1 steam engine	1000	

Date/firm	Machines insured	Values	Total insured
Rosendahl & Fane			
15 September 1848	26 prep&fin	3600	12740
	4 spin.mch.	1850	
	6 looms	120	
	1 water wheel	1600	
5 March 1856	16 prep&fin	4410	16320
	3 spin.mch.	1980	
	28 looms	1200	
	1 water wheel	1650	
21 July 1857	6 prep&fin	2580	n.a.
(added)	1 spin.mch.	550	
29 December 1866	prep&fin	4990	28020
	6 spin.mch.	3300	
	1 water wheel	1500	
31 August 1867	51 prep&fin	13220	38080
	10 spin.mch.	6440	
	2 water wheels	3600	
Solberg			
29 May 1856			7850
Lower			
26 October 1846			20050
Upper			
19 March 1853	16 prep&fin	1050	
Upper	8 spin.mch.	5600	
8 June 1853	15 prep&fin	9950	
Upper	8 spin.mch.	5600	
5 January 1854	14 prep&fin	6110	12220
Lower	4 spin.mch.	1740	
30 October 1854	19 prep&fin	7220	17360
Lower	9 spin.mch.	4060	
8 December 1856	19 prep&fin	9260	21360
Upper	8 spin.mch.	4800	
	1 water wheel	400	
8 December 1856	20 prep&fin	9590	23910
Lower	9 spin.mch.	4760	
	1 water wheel	1900	
	1 steam engine	1000	
2 November 1859	20 prep&fin	9590	23550
Lower	9 spin.mch.	4760	
	1 water wheel	1600	
	1 steam engine	1000	
10 November 1868	18 prep&fin	7250	17080
Upper	8 spin.mch.	3200	
	1 water wheel	1550	

Date/firm	Machines insured	Values	Total insured
10 November 1868	22 prep&fin	8640	20470
Lower	9 spin.mch.	4350	
	1 water wheel	1500	
Vøien			
22 September 1845			28200
11 February 1847	27 prep&fin	16800	37390
	9 spin.mch.	9000	
29 November 1854	14 prep&fin	8160	73770
(added)	5 spin.mch.	5000	
	1 water wheel	4500	
16 May 1856	56 prep&fin	34420	79310
	21 spin.mch.	21000	
	1 water wheel	4500	
6 August 1857	1 prep&fin	1600	n.a.
(added)	2 spin.mch.	2000	
10 July 1860	1 water wheel	4500	32020
29 September 1860	49 prep&fin	30045	83980
	32 spin.mch.	18560	
	1 water wheel	4500	
8 November 1861	5 prep&fin	1455	106855
(added)	6 spin.mch.	4530	
9 March 1864	6 prep&fin	1455	112053
(added)	2 spin.mch.	2210	
16 August 1866	9 prep&fin	5195	119985
(added)	4 spin.mch.	2320	
1–4 September	75 prep&fin	42475	119740
1868	24 spin.mch.	27620	
	1 water wheel	3600	
12 February 1873	14 prep&fin	3150	129800
(added)	6 spin.mch.	4100	
Wallem			
17 September 1846	13 prep&fin	3970	12980
	2 spin.mch.	1180	
	1 steam engine	1320	

Appendix B

BRITISH FIRMS ACTIVE IN NORWAY, 1845–1870

This Appendix lists all British firms which left some trace – invariably either in the correspondence archives or in invoice files – in the records of the Norwegian textile enterprises researched in this study. The heading 'Activity' lists their principal line(s) of business. 'Machines' indicates that the firm is a textile engineering enterprise selling machinery and equipment, or a firm supplying machinery and equipment; 'RM' indicates raw material suppliers (i.e. of raw cotton, yarn, etc.); 'Ancil' indicates suppliers of ancillary equipment such as oil, dyestuffs, cards, machine parts, and so on; 'Agent' indicates that the firm acts as an agent on behalf of Norwegian firms, dealing with any of the above category of firms, and arranging shipping and so on; 'Finance' indicates a financial institution which may have been a bank, or some other firm arranging finance and payment. Other categories are self-explanatory. Where firms have multiple activities, the primary activity is listed first.

Firm	Location	Activity	Dates
John Abbot & Co.		Ancil.(rollers)	1845
Alders, Preyer & Co.	Manchester	Machines	1867–70
John Albot & Co.	Gateshead-upon-Tyne	Ancil.(gas meter)	1860
E. and H. Allison	Hull	Ancil.(soda)	1863
J.A. Amberley & Co.	Hull		1866
A. Andersen	Elland	Agent	1867
Andersen & Co.	Manchester	RM	1867
Anderston Foundry	Glasgow	Machines	1859–70
R. Armitage & Co.	Huddersfield	Machines	1845
Ashworth & Slater	Haslingdon	Machines Ancil.(combs)	1869
Asquith Bros. (Providence Foundry)	Morley nr.Leeds	Machines	1863
James Atkinson	Newcastle		1862
Baerlein	Manchester		1870
Bagshaw & Sons (Victoria Foundry)		Machines Ancil.	1863
Thos Baker			1862
A. Barber & Co.	London, Hamburg		1868
Baring Bros.	London	Finance	1858
Wm Barker	Leeds	Ancil.(brands)	1847
Samuel Barnes	Oldham	Machines Ancil.(rings)	1853
Timothy Bates & Co.	Sowerby Bridge	Machines Ancil.(keys)	1864–7

Firm	Location	Activity	Dates
Thos Baxter	Manchester	Ancil.(reeds)	1853–64
Bell & Wright	Glasgow	Ancil.(hooks)	1866–7
Benecke Souchay & Co.	London	Agent	1866–70
Bentley & Sons	Leeds	RM	1870
Berend & Levy	Leeds	RM	1864
Birch (Pump Street Mill)	Manchester	Ancil.(bobbins)	1852–64
John Blackburn	Batley	Ancil.(rings)	1864
Wm Blakely & Co.		RM	1863
Bluhm & Co.	Manchester	Agents	1858–70
Leonard Bock			1840–50s
Boldemann, Borris & Co.	Newcastle-upon-Tyne	RM	1856–69
Borries Craig & Co.	Newcastle	Ancil.(acid)	1868–70
	Bottomley	Machines	1867
Boulton & Pelly		Machines	1816
E. Bower & Co.	London	RM	1867–8
Bowers		Machines	
D. Bowlas & Co. (Victoria Mill)	Stockport	Ancil.(healds)	1851–69
Boyson.. & Tag ...	London	RM	1858
Branridge	Leeds	Machines Ancil.(slide rest)	1846
Breslauer & Thomas	London, Cardiff	RM	1865
Bridgeton, Heddle Co.	Glasgow	Ancil.(healds)	1867
Thos Broadbent	Cleckheaton	Ancil.(oil)	1855–9
Ch. Brocklehurst & Son		Machines Ancil.	1857–70
H. Bromet	Spitalfields London	Ancil.(rags)	1869–70
J. Brooke	Spitalfields London	Ancil.(rags)	1869–70
Brown		Ancil.(bobbins)	1845
E. Burman's Executors	Dewsbury	Machines	1865–7
Burridge & Son	Portsmouth		1816–17
Jonathan Buckley			1845
Thos Campbell (Dolphine Foundry)	Leeds	Machines Ancil.(fittings)	1863–5
Wm Carr	Bramley nr Leeds	Ancil.(bands)	1866
Cass	Bradford	RM	1867–9
J. Chapman & Co.	London		1861
Geo. Clarke	Hull	Shippers	1866
Colbeck Bros. (Cheapside Mill)	Dewsbury	RM	1863
Cooper	Birmingham		1845
D. Coopland	Yeadon nr Leeds	Ancil.	1868
T.B. Cornock	Leeds	Ancil.(teazles)	1863–9
W. Coulthurst	Old Accrington	Ancil.(soap)	1869
Crabtree & Stead	Leeds	Machines	1870
Crawford & Barnett		RM	1862
Crawshaw & Sons	Dewsbury	Ancil.(leather)	1863–7
Curtis & Son (Leather Warehouse Co.)	Manchester	Machines Ancil.(brands)	1859
Delius, Jacobs & Co.	Bradford	RM	1870
G. Denton	Leeds	Agent	1863–4
J. Denton	Leeds	Ancil.(straps)	1857–70
Wm Dickinson & Sons (Phoenix Iron Works)	Blackburn	Machines	1862–5

Firm	Location	Activity	Dates
E.P. Dixon			1859
Dobson & Co. (& Barlow)		Machines	
Jacob Dockray	Leeds	Machines Agent	1846–7
W. and G. Dorville		Agent Finance	1810–18
Drake, Kleinworth & Cohen	Liverpool	RM	1868
Dunkerley & Co.	Hull	Shippers RM Ancil.(coal)	1862
Dyson & Shaws	Elland	RM	1863–70
Easton, Amos & Son (Grove Iron Works)	London	Machines	1859–60
Thos Eddison	New Wortley nr Leeds	Ancil.(slays)	1866
Wm Fairbairn	Manchester	Machines	1846–61
Farmer & Son			1818
I. and I. Farrar	Elland	Ancil.(cards)	
Fawcett and Shackleton (Victoria Works and St Andrews Foundry)	Leeds	Machines	1868
du Fay & Co.	Manchester	Agent	1847–70
Wm Fearnley	Farnley Nr Leeds	Ancil.(plates)	1863
Fedden Bros & Co.	Newcastle-upon-Tyne	RM	1868–70
John Finlay	Belfast	RM	1863–9
Isaac Firth & Son	Halifax		
Thos Firth (Engine Bridge Works) or Tomlinson. See below.	Huddersfield	Machines	1863
G. Fisher & Co. (Hoyle St Works)	Sheffield	Ancil.	1857
Salomon Flatow	Leeds	Agent	1845–8
Fleming, Watson & Nairn	Glasgow	RM	
Edward Flint		Ancil.(cans)	1845
D. Foxwell	Manchester	Machines Ancil.(cards)	1853–70
Frühling & Goschen	London	Agent Finance	1855–70
Fullerston & Davidson	Dundee		1865–7
John Fe..ck		Ancil.(glass)	1859
Gachen, Ashton & Trier	Liverpool	RM	1846–8
P. and C. Garnett (Wharfe Works)	Cleckheaton	Machines	1863–8
Gaukroger Bros.	Halifax	Ancil.(cards)	1864
Wm Gibson & Co. (Silvan Works)	Glasgow	Ancil.(shuttles)	1868
Good..admann & Co.	Hull	Shippers	1855
James Greenhaigh	Rochdale	Ancil.(cistern)	1863
Greening & Co. (Victoria Iron & Wire Works)	Manchester	Ancil.(netting)	1864–5
Fried. Greenwood	Rochdale	Machines Ancil.(plates)	1867–9
John Greenwood		Ancil.(shuttles)	1870

Firm	Location	Activity	Dates
Haigh & Heaton	Milne's Bridge nr Huddersfield	RM	1868
R. Halliday & Co.	Huddersfield	Ancil.	1846
R. Hallmaker		Machines	
H.E.J. Hambro & Co.	Newcastle-upon-Tyne	Agent	1845
C.J. Hambro	London		1862
B. Hamilton	Rochdale	Ancil.(oil cans)	1867
Haggre Bros.	Newcastle	Ancil.(chains)	1845
A. Hardman (Coronation Foundry)	Bolton	Machines	1851
Benjamin Hargreave & Son	Leeds	Ancil.(bands)	1863
Simon Harker	Leeds	Machines	1862–3
Anthony Harris & Co.	Newcastle-upon-Tyne	Ancil.(soda)	1860
Harrison & Sons (Bank Foundry)	Blackburn	Machines Ancil	1855–61
G.W. Hart	Hull	Ancil.(vitriol)	1864
Hastings & Mellor (Bradley Mills)	Leeds	Ancil.(press paper)	1863
John Hetherington & Sons (Vulcan Works)	Manchester	Machines	1850–60
Edward Hey (Victoria Foundry and Providence Works)	Batley nr Leeds	Ancil.(shuttles)	1866–70
Heymann & Alexander	Bradford	RM	1855
James Higginbottom (Albert Mills)	Manchester	Other	1861–2
Wm Higgins & Son	Manchester	Machines	1874
Robert Hilt & Sons	Halifax	Ancil.(lacis)	1867
Hirst Bros.	Batley	RM	1867
Thos Hitchings (Newton Picker Works)	Manchester	Ancil.(pickers)	1852–60
Hobson Bros. & Co.	Newcastle	Ancil.(oil)	1857–61
George Hodgson (Beehive and Laycock's Mills)	Bradford	Machines Ancil.(temples)	1867–8
Hollingdrake & Hickman	Stockport	Ancil.(gas tubes)	1857–9
Samuel Holt (New Mills)		Machines	1869
J.P. Hornung	Middlesbrough	Ancil.(pipes)	1765–9
John Horrocks	Pilkington nr Manchester	Machines	1855
Horsfield & Barras		Machines	1845
G.and J. Howard	Burnley	Machines	1863–70
Howard & Bullough		Machines	
G. and J. Howorth	Burnley	RM	1863–70
Hull Flax and Cotton Mill Co.	Hull	RM	1840–50s
James Hunt		Ancil.(oil)	1859
W. Hunter & Co.	Glasgow	Agent	1865
James Hurst and John Lord	Manchester	Ancil.(oil)	1857–65
Huth & Co.	Liverpool	RM	1854–70
Geo. Hutchinson	Manchester	Ancil.(oil)	1867
H. Hutchinson Bros.	Leith		1859–61
Hutchinson & Hollingworth (Dobcross Iron Works)	Manchester	Machines	1866–70
Hutter & Co.		RM	1850s
Hvistendahl & Co.	Liverpool	RM	1869–70
Hvistendahl, Holst & Co.	Manchester	Agent	1863–70

Firm	Location	Activity	Dates
Irving & Co.		Other	1848
Irving, Ebsworth, Holmes	London		1862
Jaffe Bros. & Co.	Dundee, Hamburg	RM	1867–70
Joseph Jebb & Son	Batley	Ancil.(tenters)	1863
T. and E.G. Jepson	Leeds	Ancil.(soap) Ancil.(spindles)	1863
R. Johnson, Clapham & Morris	Manchester Liverpool	Ancil.(iron tubes)	1867
Johnston Harlisle (Brookfield Flax Spinning Mill)	Belfast	RM	1862
E. Jones & Son	Manchester	Machines	1856
Kamcke & Co.	Belfast	RM	1863–8
Thos Kenyon		Machines	1869
John Kerr & Co.	Dundee		1862
Robert Kerschaw	Rochdale	Machines	1862
Kessler & Co.	Manchester Bradford	RM	1855–70
Ch. King	Halifax	RM	1868–70
John King & Co.	Hull	Shippers	1868
Kington & Co.	London	Agent	1854–61
Kirkstall Forge		Machines	1846
Kirkwood & Co.	London		1852
Knoop & Co.	Manchester	Agent	1858–62
Knowles, Houghton & Co. (& Leach) (California Works)	Gomersal nr Leeds	Machines Ancil.	1863–8
Krighton & Co.		Machines	pre 1853
Samuel Lamb	Leeds	Machines	1863
Thos. Lancaster	Brighouse	Machines	1863
Landell, Gibson & Co. (Silvan Works)	Glasgow	Ancil.(shuttles)	1863–70
Samuel Law (West Town Doffing and Cleaning Plate Works)	Dewsbury	Ancil.	1864–7
Lawson & Sons	Leeds	Machines	1859–70
R. Lawton		Agent	
Edm. Leach & Son (Castle Works)	Rochdale	Machines	1862–70
Asa Lees (Soho Iron Works)	Oldham Manchester	Machines	1857
Lees and Barnes (Soho Iron Works)	Manchester Oldham	Machines	1840–50s
Leisler, Bock & Co.	Glasgow	RM	1863–70
Lemonius & Co.	Liverpool	Agent	1865–73
R. Levig & Co.	Bradford, Leeds	RM	1870
Levin & Adler		Ancil.(oil)	1859
Levin & Co.	London		1861–2
Thos Lewthwait		Ancil.	1867
Liebert	Manchester	RM	1850s
David Liepmann	Manchester	Agent	1859–65
James Lille & Son	Manchester	Machines	1846
Lindberg & Hornung	Newcastle	Shippers	1855
Lister	Leeds	RM	1863
Ludvigsen	Liverpool	RM	1859–65
Luhm	Manchester	RM	1863
Maclea & March	Leeds		1845
J. Magnus & Nephew	Manchester		1863–9
Malcolm	Glasgow	RM	1854

Firm	Location	Activity	Dates
Marschall & Co.			1845
S. Marschland	Bradford	RM	1868–70
Mather & Platt	Manchester	Machines	1857–68
(Salford Iron Works)			
Benj. Matthews	Elland	Machines	1867
Maud & Son	London	RM	1869–70
Mellor, Bromley	Leicester	Machines	
& Co. (Minotaur Works)			
Mellor & Waddington	Leeds	Ancil.(press paper)	1868
(Hunslet Paper Mills and	Halifax		
Bradley Mills)			
Merck & Co.	Manchester	Agent	1849–58
John Metcalf	Bradford	RM	1867–70
John Middle	Leeds	Ancil.(rags)	1870
Joseph Millner	Halifax	Ancil.(cards)	1857–69
Edwin Mills	Huddersfield	Machines	1866
(Aspley Iron Foundry)			
John Mills	Bradford	RM	1868
Mill.. & Leidhold	Manchester	Ancil.(oil)	1866
Mitchell & Son	Stocksteads	Ancil.(felt)	1868
Edwin Moorhouse	Ashton-under-Lyne	Ancil.(reeds)	1856–9
T.B. Morley & Co.	Hull	Shippers	1853–66
Mortimer		Ancil.(rollers)	1846
G.& R. Mortimer	Leeds	Ancil.(bobbins)	1866–70
(Monk Bridge Bobbin and			
Shuttle Works)			
G. Mosley	Manchester	Ancil.(copperas)	1860
Mynssen	Manchester	Machines	1870
John Neck & Sons	London	Agent	1867–70
(late Sewell & Neck)			
Neuth & Co.	Leeds	Ancil.	1866–74
Henry Newall & Co.	Littleborough	Ancil.(flannel)	1863–6
(Patent Candle Company)	nr Manchester		
J.B. Newsome	Batley	RM	1863
T. Nicholson	Leeds	Machines	1863–70
North British	Edinburgh	Ancil.	1865
Rubber Company Ltd			
North Brothers	Leeds	Ancil.(teazles)	1869–70
The North Moor	Oldham	Machines	1863–9
Foundry & Co.			
Oelrichs & Co.	Liverpool	Agent	1863
Oetling, Flohr & Co.	Manchester		
Okenayd & Sons	Halifax		1845
Parker		Ancil.(heckles)	1845
Parker & Son	Sheffield		1863–5
Parr, Curtis & Co.	Manchester	Machines	1853–66
(later Parr, Curtis & Madeley)		Ancil	
(Phoenix Works)			
Parry & Co.	Birmingham	Ancil.	1870
Patent Heddle Company	Glasgow	Ancil.	1867
Pearson & Co.	Hartlepool	Shippers	1865
Pearson & Spurr	nr Leeds	Machines	1863
(Briston Foundry)			
Joseph Peel	Yeadon	RM	1869–70
	nr Leeds		
Alb Pelly		Ancil.	1859
John Petrie	Rochdale	Machines	1864–8
Philips & Co.	Manchester		1863
Platt Bros. & Co.	Oldham	Machines	1865

British firms active in Norway, 1845–1870

Firm	Location	Activity	Dates
G. Pregel & Co.	Bradford	RM	1854–60
Prescott & Co.	London	Agent	1947–57
Preston & Dania	Rochdale	Ancil.(lags)	1863
Wm Priest & Co.	Hull	Shippers	1855–6
Proctor	Newcastle-upon-Tyne		1845
G. Ramsden	nr Leeds	Machines	1864
J. Ratcliff		Ancil.	1865
J. Rhodes & Son	Morley	Machines	1863–70
	nr Leeds		
Richardson Bros. & Co.	Leeds	Agent	1865–70
	Hunslet	Ancil.(potash)	
Rigm.. & Son		Machines	pre 1853
T. Riley	Gretland	Machines	1862–63
Robert & Platt		Machines	pre 1853
Robinson & Co.	Salford	Ancil.(rollers)	1865
A. Robinson & Son	Hebden Bridge	RM	1867
Rohr & Randrup	Manchester	RM	1868–70
		Ancil	
Roper & Frerich	Bradford	RM	1863
Rothwell & Co.	Bolton	Machines	1866–7
(Union Foundry)			
E. Scharff & Co.	Bradford	Agent	1863–9
	Leeds		
J. Schoefield & Son	Huddersfield	RM	1863
(Commercial Mills)			
Schoefield & Son	Hulme	Ancil.(grooms)	1866
	nr Manchester		
F. Schwann	Leeds		1864–9
Schwann, Kell & Co.	Dundee		1863–4
David Scott	Halifax		
Seaward, Bell & Co.	London	Shippers	1870
Sewell, Norman & Sewell	London	Agent	1810–68
(later Sewell, Hanbury &		Finance	
Sewell)			
(later Sewell & Neck)			
A. Sharpe	Cleckheaton	Shippers	1862
	nr Normantown		
Sharp & Son	Cleckheaton	Agent	1863–70
	nr Leeds	Ancil.(cards)	
Benjamin Shaw	Radcliffe	Ancil.(hooks)	1863
Luke Shaw	Elland	Ancil.(cases)	1868
Shuttleworth		Ancil.	1856
R. Simpson & Co.	Rochdale	Ancil.(bands)	1863
Skilton, Hill & Co.	Hull	Shippers	
W.R.W. Smith	Glasgow	RM	1860–3
Smith & Brothers	Heywood	Ancil.	1855
Squire Diggles	Radcliffe	Machines	1855–57
(Atlas Works)	nr Manchester		
J. Standring	Rochdale	RM	1863–70
Ch. Stanley	Wath-on-	Ancil.(oil)	1867
	Dearne, Yorkshire		
Stead & Simpson		Ancil.	1846
J. Steedman	Charlestown	Ancil.(coal)	1863–5
(Elgin Colliery)			
Steinthal & Co.	Bradford	RM	1856–7
Duncan Stewart	Glasgow	Machines	1865–7
		Ancil.(steam traps)	
Daniel Stockwell	Manchester	Ancil.(oil)	1869
John Stockwell	Morley	Other	1870
Samuel Stone	Leeds	Ancil.(line)	1868

Firm	Location	Activity	Dates
H. Sugden & Sons (Victoria Foundry)	Bramley, nr Leeds	Machines	1866–70
John Sykes & Son (Turnbridge Machine Works)	Huddersfield	Machines	1866–7
John Tatham (Moss Lane Works, Milnow Road Works)	Rochdale	Machines	1867–70
James Taylor	Leeds	Machines Ancil.(heckles)	1866
Wm. Taylor	Upper Batley nr Leeds	Ancil.(rags)	
Thos Taylor	Bradford		
Taylor, Wordsworth & Co. (Midland Junction Foundry)	Leeds	Machines Ancil. Agent	1845–72
Tennant & Co.	Glasgow		1862
Thornton Bros (Marsh Mill Foundry)	Cleckheaton nr Leeds nr Normantown	Machines Ancil.(cards)	1863–5
C.T. Tiffany	Leeds	Machines	1867
Tobler & Co.	Manchester	Ancil.(rubber)	1866
G.W. Tomlinson (late Firth) (Engine Bridge Works)	Huddersfield	Machines Ancil.(blades)	1864–70
James Townson	Manchester	Other	1854
E.C. Travis	Manchester	Ancil.(glass)	1859–60
J. Trescott & Co.	Manchester		
John Tullis & Son	Glasgow	Ancil.(leather)	1867–70
Turnbull, Salvessen & Co.	Leith	Ancil.(coal)	1864–6
Voss & Delius	Manchester	Agent Finance	1854–69
Daniel Wade	Farsley Leeds	Ancil.(slays)	1863–70
James Walker	Elland	Machines	1867
Walton, Walker & Co./& Son			1859
S. and J. Watts & Co.	Manchester		1863–6
Welsh Slate Company	Port Madoc	Ancil.(slates)	1854
Westerman	Leeds	Ancil.(bobbins)	1863
G. Westwood	Halifax	Machines	1868
John White	Manchester	Ancil.(pickers)	1851–9
Whitehead	Leeds	Agent	1845
Whitehead & Meyer	Liverpool	Agent	1851–9
Isaac White & Son	Bradford	RM	1867–70
Whiteley	Lockwood nr Huddersfield	Machines	1863–4
W. Whiteley & Son	nr Leeds	Ancil.(paper)	1869–70
Samuel Whiteworth	Rochdale	Ancil.(shuttles)	1863–9
S. and J. Whitham (Perseverance Foundry)	Leeds	Machines Ancil.	1846–7
Whitworth, Lord & Co.	Manchester	RM	1868
Wichenhaus & Busch	Liverpool	RM	1856–62
E. Wilkinson (Providence Work)	Isle of Cinder	Ancil.(oil)	1869
Wilkinson & Wallace	Halifax	RM	1867–70
Willis & Chell (Victoria Works)	Manchester	Machines	1856–9
John Wilson		Ancil.(leather)	1859–60
Wilson, Sons & Co.	Hull	Shippers	1842–70

British firms active in Norway, 1845–1870

Firm	Location	Activity	Dates
Wilson, Walker & Co.		Ancil.	1859
H. Wingard & Co.	Newcastle-upon-Tyne	Agent	1846–50s
Wolff	Hull		1866
Wolff, Hasche & Co.	Manchester	RM	1855–6
Wood	Manchester	Ancil.(lamps)	1846
G. Wordsworth	Manchester		1845
Wren & Berend	Manchester	Machines	1846
Ernest Zachrisson	Liverpool	RM	1859
E. Zwilchenbart & Co.	Liverpool	RM	1852–60

Appendix C

NORWEGIAN FIRMS AND BRITISH MACHINERY MAKERS: CONTACTS TO 1870

	Halden	Solberg	Nydalen	Wallem	Rosend	Arne	Br.Vei. Hjula	Christiania Sailcloth	Others/ unknown
Aders, Preyer & Co.							1867–70		
Anderston Foundry							1859–70		
Armitage & Co.			1845						
Ashworth & Slater						1869			
Asquith Bros.							1863		
Bagshaw & Sons							1863		
S.Barnes							1853		
T.Bates & Co.						1864–7			
Bottomley							1867		
Boulton & Pelly	1816								
Bowers						18..			
Branridge					1846				
Brocklehurst & Son						1857–70			
Burman's Exec.							1865–7		
Thos Campbell							1863–5		
Crabtree & Stead							1870		
Curtis & Son			1859						
Dickinson & Son							1862–5		
Dobson & Co. (& Barlow)				18..					pre 1853
J.Dockray				1846–7					
Easton, Amos & Co.							1859–60		
Wm. Fairbairn				1846			1850–61		
Fawcett & Shackleton							1868		
T.Firth							1863		
D.Foxwell	1866–7	1853–68					1867–70		
P. and C. Garnett						1863–8			
F.Greenwood							1867–9		
R.Hallmaker			18..						
A.Hardman							1851		
S.Harker						1862–3			
Harrison & Sons			1859				1855–61		

Contacts with British machinery makers in 1870

	Halden	Solberg	Nydalen	Wallem	Rosend	Arne	Br.Vei. Hjula	Christiania Sailcloth	Others/ unknown
Hetherington & Son	1859		1859–60				1850–9		
Higgins & Son						1874			
G.Hodgson							1867–8		
S.Holt						1869			
J.Horrocks							1855		
Horsefield & Barras				1845					
G. & J. Howard						1863–70			
Howard & Bullough						18..			
Hutchinson & Hollingworth							1866–70		
E.Jones & Son						1856	1856		
T.Kenyon						1869			
T.Kerschaw						1862			
Kirkstall Forge					1846				
Knowles, Houghton & Co. (& Leach)							1863–8		1866
Krighton & Co.									pre 1853
S.Lamb						1863			
T.Lancaster							1863		
Lawson & Sons								1859–70	
Leach & Son						1862–70	1863		
Asa Lees						1857			
Lees & Barnes						1840s–50s	1851–2		
J.Lille & Son				1846					
Mather & Platt		1857					1857–68		
B.Mathews						1867			
Mellor, Bromley & Co.		18..							
E.Mills							1866		
Mynssen							1870		
T.Nicholson						1869	1863–70		
North Moor Foundry & Co.						1863–9			
Parr, Curtis & Co. (later Parr, Curtis & Madeley)	1853–62	1855–9					1855–9	1857	1855–66
Pearson & Spurr							1863		
J.Petrie						1864–8			
Platt Bros. & Co.						1865			
G.Ramsden							1864		
Rhodes & Son						1866	1863–70		
Rigm.. & Son									pre 1853
T.Riley						1862–3			
Robert & Platt									pre 1853
Rothwell & Co.						1866–7			
Squire Diggles							1855–7		1856

	Halden	Solberg	Nydalen	Wallem	Rosend	Arne	Br.Vei. Hjula	Christiania Sailcloth	Others/ unknown
D.Stewart							1865–7		
Sugden & Sons							1866–70		
J.Sykes & Son							1866–7		
J.Tatham							1867–70		
J.Taylor					1866				
Taylor, Wordsworth & Co.			1845		1846–72		1864		
Thornton Bros						18..	1863–5		
C.T.Tiffany						1867			
G.W.Tomlinson						18..	1864–70		
J.Walker						1867			
G.Westwood						1868			
Whiteley						1863–4			
S. and J. Whitham				18..	1846–7				
Willis & Chell							1856–9		
Wren & Berend					1846				

Sources: Correspondence records, *Faktura* [invoices], account books.

The dates show the first and the last traceable contacts, and thus do not necessarily indicate that contact was maintained between the two dates. The Vøien enterprise is not included because none of the available records indicate which firms they were dealing with. When 18.. only is entered, it is not possible to get exact year of contact from the records.

Appendix D

BRITISH WORKERS IN NORWEGIAN TEXTILE ENTERPRISES

This appendix summarizes available information on workers of British origin in the Norwegian textile industry during the period of this study. For various firms I give (1) names, (2) dates when workers either were first engaged or are known to have been at work in Norway – where details of recruitment are known, this is indicated, (3) functions or occupation, where known, (4) wages – these are taken not from tax records, but from contracts or letters of agreement prior to employment, (5) details of any relevant family accompanying the worker/manager, or being supported in Britain, (6) brief comments on performance, reasons for dismissal, post-Norway destinations, etc., (7) sources – these are first and foremost firm records, either correspondence files or wages lists. The other important sources are central government taxation records, and the Censuses of 1865 and 1875.

Name	Year	Function	Wage	Family/age	Comments	Sources
Akersekven Cloth factory						
Dilling	1857	Spinning-master				Tax 1857
Gray	1861	Foreman				Correspondence
Studsky	1857	Weaving-master				Tax 1857, 1858

Name	Year	Function	Wage	Family/age	Comments	Sources
Arne						
Brandwood	1847					S.Grieg, *Arne Fabrikker*, p.59
Lawrence Nelson	1869 1846					Account books S.Grieg, *Arne Fabrikker*, p.59
Nuttel	1846					S.Grieg, *Arne Fabrikker*, p.59
John Shaw	1860 1874	Machine-master		Wife and children in Norway in 1869. Born 1838		Census 1875
Elay Shaw		Spinner		Son of John Shaw. Born 1860 England		Census 1875
Abraham Sutcliffe	1863 1867	Machine-master		Married 50 years		Accounts books. Census 1865, 1875
Christiania Sailcloth factory						
Helen Browson	Sept. 1859 to May 1860	Weaver				Wage lists Tax 1860
Kathrine Browson	1860	Factory-girl Factory-girl				Wage lists Tax 1860 Wage lists
Katie Cunningham	Apr. 1861 to Dec. 1870	Spinner				Wage lists
Dishart	Sept. 1859 to May 1860					Wage lists
son of Dishart	Sept. 1859 to May 1860					Wage lists
Martha Donnel	Sept. 1858 to May 1860	Spinner Weaving-girl				Wage lists Tax 1860

Name	Dates	Occupation	Source
Donaldson	Sept. 1858 to May 1860	Weaver	Wage lists
David Duhart	1860	Smitter	Tax 1860
		Factory-master	Tax 1860
Ann Duff	Apr. 1859 to May 1860(61?)	Spinner	Wage lists
Wallace Fairweather	1868	Factory-master	Tax 1868
Cathrine Farmer	Sept. 1858 to May 1860	Spinner	Wage lists
Jessie Flint	1860	Weaving-girl	Tax 1860
James Fotheringham	1860 to 1870	Factory-girl	Tax 1860
		Bleaching-master	Tax 1860
Ann Gibbs	Sept. 1859 to May 1860	Weaver	Wage lists
William Greenhill	1859	Factory-girl	Tax 1860
	1860	Weaving-master, Spinning-master	Tax 1859, 1860
John Grieves	1861 to 1866	Weaving-master	Tax 1861–6
Johnston	Sept. 1859 to May 1860	Tenter	Wage lists
Jane (Jenny?) Lawson	Apr. 1859 to Sept. 1859	Spinner	Wage lists
Agnes Stephenson	Sept. 1858 to Sept. 1859(61?)	Spinner	Tax 1860
Anna Stewart	Sept. 1858 to May 1860	Weaving-girl	Wage lists
		Spinner	Tax 1860
Jane Stewart	Sept. 1859 to May 1860	Weaving-girl	Wage lists
Ratcliffe Mary	Sept. 1858 1871	Weaver	Wage lists

J.Ramstad, *Kvinnelønn og Pengeøkonomi*, Vol. 11, Appendix 4

Name	Year	Function	Wage	Family/age	Comments	Sources
Foss						
Jonathan Ballard	1860 1863	Spinning-master			Takes out patent in 1862	Hjula *Kopibok* 3 Nov. 1859 Tax 1860–3
Thomas Dean	1866 to 1875	Spinning-master		British wife in Norway in 1875. Son Joseph, Born 1822		Bill in Hjula archives: 1866 box. Tax 1866–70 Census 1875
Joseph Dean		Spinning-foreman		Son of Thomas. Born 1852 in England		Goes on to Census 1875
William Dean	1867 1875	Foreman		Son of Thomas. Norwegian wife in 1875. Born 1844 in England		Tax 1867–9; Census 1875
Leerfossen/Grorud						
J W Dockray	1870	Finisher				Tax 1870
Stephen Marmont	1869 to 1871?	Technical leader		Previously at Hjula. Returns to Hjula		See Hjula
George Richardson	1869 to 1871?			Previously at Hjula		See Hjula
Halden						
Stoker	1852	Master				S.Grieg, *Norsk Tekstil, Vol 1*, p.278
Hjula						
Thomas Barrat	by PCM Aug. 1856 to July 1857	4-loom weaver	£1 10s 0d 12 months contract	Wife and mother in UK, paid by PCM	Recommended by Pollit Drinks Nearly sacked	Correspondence Tax 1857

Name	Employed	Position	Wage	Family	Remarks	Source
Harry Baxter	by PCM Aug. 1856	Overlooker			Recommended by Pollit	Correspondence
James Brierly	by PCM May 1857 to 1862	To replace Murray Loom-mechanic Overlooker	50 sh	Wife in UK, paid by PCM and Bluhm & Co. Wife destitute in 1862	'Very useful' Laid off Wants employment abroad	Correspondence Tax 1858, 1861, 1862
Andrew Clarke	by Anderston Foundry Oct. 1859 to March 1860	Foreman Tenter	£3 0s 0d 12 months contract	Wife in UK, paid by Anderstons	Learns dressing before arrival Drinks Sacked	Correspondence
Sam Clegg	by Sharp & Son May 1865 to May 1869	Finisher	£3 0s 0d	Wife in UK, paid by Sharp & Son	Returns UK	Correspondence
Wright Farrington	by Hvistendahl & Holst Sept. 1864 to Dec. 1864	Finisher	45 sh 3 months contract	Wife and children in UK, paid by Hvistendahl Holst	Temporary	Correspondence
William Harrison	by Richardson & Co Nov. 1868 to June 1870	Foreman carder and spinner	£3 0s 0d	Wife in UK, paid by Richardson & Co	Recommended by Hudson 'Incompetent' Nearly sacked	Correspondence Tax 1870
William Heywood	May 1860 to Aug. 1860		£2 0s 0d			Account books
Frederick Holt	by PCM July 1857 to ca June 1858	Overlooker To replace Pollit	£2 0s 0d	Brings wife	Drinks Not kept on	Correspondence
Thomas Horrebin	by PCM 1859 to 1862	Weaving-master		Wife in UK, paid by Bluhm & Co	In Germany 1865 Wants reemployment with wife and children	Correspondence Tax 1861, 1862
James Horton	by Richardson & Co March 1870 to Sept. 1870	Wool dyer	£3 0s 0d 6 months contract £25 gratuity	Wife in UK, paid by Richardson & Co	Drinks	Correspondence
Alfred Hudson	Nov. 1868 to Aug. 1870	Foreman		Wife in UK, paid by Richardson & Co., then in Norway. Three children and Waddington's son	Goes on to Christiania Cloth Factory; agent in 1875	Correspondence Tax 1870 Census 1875

Name	Year	Function	Wage	Family/age	Comments	Sources
John Hunt	Sept. 1856 to Oct. 1862	Foreman		Wife, father and mother in UK, paid by PCM	Sacked twice	Correspondence Tax 1857, 1858, 1861, 1862
Jackson	1851? Before Aug. 1855 to before August 1856	Foreman				Correspondence
John Kellett	By 1865 to past 1866	Dyer	£3 0s 0d	Wife and 3 children in UK, paid by Sharp & Son		Correspondence Tax 1866, 1867
John Kingston	1852 1853			Brother of Joseph		Correspondence
Joseph Kingston	1849 to May 1853	Weaving-master		Brother wants to come 1854. Wife in UK? Father of Jonathan and 'daughter(s)'	Goes on to America	Correspondence Account books Tax 1851, 1852, 1853
Jonathan Kingston	1849 to 1853			Son of Joseph		Account books Tax 1851, 1852
Kingston daughter	Sept. 1850 to May 1851			Daughter of Joseph		Account books
James Maiden	by J.Tatham May 1870 to Aug. 1870	Set up machinery	£3 10s 0d	Wife in UK, paid by Tatham		Correspondence
Stephen Marmont	by G.Denton Nov. 1863 to Jan. 1869	Manager	£200 per annum	Wife in UK, paid by Denton, then Norway 36 years in 1863	Sets up Leerfossen with Richardson. Machines from Schou. At Hjula in 1875	Correspondence Tax 1865–70 Census 1875
John Marmont	Nov. 1863 to ?	Foreman in 1875	15 sh	Son of Stephen 13 years		Correspondence Census 1875
George Murray	by Squire Diggles July 1856 to Oct. 1856	Overlooker	£2 10s 0d 12 months contract	Wife in UK, paid by Merck & Co	Incompetent. Drunkard. Sacked. Reemployment refused	Correspondence

Name	Employment	Job	Wage	Family	Notes	Sources
Oall		Weaver				Tax 1858
Joseph Oddy	1857/8 March 1850 to May 1850	Set up machinery			On to Germany	Correspondence Account books
John Orme	Before 1860	Weaver			Returns to Armitage. Wants reemployment	Correspondence
James Pollard	by Richardson & Co May 1869 to past 1870	Foreman-finisher	£3 0s 0d	Wife and children in UK	Brings wife and children. 41 years in 1869	Correspondence Census 1875
Thomas Pollit	by PCM June 1856 to June 1857	Foreman	12 months contract	Wife in UK, paid by PCM	'good worker' Drinks	Correspondence Tax 1857
George Richardson	by G.Denton Aug. 1863 to 1869	Power-loom overlooker	£2 10s 0d		Returns UK Sets up Leerfossen with Marmont	Correspondence Tax 1868
William Roebuck	by Richardson Aug. 1870	Foreman. Manufacturer. To replace Hudson	£3 0s 0d	Wife in UK, paid by Richardson & Co		Correspondence
David Rorison	by Anderston Foundry Aug. 1859 to 1867–9?	Tenter, Overlooker	£3 10s 0d	Wife in UK, then Norway	Arrives via St Petersburg. Leaves Anderstons for Hjula	Correspondence Tax 1861–5
William Stead	by Sharp & Son From May 1865, 1868	Fulling miller	£1 10s 0d			Correspondence Tax 1867, 1868
Elisabeth Stocks				Comes with husband William, and two daughters		Correspondence Tax 1865
William Stocks	by G.Denton July 1863 to past April 1968	Finisher	£3 0s 0d	Brings wife Elisabeth, and two daughters		Correspondence Tax 1865
Abraham Taylor		Spinning master		born 1841 Married		Census 1875
Taylor Wade	by G.Denton 1863	Weaver				Correspondence
John Waddington	by PCM Sept. 1856 to June 1858	Sizer		Son Arthur, born 1864 in UK, is foster-child with Hudson in 1875	'very useful'. Laid off. Wants employment abroad	Correspondence Tax 1857, 1858 Census 1875

Name	Year	Function	Wage	Family/age	Comments	Sources
John Warrington	by PCM From Aug. 1856	Heald knitter and dyer			Recom. by G.Murray	Correspondence
Nicolaysen Charles Collony	1860 1861	Spinning-master				Tax 1860, 1861
Nydalen Johan Hurst	1859	Factory-master				Tax 1859
Hargreave Jameson	by Hiorth 1847 to 1870 (dies 1870)	Spinning-master		Father of Joseph	Brings skilled workers	Tax most years 1859–70 *Nydalens Compani 100 år*, p.26 Correspondence; also in Hjula archives
Joseph Jameson		Spinning-master Director in 1889		Son of Hargreave		*Morgenbladet Nydalen Comapni 100 år*, p.37
Rosendahl & Fane Thomas Booth	Oct. 1845, 1846	Master		Wife in UK, paid by Flatow, son to Norway	Previously at Wallem	Correspondence Account books
son of Booth	June 1846					Correspondence Account books
Anna Chadwick	Aug. 1846	Spinner				Correspondence
daughter Chadwick	Aug. 1846	Spinner		Brings daughter		Correspondence
Flood	July 1846	Smith				Account books

Name	Date	Role	Wage/Contract	Personal/Family	Activity	Source
Voien						
J. Crowland	1855	Spinning-master				Tax 1855
James Lindley	1855 to 1875	Spinning-master		Norwegian wife born 1812		Tax 1857 to 1861; Census 1875
H. Morris	1846; 1858	Factory-master				Tax 1859; O.Morch *A.S.Knud Graah & Co.* p.41
Andrew Scobie				Norwegian wife. Born 1829. Son born 1866 in Glasgow		Census 1875
Wallem						
Thomas Booth	by Wallem 1845	Workshop-master	£2 2 year contract	Wife in UK, paid by Taylor, Wordsworth & Co. and Hambro	Goes on to Rosendahl & Fane	Wallem papers
James Fothergill	1845					Wallem papers
'the girls' (Jane...)	1845				Return Leeds with Robinson Aug. 1846	Wallem papers
John Robinson	1846	Mechanic and workshop-master	£2½ 6 months contract		To Leeds for Wallem	Wallem papers
Andrew Yardley	by Wallem May 1845				Drinks Buys in UK for Wallem	Wallem papers
W. Yearley	1846					Wallem papers; Correspondence in, 1 March 1848

BIBLIOGRAPHY

MANUSCRIPT SOURCES

Bergen Byarkiv [Bergen City Archives]
   Arne Fabrikker Papers
   Rosendahl and Fane Spinnery Papers
Bergen University Library. MS 1589
   Wallem Papers
Brankasse [State Fire Insurance Corporation], Statsarkiver [State Archives], Oslo and
   Bergen.
   Branntakstprotkoller [Fire Insurance Records]
Norsk Teknisk Museum [Norwegian Technical Museum], Oslo.
   Hjula Weavery Papers
   Halvor Schou Papers
Nydalens Compagnie, Oslo.
   Nydalen Papers
Oslo Byarkiv, Rådhuset [Oslo City Archives, Town Hall]
   Ligningsprotokoller [Personal Taxation Records]
Lancashire Record Office, Preston.
   Platt-Saco-Lowell Archives
Riksarkivet [National Archives], Oslo.
   Private Archive No. 332 Fortex: *Christiania Sailcloth Factory Papers*
Solberg Spinnery A.S. (Nedre Eiker)
   Solberg Spinnery Papers
Statsarkiver, Oslo and Bergen [State Archives]
   Folketellinger [Population Censuses], 1865 and 1875
   (Bergen) *Ligningsprotokoller* [Personal Tax Records].

PRIMARY SOURCES (PRINTED)

Polytechnic society, Oslo: *Oppgave Over Foredrag og Diskussioner. Den Polytekniske
   Forening (1854–1905)*, Oslo, 1952.
Parliamentary Papers:
Report of the Select Committee Appointed to Inquire into the Export of Machinery, 1841, Vol.
   VII.
Board of Trade, 1854–55, LII, 1–505.

Frederikshald Budstikke.
Polyteknisk Tidsskrift, various issues.
Smaalenenes Amtstidene, 1854.
Teknisk Ugeblad (8 April 1902).

SECONDARY SOURCES: BOOKS

Berend, I. T. and Ranki, G. (1982): *The European Periphery and Industrialization 1780–1914*. Cambridge University Press/ Editions de la Maison des Sciences de l'Homme.

Berg, M. (1980): *The Machinery Question and the Making of Political Economy 1815–48*. Cambridge University Press.

Bergh, T., Hanisch, T. J., Lange, E. and Pharo, H. Ø. (1980): *Growth and Development: the Norwegian Experience 1830–1980*. Oslo: Norwegian Institute of International Affairs.

Burstall, A. F. (1963): *A History of Mechanical Engineering*. London: Faber and Faber.

Catling, H. (1970): *The Spinning Mule*. Newton Abbot: David and Charles.

Chapman, S. (1984): *The Rise of Merchant Banking*. London: Allen and Unwin.

Church, R. (1980): *The Dynamics of Victorian Business. Problems and Perspectives to the 1870s*. London: Allen and Unwin.

Cipolla, C. (ed.) (1977): *The Fontana Economic History of Europe. Volume 4: The Emergence of Industrial Societies, Part Two*. London: Fontana.

Crafts, N. F. R. (1986): *British Economic Growth During the Industrial Revolution*. Oxford University Press.

Crisp, O. (1978): *Studies in the Russian Economy Before 1914*. London: Macmillan.

David, P. (1969): *A Contribution to the Theory of Diffusion*. Stanford Centre for Research in Economic Growth. Memorandum 71, Stanford University.

Davies, S. (1979): *The Diffusion of Process Innovations*. Cambridge University Press.

Deane, P. and Cole, W. A. (1978): *British Economic Growth 1688–1959*. Cambridge University Press.

Derry, T. K. (1973): *A History of Modern Norway 1814–1872*. Oxford: Clarendon Press.

Dyrvik, S., Fossen, A. B., Grønlie, T., Hovland, E., Nordvik, H. and Tveite, S. (1979): *Norsk Økonomisk historie 1500–1970, Band 1: 1500–1850*. Bergen: Universitetsforlaget.

Fairbairn, W. (1877): *The Life of Sir William Fairbairn, Bart.*, edited and completed by William Pole. London: Longmans.

Farnie, D. A. (1979): *The English Cotton Industry and the World Market, 1815–1896*. Oxford University Press.

Fasting, K. (1952): *Teknikk og Samfunn. Den Polyteknisk Forening 1852–1952*. Oslo: Polyteknisk Forening.

Foster, J. (1974): *Class Struggle and the Industrial Revolution: early industrial capitalism in three English towns*. London: Weidenfeld and Nicolson.

Gerschenkron, A. (1962): *Economic Backwardness in Historical Perspective*. Cambridge, Mass.: Harvard University Press.

Grieg, S. (1946): *A. S. Arne Fabrikker 1846–1946*. Bergen: A. S. Arne Fabrikkers Direksjon.

(1948): *Norsk Tekstill*, Vol. I. Oslo: De Norske Tekstilfabrikers Hovedforening.

Bibliography

Harris, J. R. (1971): *Industry and Technology in the Eighteenth Century: Britain and France.* (Published Inaugural Lecture, University of Birmingham).

Helseth, H. (1923): *Hovel Helseths Selvbiografi.* Kristiania: Grøndahl & Søns Boktrykkeri.

Henderson, W. O. (1965): *Britain and Industrial Europe 1750–1870. Studies in British Influence on the Industrial Revolution in Western Europe.* Leicester University Press.

(1967): *The Industrial Revolution on the Continent. Germany, France, Russia, 1800–1914.* London: Frank Cass.

Higgins, J. P. P. and Pollard, S. (eds.) (1971): *Aspects of Capital Investment in Great Britain, 1750–1850. A Preliminary Survey.* London: Methuen.

Hodne, F. (1975): *An Economic History of Norway 1815–1970.* Bergen: Tapir.

Jeremy, D. J. (1981): *Transatlantic Industrial Revolution. The Diffusion of Textile Technologies Between Britain and America, 1790–1830s.* Oxford: Basil Blackwell.

Kenwood, A. G. and Lougheed, A. L. (1982): *Technological Diffusion and Industrialization Before 1914.* London: Croom Helm.

Landes, D. S. (1969): *The Unbound Prometheus. Technological Change and Industrial Development in Western Europe from 1750 to the Present.* Cambridge University Press.

Lee, W. R. (ed.) (1979): *European Demography and Economic Growth.* London: Croom Helm.

Mansfield, E. (1968): *The Economics of Technological Innovation.* New York: Norton.

Mansfield, E., Rapoport, J., Romeo, A., Villani, E., Wagner, S. and Husie, F. (1977): *The Production and Application of New Industrial Technology.* New York: Norton.

Marriner, S. (ed.) (1978): *Business and Businessmen. Studies in Business, Economic and Accounting History.* Liverpool University Press.

Mathias, P. (1979): *The Transformation of England. Essays in the Economic and Social History of England in the Eighteenth Century.* London: Methuen.

(1983): *The First Industrial Nation. An Economic History of Britain 1700–1914.* Second edition. London: Methuen.

(1986): *The Industrial Revolution and the Creation of Modern Europe.* Oxford.

Mathias, P. and Postan, M. (1978): *The Cambridge Economic History of Europe, Vol. VII, The Industrial Economies: Capital, Labour and Enterprise.* Parts 1 and 2. Cambridge University Press.

Maurseth, P. (1982): *Sentraladministrajonens Historie 1814–1844.* Oslo: Universitetsforlaget.

Melby, B. (1952): *Oslo Håndverks- og Industriforening 1838–1938.* Oslo Håndverks- og Industriforening.

Milward, A. and Saul, S. B. (1979): *The Economic Development of Continental Europe 1780–1870.* London: Allen and Unwin.

Mokyr. J. (ed.) (1985): *The Economics of the Industrial Revolution.* London: Allen and Unwin.

Mørch, O. (1921): *A/S Knud Graah & Co og A/S Vøiens Bomuldsspinderi 1846–1921.* Kristiania: Fabritius & Sønner.

Musson, A. E. and Robinson, E. (1969): *Science and Technology in the Industrial Revolution.* Manchester University Press.

Myhre, J. and Østberg, J. (eds.) (1979): *Mennesker i Kristiania.* Oslo: Universitetsforlaget.

Bibliography

Nelson, R. and Winter, S. (1982): *An Evolutionary Theory of Economic Change*. Cambridge, Mass: Harvard University Press.

O'Brien, P. and Keyder, C. (1978): *Economic Growth in Britain and France, 1780–1914*. London: Allen and Unwin.

Pollard, S. (1965): *The Genesis of Modern Management*. London: Edward Arnold.

(1981): *Peaceful Conquest. The Industrialization of Europe 1760–1970*. Oxford University Press.

Pollard, S. and Holmes, C. (eds.) (1968): *Documents of European Economic History. Vol. 1: The Process of Industrialization, 1750–1870*. London: Edward Arnold.

Prude, J. (1983): *The Coming of Industrial Order. Town and Factory Life in Massachusetts, 1810–1860*. Cambridge University Press.

Ratcliffe, B. M. (ed.) (1975): *Great Britain and Her World 1750–1870*. Essays in Honour of W. O. Henderson. Manchester University Press.

Rosenberg, N. (1977): *Perspectives on Technology*. Cambridge University Press.

(1982): *Inside the Black Box. Technology and Economics*. Cambridge University Press.

Saul, S. B. (ed.) (1970a): *Technological Change: the United States and Britain in the 19th Century*. London: Methuen.

Schweigaard, A. (1840): *Norges Statistikk*. Christiania: J. Dahl.

Sejersted, F. (1973): *En Teori om den Økonomiske Utvikling i Norge i det 19 Århundre*. Oslo.

(1974): *Fra Linderud til Eidsvold Værk*, Vol. III. Oslo: Mathiesen-Eidsvold Værk.

Sejersted, F. and Schou, A. (1972): *Fra Linderud til Eidsvold Værk*, Vol. II. Oslo: Mathiesen-Eidsvold Værk.

Solhaug, T. (1976): *De Norske Fiskeriers Historie*. Oslo: Universitetsforlaget.

Statistisk Sentralbyrå (1969): *Historisk Statistikk 1968*. Oslo.

Stewart, F. (1978): *Technology and Underdevelopment*. London: Macmillan.

Stoneman, P. (1983): *The Economic Analysis of Technological Change*. Oxford University Press.

Sundt, E. (1975): *Om Husfliden i Norge*. Oslo: Gyldendal.

Trebilcock, C. (1981): *The Industrialization of the Continental Powers 1780–1914*. London: Longman.

von Tunzelmann, N. (1978): *Steam Power and British Industrialization to 1860*. Oxford University Press.

Wicken, O. (1982): *Mustad Gjennom 150 År, 1832–1982*. Oslo.

Wiesner, A. Mohr (1918): *Bergens Forelæsningsforening, 1868–1918. En femitårsberetning*. Bergen.

SECONDARY SOURCES: ARTICLES

Birch, A. (1955): 'Foreign observers of the British iron industry during the eighteenth century', *Journal of Economic History*, 25, pp. 23–33.

Blaug, M. (1961): 'The productivity of capital in the Lancashire cotton industry during the nineteenth century', *Economic History Review*, Second Series, 13, pp. 358–81.

Bruland, K. (1982): 'Industrial conflict as a source of technical innovation: three cases', *Economy and Society*, 11, 2, pp. 91–121.

(1986): 'The coming of industrial order', *Comparative Studies in Society and History*, 30, 2, pp. 388–93.

Buchanan, R. A. (1986): 'The diaspora of British engineers', *Technology and Culture*, 27, 3, pp. 501–24.

Cameron, R. (1985): 'A new view of European industrialization', *Economic History Review*, Second Series, 38, 1, pp. 1–23.

Chapman, S. D. (1971): 'Fixed capital formation in the British cotton manufacturing industry', in Higgins, J. P. P. and Pollard, S. (eds.) (1971), pp. 57–107.

(1971a): 'The reliability of insurance valuations as a measure of capital formation' in Higgins, J. P. P. and Pollard, S. (eds.) (1971), pp. 89–91.

Crafts, N. F. R. (1983): 'Gross national product in Europe 1870–1910: some new estimates', *Explorations in Economic History*, 20, pp. 387–401.

(1984): 'Patterns of development in nineteenth-century Europe', *Oxford Economic Papers*, 36, pp. 438–58.

Crisp, O. (1976): 'French investment and influence in Russian industry, 1894–1914', in Crisp (1976), pp. 174–8.

(1976a) 'The pattern of industrialisation in Russia, 1700–1914', in Crisp, O. (1976), pp. 5–54.

(1978): 'Labour and industrialization in Russia', in Mathias, P. and Postan, M. (1978), pp. 308–415.

Drake, M. (1979): 'Norway', in Lee, W. R. (1979), pp. 284–318.

Farnie, D. A. (1981): 'Platt Bros. and Co. Ltd of Oldham, machine makers to Lancashire and the world', *Business History*, 23.

Flinn, M. W. (1957–9): 'The travel diaries of Swedish engineers of the eighteenth century as sources of technological history', *Transactions of the Newcomen Society*, 31, pp. 95–115.

Harris, J. R. (1978): 'Attempts to transfer English steel techniques to France in the eighteenth century', in Marriner, S. (1975), pp. 199–233.

(1985): 'Industrial espionage in the eighteenth century', *Industrial Archeological Review*, 7, 2, pp. 127–38.

(1988): 'The diffusion of English metallurgical methods to eighteenth-century France', *French History*, 2, 1, pp. 22–44.

Henderson, W. O. (1972a): 'English influence on the development of the French textile industries, 1750–1850', in Henderson, W. O. (1972), pp. 10–36.

Hovland, E., Nordvik, H. V., Tveite, S. (1982): 'Proto-industrialization in Norway, 1750–1850: fact or fiction?', *Scandinavian Economic History Review*, 30, 1, pp. 45–56.

Jörberg, L. (1977): 'The Nordic countries. 1850–1914', in Cipolla, C. (ed.) (1977), pp. 375–485.

Lee, J. (1978): 'Labour in German industrialization', in Mathias, P. and Postan, M. M. (1978), pp. 442–91.

Lévy-Leboyer, M. (1978): 'Capital investment and economic growth in France, 1820–1930', in Mathias, P. and Postan, M. M. (1978), pp. 226–7.

Mathias, P. (1979a): 'Skills and the diffusion of innovations from Britain in the eighteenth century', in Mathias, P. (1979), pp. 21–44.

(1986): 'The industrial revolution and the creation of modern europe', Mimeo.

Moe, T. (1970): 'Some economic aspects of Norwegian population movements 1740–1940: an econometric study', *Journal of Economic History*, 30, 1, pp. 267–70.

Musson, A. E. (1980): 'The engineering industry', in Church, R. (1980), pp. 87–106.

O'Brien, P. K. (1986): 'Do we have a typology for the study of European industrialization in the nineteenth century?', *Journal of European Economic History*, 25, 2, pp. 291–334.

Parmer, T. (1981): 'Mads Wiels bomuldsfabrik, 1813–1835. Norges første moderne industribedrifte?', *Volund 1981*, pp. 7–76.

Pollard, S. (1985): 'Industrialization and the European Economy', in Mokyr, J. (1985), pp. 165–76

Robinson, E. H. (1974): 'The early diffusion of steam power', *Journal of Economic History*, 24, pp. 91–107.

'The transference of British technology to Russia, 1760–1820', in Ratcliffe, B. M. (1975).

Rosenberg, N. (1982a): 'Marx as a student of technology', in Rosenberg, N. (1982), pp. 34–54.

(1977a): 'Factors affecting the diffusion of technology', in Rosenberg, N. (1977), pp. 189–210.

(1977b): 'Economic development and the transfer of technology', in Rosenberg, N. (1977), pp. 151–72

(1977c): 'Problems in the economist's conceptualization of technological innovation', in Rosenberg, N. (1977), pp. 61–84.

Sandberg, L. (1982): 'Poverty, ignorance and backwardness in the early stages of European industrialization. Variations on Alexander Gerschenkron's grand theme', *Journal of European Economic History*, 11, 3, pp. 675–8.

Saul, S. B. (1970): 'The market and the development of the mechanical engineering industries in Britain 1860–1914', in Saul, S. B. (1970a), pp. 141–70.

Saxonhouse, G. (1974): 'A tale of Japanese technological diffusion in the Meiji period', *Journal of Economic History*, 39, pp. 149–65.

Saxonhouse, G. and Wright, G. (1984): 'New evidence on the stubborn English mule and the cotton industry, 1878–1920', *Economic History Review*, Second Series, 37, 4, pp. 507–19.

Sejersted, F. (1968): 'Aspects of the Norwegian timber trade in the 1840s and 1850s', *Scandinavian Economic History Review*, 16, 2, pp. 137–54.

Tann, J. (1978): 'Marketing methods in the international steam engine market: the case of Boulton and Watt', *Journal of Economic History*, 38, 2, pp. 363–91.

Tann, J. and Brechin, M. (1978): 'The international diffusion of the Watt engine, 1775–1825', *Economic History Review*, 31, pp. 541–64.

Thue, L. (1979): 'Fattiggutter med to tomme hender?', in Myhre, J. and Østberg, J. (1979).

Uselding, P. (1980): 'Business history and the history of technology', *Business History Review*, 54, 4, pp. 443–52.

Wilkins, M. (1974): 'The role of private business in the international diffusion of technology', *Journal of Economic History*, 39, pp. 166–88.

UNPUBLISHED THESES

Kirk, R. M. (1983): *The Economic Development of the British Textile Machinery Industry c. 1850–1939*, 2 Vols., University of Salford.

Ramstad, J. (1981): *Kvinnelønn og Pengeøkonomi*, 2 Vols., Norges Handelshøyskole, Bergen.

Thue, L. (1977): *Framveksten av et Industriborgerskap i Kristiania, 1840–1875*, University of Oslo.

Index

188

Printed in the United States
By Bookmasters